M000220527

Getting Started with React VR

Build immersive Virtual Reality apps for the web with React

John Gwinner

BIRMINGHAM - MUMBAI

Getting Started with React VR

Copyright © 2017 Packt Publishing

All rights reserved. No part of this book may be reproduced, stored in a retrieval system, or transmitted in any form or by any means, without the prior written permission of the publisher, except in the case of brief quotations embedded in critical articles or reviews.

Every effort has been made in the preparation of this book to ensure the accuracy of the information presented. However, the information contained in this book is sold without warranty, either express or implied. Neither the author, nor Packt Publishing, and its dealers and distributors will be held liable for any damages caused or alleged to be caused directly or indirectly by this book.

Packt Publishing has endeavored to provide trademark information about all of the companies and products mentioned in this book by the appropriate use of capitals. However, Packt Publishing cannot guarantee the accuracy of this information.

First published: November 2017

Production reference: 1281117

Published by Packt Publishing Ltd.
Livery Place
35 Livery Street
Birmingham
B3 2PB, UK.

ISBN 978-1-78847-660-7

www.packtpub.com

Credits

Author
John Gwinner

Reviewers
Jerry Isdale
Sharan Volin

Commissioning Editor
Kunal Chaudhari

Acquisition Editor
Akshay Ghadi

Content Development Editor
Gauri Pradhan

Technical Editor
Surabhi Kulkarni

Copy Editor
Charlotte Carneiro

Project Coordinator
Sheejal Shah

Proofreader
Safis Editing

Indexer
Aishwarya Gangawane

Graphics
Jason Monteiro

Production Coordinator
Nilesh Mohite

About the Author

John Gwinner is a chief technology officer with nearly 2 decades of experience in VR. He developed a VR interface for CompuServe during the last wave of VR. He helped develop **Virtual Reality Markup Language (VRML)** and Web3D with a focus toward PCs and put early versions of XML on the web. While VR got quiet, as the Director of Technology, later CTO, he helped build a consulting company from 16 people to over 350. He was a returning speaker at the Game Developer Convention on 3D toolkits, AI, and VR. He was an early kick-starter of a new VR Headset in 2014 when VR started taking off again. Now that Virtual Reality is definitely real, John is once again at the forefront, with Vontic-developing VR interfaces to data, and a bowling game that pits you against garden gnomes. He is among the most-viewed writers on virtual worlds and Augmented Reality on Quora, answering questions about VR and its future direction.

Acknowledgements

First, I want to acknowledge and dedicate this book to my mother and father. Mom is the most emotionally intelligent person I know, and Dad is the most "Engineer's Engineer" that I know. A friend of theirs once said that I was the combination of the best of them. I've never been prouder than to hear that. This book is dedicated to all those who have started with me on my journey. A long time ago, on a computer system far, far away (CompuServe), there was a forum called Cyberforum. A meeting place for information, files, pictures, and discussions. We were inventing Cyber Space. All of that is gone now. We were there, we were the pioneers, but time went on and VR essentially collapsed, except for a few small islands. It's never really been gone, but it's been in the sunset. CompuServe also disappeared. Long live the Web. Now, VR is taking off again. I wouldn't be here if it wasn't for my friends. Paul and Mary Summit, for being the first to write about this brave new 3D world. Jerry Isdale, who's seminal paper on "What is VR" really broke it down for all of us. Jerry, this book wouldn't exist without you, thank you for all of your help. Phillpe Van Nedervelde, for getting CompuServe's attention on our little forum, and getting the rendering software that would allow me to make VR worlds based on CompuServe's protocols. To Karen Weatherbee, or WeeBee, for providing an artistic viewpoint; Mike "Mstripe", for knowing high performance code and getting me into Game Dev; Doug Faxon, Bernie Roehl for building some of the first public PC VR that didn't take a quarter of a million dollars, and showing people that you could walk around in alternate universes. And all of the others whose names I have forgotten. I'd also like to acknowledge the early VRML pioneers, Mark Pesce, Tony Parisi, Gavin Bell, and others; Len Bullard, Cindy Ballreich, Justin Couch, Don Brutzman, and everyone else on the old VRML list and the new X3D list. Also, thank you to the people at Facebook who are once again making Cyberspace real. Finally, to my brother Jim and his wife Margaret, who have always been there—even though, for the first few years on the planet, Jim was a bit of a pest. Sorry, I missed Thanksgiving this year, Margaret!

About the Reviewers

Sharan Volin has worked as a game programmer for the past decade, for companies such as Electronic Arts and Sony Online Entertainment. Before that, she spent 8 years doing frontend web development and was a copy editor for about 4 years. In the process of all those career changes, she collected two bachelor degrees and three masters degrees. In addition, Sharan helped out with *The Official GameSalad Guide to Game Development* by *Jeannie Novak* (Cengage Learning) and is currently writing an urban fantasy novel.

I'd like to thank my mother, Linda Volin, who, as an English teacher, always encouraged my love of books and has also supported me in my programming career.

Jerry Isdale has a long career on the bleeding edge of Art and Technology. He helped develop Oscar winning software for Computer Animation (PRISMS – Omnibus Computer Graphics), ground breaking multimedia CD-ROM edutainment titles (Xiphias), location based VR entertainment installations (SpeedSports at Sahara hotel, Las Vegas), and military/industrial AR/VR projects (HRL Laboratories). He wrote the *Technology Review* column for VR News, and served as technical editor for *Adventures in Virtual Reality* (Que Corp.), *Virtual Reality Creations* (The Waite Group), *Virtual Reality and The Exploration of Cyberspace* (Sams). He has been a serial makerspace founder, most recently with Maui Makers (Hawaii). He is founder (with Lorayne Lipps) of the Maui Institute of Art and Technology where he works on wearable technology, IoT, fashion technology, and Virtual/Augmented Reality projects.

I would like to thank John Gwinner for decades of friendship and including me in this book project and my lovely partner Lorayne Lipps for creative direction in our MIOAT projects and our travels and life together.

www.PacktPub.com

For support files and downloads related to your book, please visit www.PacktPub.com.

Did you know that Packt offers eBook versions of every book published, with PDF and ePub files available? You can upgrade to the eBook version at www.PacktPub.com and as a print book customer, you are entitled to a discount on the eBook copy. Get in touch with us at service@packtpub.com for more details.

At www.PacktPub.com, you can also read a collection of free technical articles, sign up for a range of free newsletters and receive exclusive discounts and offers on Packt books and eBooks.

https://www.packtpub.com/mapt

Get the most in-demand software skills with Mapt. Mapt gives you full access to all Packt books and video courses, as well as industry-leading tools to help you plan your personal development and advance your career.

Why subscribe?

- Fully searchable across every book published by Packt
- Copy and paste, print, and bookmark content
- On demand and accessible via a web browser

Customer Feedback

Thanks for purchasing this Packt book. At Packt, quality is at the heart of our editorial process. To help us improve, please leave us an honest review on this book's Amazon page at https://www.amazon.com/dp/1788476603.

If you'd like to join our team of regular reviewers, you can email us at customerreviews@packtpub.com. We award our regular reviewers with free eBooks and videos in exchange for their valuable feedback. Help us be relentless in improving our products!

Table of Contents

Preface	1
Chapter 1: What is Virtual Reality, Really?	7
What Virtual Reality is and how it works	8
Use of stereo and parallax in Virtual Reality	15
Why does Virtual Reality work if it doesn't look 100% real?	17
Other types of VR; AR, XR, SR/FR	18
History of VR	20
User agency - interacting with the world through controllers	20
High-end controllers for PC, Mac, and Linux	21
HTC Vive	22
Oculus Rift	23
Mobile VR	26
Rendering hardware	27
How to view VR?	28
VR can be dangerous	28
VR Headset options	29
Types of headsets	30
Mobile headsets	30
PC, Mac, and Linux headsets	31
Summary	32
Chapter 2: Flatland and Beyond: VR Programming	33
HTML and ways to move beyond the 2D internet	33
Background of Node.js and JavaScript	35
Making servers React	35
Graphics libraries — OpenGL and WebGL	36
Installation of Node.js and React VR	37
Installation of Node.js	38
Post Node.js installation — installing React VR	39
Installation of a WebVR browser	45
Summary	48
Chapter 3: 3D or Reality in Dimensions Other than X and Y	49
Beyond flatland - 3D concepts	50
Coordinates	50
What about rotations?	53
Points	54

Vectors   54
Transforms   55
    What about the matrix?   58
Rendering   60
    Testing how it looks   61
    How rendering works   62
Summary   63

Chapter 4: The React VR Library   65

JSX - the syntax of React VR   66
Differences between React VR and React   66
Core Components   67
VR Components   68
Props   68
State   69
Events   69
Layout and style   70
The next level - the details   71
Stuff (objects, whether visible or not)   71
    Primitives   72
        Box   72
        Cylinder   72
        Plane   73
        Sphere   74
    Model   74
    CylindricalPanel   75
    VideoControl   77
    VrButton   77
Lights   78
    Common light properties   79
    AmbientLight   79
    DirectionalLight   81
    PointLight   82
    SpotLight   83
Multimedia - sound and video   84
    Sound   84
    Video   86
Cameras and viewing   87
    LiveEnvCamera   87
    View   88
Summary   88

Chapter 5: Your First VR App   89

Moving beyond hello world - our first VR world   89

VR world design - or, congrats, you are the new Astronomy Museum curator!   89
Creating the base React VR components   90
Creating the larger world - background image   93
Cluttering up the world - adding our first VR components   98
    Lighting up the world   100
    Why did I have you paste in both a Plane and a Box?   102
Got Class - consolidating objects as new keywords   103
Putting it all together   105
Adding the pedestals   107
Summary   111

Chapter 6: Working with Poly and the Gon Family   113
Polygons and why we like them   114
    Why doesn't VR use some of these techniques?   116
What is a polygon? discussion of vertices, polygons, and edges   120
Where to get 3D models   130
Summary   132

Chapter 7: Sitting Down with a (Virtual) Teapot   133
The teapot in Blender   134
    Fixing the UV maps for the teapot   143
Importing materials   152
Fixing the deck plates   154
    The finished VR world   158
Summary   164

Chapter 8: Breath Life in Your World   165
The Animated API   165
    Flying teapots   167
    Spinning once and forever   170
    The final code   172
Sound   177
    Putting sound in our world   178
Summary   180

Chapter 9: Do It Yourself – Native Modules and Three.js   181
Native modules and views   181
    Making a three.js cube demo   182
    Making native code interact with React VR   185
    Summing up the code so far   188
Something more visual   191

Next steps   196
Extending React VR — Native Views   196
Extending the language   196
Summary   197

Chapter 10: Bringing in the Real Live World   199

Going to Mars (the initial world creation)   199
Creating the initial world   200
Jason and JSON   200
Why JSON has nothing to do with React   201
Finding the API -- All the way from Mars   202
A better API from NASA   208
Everyone needs a style(sheet)   211
Building the image and status UI   212
How (not to) to make people sick   216
Summary   217

Chapter 11: Take a Walk on the Wild Side   219

Going loco–VR locomotion   219
Types of VR locomotion   220
Avoiding the ghost effect   223
Building a maze   224
Almost random–pseudo random number generators   225
Including library code from other projects   225
The Maze render()   226
Adding the floors and type checking   228
Using the glTF file format for models   232
Animation — VR Buttons   237
Raycasters   239
Props, state, and events   241
Making updates flow up river   242
Where to go from here?   244
Summary   245

Chapter 12: Publishing Your App, and Where to Go from Here   247

Upgrading React VR   248
Upgrading in place   249
Third-party dependencies   250
Really broken upgrades – rip and replace   252
The best time to do an upgrade   253
Getting your code ready to publish   253

Good code organization   254
Cleaning the lint trap (checking code standards)   255
React VR coding style   256
Third-party dependencies   257
Bundling for publishing on the web   258
Packaging React VR for release on a website   259
Obtaining releases and attribution   261
Checking image sizes and using content delivery sites   261
Optimizing your models   262
Now that we've gotten it published, what's next   262
Physics – making the world interact with itself   263
Game play engines – letting you interact with others   263
Monetizing VR   264
Where VR will go in the next five years   266
Do not wait for next year's technology   267
Better HMDs   268
Better and more realistic graphics   268
Easier content creation and more high-end content   269
Eye tracking   269
Audio improvements   270
Controlling VR   271
Social and legal issues and solutions   272
Summary   272
Index   275

Preface

Virtual Reality, from a computer standpoint, has been around since the 1960s. It started up again in a big way in the late 90's, and then mostly collapsed for a while—although it's never really gone away. It is back now, and, this time, it is here to stay.

What has made this change is the cell phone—the large, high-resolution display technology used in cell phones has helped created HMDs (Head Mounted Displays, or VR Goggles). Circuits and computers are also vastly faster than they used to be; computer graphics that used to cost a quarter of a million dollars in 1998 now costs less than two thousand and is even faster.

Building VR worlds has always been difficult, however. You had to be a C++ programmer and know an immense amount about high speed programming, real-time graphics, geometry, and other complex topics. This has been simplified in the last few years with game development engines—simplified, but only to a point.

With React VR, it is even simpler. You can code a VR world now using React syntax, a simple declarative HTML-like language. If you want to create a box, you just declare a box with the right width, height, and so forth, instead of having to write procedural code. The syntax may be simple, but these worlds can be event driven, animated, and responsive to user input as well as obtaining information from the web.

This will enable you to build complex virtual worlds with simple JavaScript and HTML-like code. This uses a new browser-based programming paradigm called WebVR; regular browsers on PCs and on mobile devices can now view worlds in VR.

You can do this too, and this book will show you how.

What this book covers

Chapter 1, *What is Virtual Reality, Really?*, shows what Virtual Reality really is—how the right combination of movement and images makes things look real, even if they aren't completely realistic.

Chapter 2, *Flatland and Beyond: VR Programming*, is about the different ways that we can program VR and gets us started with React VR and Node.js.

Chapter 3, *3D or Reality in Dimensions Other than X and Y*, introduces us to 3D math, coordinates, and how to describe objects in React VR.

Chapter 4, *The React VR Library*, describes the major components and objects in the React VR library.

Chapter 5, *Your First VR App*, shows us how to create our first major VR world, including downloading and using photo-realistic background images.

Chapter 6, *Working with Poly and the Gon Family*, introduces us to polygon modeling, and the free software program called Blender, for doing 3D modeling.

Chapter 7, *Sitting Down with a (Virtual) Teapot*, continues our introduction to Blender, showing how to texture map and include these 3D objects into our VR world.

Chapter 8, *Breath Life in Your World*, introduces the Animation API and ways to make our objects move and sound real.

Chapter 9, *Do It Yourself – Native Modules and three.js*, demonstrates how to stay within React VR and build even more complex worlds.

Chapter 10, *Bringing in the Real Live World*, connects our VR worlds to real-world APIs and enables us to bring in graphical data all the way from Mars.

Chapter 11, *Take a Walk on the Wild Side*, develops code and user interface to let us walk around in VR and then promptly end up in a (constructed for fun) maze.

Chapter 12, *Publishing Your App, and Where to Go from Here*, shows us how to upgrade and publish our worlds; we also discuss monetization and where VR could go in 5 years.

What you need for this book

You will need a Windows PC, of nearly any type; for maximum enjoyment, you will need VR rig. Either an HTC Vive, Oculus Rift, a Samsung Gear VR, Google Daydream, or other VR goggles (including the Google Cardboard) and a cell phone.

You can develop these WebVR worlds even if you don't have a sophisticated **Head Mounted Display** (**HMD**) or **VR Headset** ; you can view them in flat mode on your regular computer screen. You can pick up a simple VR cell phone holder/headset (Google Cardboard or similar) for less than 20 dollars or even free in many places, so don't let hardware be a barrier to learning about the next great thing.

Who this book is for

This book is for anyone who wants to learn Virtual Reality on the web and create engaging 3D websites with WebVR through React VR. You will pick this up quickest if you have already known some JavaScript, and even faster if you already know React or React Native. Even if you don't, the book will show you step by step what to do. If you already know how to do polygon modeling, this will help, but this book will also show people how to use the free and open source Blender to do some basic modeling if needed, and where to get free downloads. You do not need a VR rig to be able to enjoy this book—you can do the samples with a regular PC and even publish it on the internet.

Conventions

In this book, you will find a number of text styles that distinguish between different kinds of information. Here are some examples of these styles and an explanation of their meaning.

Code words in text, database table names, folder names, filenames, file extensions, pathnames, dummy URLs, user input, and Twitter handles are shown as follows: "Components are real things, not just labels or placeholders, as they have built in ways to present themselves through the world via a render() function."

A block of code is set as follows:

```
<Box
  dimWidth={4}
  dimDepth={1}
  dimHeight={9}
  lit
/>
```

When we wish to draw your attention to a particular part of a code block, the relevant lines or items are set in bold:

```
f:
mkdir f:\reactVR
cd \reactVR
```

Any command-line input or output is written as follows:

```
npm install mersenne-twister --save
```

New terms and **important words** are shown in bold. Words that you see on the screen, for example, in menus or dialog boxes, appear in the text like this: "Once you have the polygons assigned, click on **View->Front** then click on **Mesh->UV Unwrap->Cylinder Projection**."

Warnings or important notes appear in a box like this.

Tips and tricks appear like this.

Reader feedback

Feedback from our readers is always welcome. Let us know what you think about this book-what you liked or disliked. Reader feedback is important for us as it helps us develop titles that you will really get the most out of.

To send us general feedback, simply e-mail feedback@packtpub.com, and mention the book's title in the subject of your message.

If there is a topic that you have expertise in and you are interested in either writing or contributing to a book, see our author guide at www.packtpub.com/authors.

Customer support

Now that you are the proud owner of a Packt book, we have a number of things to help you to get the most from your purchase.

Downloading the example code

You can download the example code files for this book from your account at http://www. packtpub.com. If you purchased this book elsewhere, you can visit http://www.packtpub. com/support and register to have the files emailed directly to you.

You can download the code files by following these steps:

1. Log in or register to our website using your e-mail address and password.
2. Hover the mouse pointer on the **SUPPORT** tab at the top.
3. Click on **Code Downloads & Errata**.
4. Enter the name of the book in the **Search** box.
5. Select the book for which you're looking to download the code files.
6. Choose from the drop-down menu where you purchased this book from.
7. Click on **Code Download**.

You can also download the code files by clicking on the **Code Files** button on the book's webpage at the Packt Publishing website. This page can be accessed by entering the book's name in the **Search** box. Please note that you need to be logged in to your Packt account.

Once the file is downloaded, please make sure that you unzip or extract the folder using the latest version of:

- WinRAR / 7-Zip for Windows
- Zipeg / iZip / UnRarX for Mac
- 7-Zip / PeaZip for Linux

The code bundle for the book is also hosted on GitHub at `https://github.com/PacktPublishing/Getting-Started-with-React-VR`. We also have other code bundles from our rich catalog of books and videos available at `https://github.com/PacktPublishing/`. Check them out!

Downloading the color images of this book

We also provide you with a PDF file that has color images of the screenshots/diagrams used in this book. The color images will help you better understand the changes in the output. You can download this file from `https://www.packtpub.com/sites/default/files/downloads/GettingStartedwithReactVR_ColorImages.pdf`.

Errata

Although we have taken every care to ensure the accuracy of our content, mistakes do happen. If you find a mistake in one of our books-maybe a mistake in the text or the code-we would be grateful if you could report this to us. By doing so, you can save other readers from frustration and help us improve subsequent versions of this book. If you find any errata, please report them by visiting http://www.packtpub.com/submit-errata, selecting your book, clicking on the **Errata Submission Form** link, and entering the details of your errata. Once your errata are verified, your submission will be accepted and the errata will be uploaded to our website or added to any list of existing errata under the Errata section of that title.

To view the previously submitted errata, go to https://www.packtpub.com/books/content/support and enter the name of the book in the search field. The required information will appear under the **Errata** section.

Piracy

Piracy of copyrighted material on the Internet is an ongoing problem across all media. At Packt, we take the protection of our copyright and licenses very seriously. If you come across any illegal copies of our works in any form on the Internet, please provide us with the location address or website name immediately so that we can pursue a remedy.

Please contact us at copyright@packtpub.com with a link to the suspected pirated material.

We appreciate your help in protecting our authors and our ability to bring you valuable content.

Questions

If you have a problem with any aspect of this book, you can contact us at questions@packtpub.com, and we will do our best to address the problem.

1

What is Virtual Reality, Really?

You are reading this book to learn to make **Virtual Reality (VR)**, but what is Virtual Reality?

It seems like a simple enough question, but the answer is all over the map. Most people think VR means virtually real or alternate reality.

That is not what Virtual Reality is.

I think this is because the word virtual can mean several different things. To a computer scientist, the word virtual means something that simulates the thing it virtualizes. In other words, a virtual hard drive pretends to be a hard drive.

The virtual object acts like it is real, but it isn't--frequently, its more flexible and easier to control, modify, and support than a physical object. In many ways, it is better than the physical object. A virtual disk, for example, acts just like a computer disk. It can store data. Yet that data could be on a physical spinning disk, in a solid-state drive, or even in memory. The virtual disk can be resized, whereas a physical disk can only be copied to a larger (or smaller) disk. A virtual disk is more flexible.

Some people think virtual means almost. If a Tesla drives by, they might say, "*That's virtually noiseless!*" People know it's not really noiseless, but it is much quieter than a big V8 driving by. Or, *that person is a virtual saint* about a person they like. In this case, it means nearly or in all but name.

Virtual can also mean someone with virtue. A person who behaves ethically is virtual, although this is not the normal usage of the word (virtuous would be). This is where the word came from; in Latin virtualis means strength or virtue. Yet, in our case, we mean something that seems real, but isn't.

I think this is the misconception about Virtual Reality. People think it means almost real. Many people think VR isn't there yet because it doesn't look nearly like the real world. It will be quite some time before the view through a VR headsets looks just like the real world; other senses, especially touch and taste may take quite a while until they can be simulated.

Yet, this is not the point; the point with Virtual Reality isn't that it's nearly real. The point is, when you are in it, it *seems* real, even if it looks nothing like reality.

I'll say this again as it's an important distinction. Virtual Reality, or for that matter Augmented Reality, doesn't need to be nearly real, but it will *seem* real when you are in it (even if it doesn't remotely look real).

By the end of this chapter, you'll learn:

- What Virtual Reality is and how it works
- Some of the history of VR -it's not new, the technology is over 50 years old!
- User agency - interacting with the world through controllers
- Rendering hardware
- How to view VR
- Types of headsets

What Virtual Reality is and how it works

We have many senses. To make us feel an alternative reality is real, we need to involve these senses to fool the brain. Most VR systems make use of two: sight and sound; touch is also used but not in a full reach-out-and-touch-someone sense (although people are working on it!).

Tor Nørretranders compiled data about the senses and their relative bandwidth, in computer terms. This is a bit like comparing apples and motor oil, although useful to see how it applies to VR.

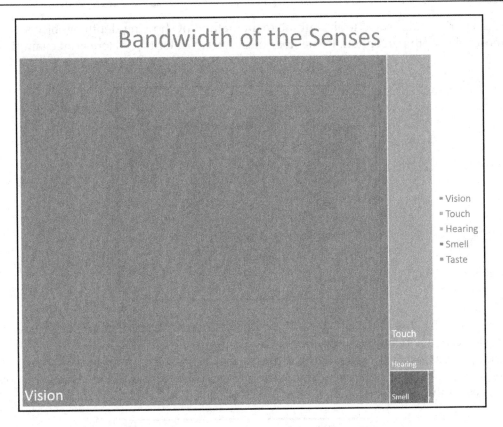

So, we can see if we make you see something that is virtually real, we may be able to convince the brain it is real. Yet, simply putting a vision screen in front of us is not the complete answer.

Giving someone depth perception is most of the answer.

This is a fairly complicated topic, but the main method of showing depth of objects is stereoscopic depth perception. Remember those ViewMaster toys? Here is an example of one:

You put in a disk that had a left eye and a right eye image. The images on the left and right nearly look identical, but they represent what the right and left eyes would see if you were standing at that location; each slightly different due to parallax. From the disk, here, we can see each of the left and right eye images. The lenses in the preceding View-Master focuses your eyes on the images.

Your brain would look at these two images and fuse the images into something that looked real. This uses a depth perception technique called **stereoscopic depth perception**.

Yes, the View-Master was an early Virtual Reality viewing device!

Now, what is really going on here? How does Stereo work?

When you look at something, perspective and separation between your eyes will make you focus your eyes differently at something closer as opposed to something far away. In this diagram, the yellow lines show our sight lines to a near object, and the orange lines show the sight lines to a distant object. Note that the angle between the yellow lines is larger than the narrow angle of the orange lines:

A friendly robot loaned us the lower half of her eyes to make this image (that's why it shows circuit boards). Your real eye is constructed somewhat similar; I omitted the light rays and where they fall on the back of the eye for illustration's sake.

Your brain will automatically figure out if your eyes are pointed at a close or far object by the difference in angles between the yellow and the orange lines.

This is just one method our brain uses to distinguish depth. Another that is also vital to Virtual Reality is the use of *parallax*.

Parallax refers to the way that, not only do the left and right android eyes point differently (as would your eyes, when they are attached to your head), but that each eye sees a slightly different view of the same objects. This will work even with one eye if you move your head to the left and right, and is how people with mono-vision perceive depth (among other ways).

This is how your left eye sees the scene:

This is how the right eye sees the same object:

Parallax refers to the way that an object that is more distant will be less to the right/left than a nearby object, when viewed with the other eye, OR (an extension) when moving your head left to right. Our brain (as well as the brains of animals) will instinctively see these as closer/further.

The red cube is either next to the blue cube or the green cube, depending on what eye sees the image. Your brain will integrate this, coupled with how the cubes move if you move your eye from side to side, to also give you a sense of depth.

 Don't despair if you are in the percentage of the population that do not perceive 3D movies. They strictly rely on stereoscopic depth perception and do not take parallax effects into account; they are pre-recorded.

With *true* VR (computer generated or light field based 360 video), if you move your head, you will see the parallax effect and the VR can seem real just like someone with stereoscopic depth perception sees.

I have mono-vision because I have a nearsighted eye and a farsighted eye, and VR works great for me. Your mileage may vary, but if you don't like 3D movies, give VR a try (then again, I really like 3D movies).

Parallax depth perception will work even if you have one eye, when you move your head right to left.

There is one additional way that your brain will use to determine depth of an object - focusing. (Actually, there are many ways other than those listed, such as blue shifting of objects in the far distance, like mountains, and other effects). Focusing on an object in the real world will make that object and other objects at roughly the same distance appear in focus, and objects both further and closer will appear blurry. Sort of like this:

Current HMD's cannot accurately show focus as an effect. You are looking at a small screen that generally has a fixed focus of about 5 feet in front of you. All objects, close and far, will appear to be focused the same as they are actually just being shown on the screen. This can cause a mild VR discomfort, called the accommodation-vergence conflict. Basically, if you focus on the far focus cube (the salmon colored one), your eyes will still focus as if the salmon cube was located where the red cube is; your eyeballs will, however, aim stereoscopically as if it was located where it should be. This effect is most pronounced with very close objects.

The accommodation-vergence conflict is most severe with close objects - so try not to have anything, such as a GUI, located too close to the user's location. You will reduce sickness this way.

This means you may need to float GUI elements out into the room instead of having them very close. This may cause overlapping UI elements.

VR design is challenging. I'm looking forward to what you design!

Use of stereo and parallax in Virtual Reality

As far back as 1968, Ivan E. Sutherland first observed that objects with stereoscopic depth perception, and that seemed to be positioned in space when the users head moved (motion parallax), seemed real.

The system that he and Bob Sproul developed, often referred to as the *The Sword of Damocles*, just displayed a handful of glowing lines in the air, yet:

> *"Even with this relatively crude system, the three dimensional illusion was real."*

> -*Ivan E. Sutherland, AFIPS '68 (Fall, part I) Proceedings of the December 9-11, 1968, fall joint computer conference, part I:* http://bit.ly/2urAV5e

Real in this instance meant that despite a total lack of realistic rendering - just a glowing cube - people thought of it as real. This is due to the stereoscopic rendering and the parallax effect. People could turn their heads and move a little bit from side to side.

They invented the first VR Headset, or **Head Mounted Display (HMD)**.

The person widely regarded as creating the term Virtual Reality, Jaron Lanier, said:

> *"It's a very interesting kind of reality. It's absolutely as shared as the physical world. Some people say that, well, the physical world isn't all that real. It's a consensus world. But the thing is, however real the physical world is – which we never can really know – the virtual world is exactly as real, and achieves the same status. But at the same time it also has this infinity of possibility that you don't have in the physical world: in the physical world, you can't suddenly turn this building into a tulip; it's just impossible. But in the virtual world you can .... [Virtual Reality] gives us this sense of being able to be who we are without limitation; for our imagination to become objective and shared with other people."*

> - *Jaron Lanier, SIGGRAPH Panel 1989, Virtual Environments and Interactivity: Windows to the Future.* http://bit.ly/2uIl0ib

A researcher named Mel Slater has performed further work on this concept, coining the further terms presence and plausibility. Some people call all of this **Immersion**. 3D images on a screen are not as compelling as when you have an HMD on and your only sight is of the constructed 3D world. You feel a sense of presence due to the audio and visual cues, even if the rendering isn't just like the real world. Plausibility means that what you see has rules and works even if it's not exactly what you see in the real world.

The combination of being limited to seeing just what is in the HMD, along with the parallax and stereoscopic views, and any audio (sounds are very important, if done well), will immerse you in the VR world. With all of these things, even if the graphics are not real, you will feel immersed, and it becomes real. For more academic detail see `http://bit.ly/2vGFso0`, although I'll explain more about this in this section.

This really works.

VR does not have to look anything like reality, but it will seem as if it is real. For example, take a look at the game *Quell4D*:

The graphics are block like, the images look nothing like reality. Yet, when the Ancient Triple Trunked Elephant Necro Shaman come at you, you will be scared. They seem real. To you, when you play the game, they are literally deadly real, meaning that your (in-game) person will die if you don't take them seriously.

VR simulations of fire will send about 10% of the people out of the room in a panic, even though the flames don't look anything like real flames.

VR is here. We do not have to wait until the graphics get better. Many people say this about VR, but it is because they haven't tried it yet and are making assumptions about what it has to be.

Dive in, the water is fine!

So, Virtual Reality is something that will seem real, not something that necessarily looks real (but it helps if it does!).

You do not have to wait until better graphics come around.

Why does Virtual Reality work if it doesn't look 100% real?

Our eyes are possibly our most important senses for showing us what the world consists of. If we substitute images and immerse someone with these images, they will start to seem real. When you first get into VR, your initial reaction is, *"that doesn't really look real"*, but with a good VR setup, you will get to a point where you think *"whoa, that was real"* even though you know you are looking at what is basically a computer game.

A fast frame rate (speed of display) and enough resolution will trick your brain into thinking what it sees visually really does exist. This is a powerful effect that most, but not all, people will have when immersed in such images (not everyone with normal eyesight sees 3D movies either).

In fact, the sense of reality is so good that people can get sick by watching VR. This happens because your eyes may say that's real, but your other senses, like your inner ear, says we aren't jumping 10 feet in the air. If your eyes think you are bouncing up in the air and your leg muscles (the sense of proprioception) say you're on the ground, your skin says you don't feel the wind and your inner ear says you are not tilting as you fly forward, your mind will be confused at a very deep level.

When your senses disagree powerfully, your body has a defense mechanism. It thinks you've been poisoned; as a result, your body will feel nausea and possibly even get sick. Your body is concerned that your eyes don't see what the rest of your body feels, so it may try to get rid of everything in your stomach, just in case something you ate had poisoned you.

Yes, it's no fun; different people will react differently.

However, not all VR does this! Generally speaking, poorly constructed VR will give you this feeling. Academic papers have been written on this effect. This book will summarize these discussions into a few simple rules that will make your VR much more comfortable for people.

Another important aspect of Virtual Reality is that it is something that you can interact with (the reality itself). This brings up mechanical difficulties; not everyone owns 3D controllers. We cover this in the section: *User Agency - interacting with the world through controllers.* True VR can be interacted with even if it is something as simple as gaze detection - look at something (gaze) and things happen - movement occurs, you're teleported, an animation plays.

Other types of VR; AR, XR, SR/FR

There is another type of imagery which is sometimes called VR, which is **360 Video**. There are special video players that record in all directions. Sophisticated software will stitch the different camera inputs together to make a video stream that playback software will project to be all around you. When you turn your head, you seem to change your point of view inside the filmed world. It's as if you're in the real world, looking around at whatever you want to see.

The 360 Video looks possibly better than most computer graphic generated VR, but to me it's not reality because, at best, you are a disembodied ghost. Sure, the world looks great, but you can't reach out and touch things, because it's been filmed. The 360 Video and systems like it are beyond the scope of this book. Having said this, I do think the 360 Video is certainly a valid art form and something to pursue--just not covered by this book.

Please understand - I don't mean this dismissively of 360 video, just because it's not *real* VR. (Pronouce that second to last word like it had air quotes around it). 360 Video can be very heart warming, intense, emotional dramas. You do get a hint of presense, and the visuals are astounding. It is an area where we should see amazing art being made as more people are familiar with it and work out the details.

I am proposing a new term for 360 Video; **Filmed Reality (FR)** or **Surround Reality (SR)**. (Although no one uses actual film for these, the phrase 'filmed' still means to record something through a lens, but maybe SR is better. You choose!)

There are other types of VR. So many that some people use the phrase **XR** which means (Anything) Reality; mainly to mean AR and VR. What is AR?

The HMD, which consists of some small displays and sophisticated optics, will allow you to see a stereo 3D image when you put the headset on. Most VR headsets intentionally block out the rest of the world while you are in them, to further immerse you in VR. This is an important component of VR, although there is a type of VR called Augmented Reality (AR) where the VR items are projected into the real world by wearing a type of HMD that is transparent. There are a number of manufacturers, although the Microsoft Hololens may be the best well known. There is also the game *Pokemon Go*, which is a type of AR. People hold up their cell phone, which shows images layered on top of reality. This is not a headset, but is still AR. Reality has been augmented with the Pokemon world.

VR systems can also be **windows on world** systems, although this is not commonly called VR today. In other words, a real, persistent 3D world that you sit at your keyboard and view through your screen. During the last wave of VR, years ago, this was referred to as VR, although today it's commonplace enough that people do not call it VR. You may have heard of **World of Warcraft**.

This is a type of Virtual Reality; although it's not (usually) in 3D, it is a persistent world in an alternate reality. It is also a full 3D world that you can see by looking at your screen; the screen transports you to a virtual reality so it's similar to a Windows on World system (although not head tracked).

Watching movies can be viewed as a valid form of VR; you are transported to another world, and, for a short time, feel as if you are immersed in the story. Television is a type of VR.

The first use of the term VR in fact referred to the theater. While many people today would say that's not VR, they spend much of their lives watching other realities and not paying attention to the people sitting next to them. How is this not Virtual Reality? You are pretty immersed with *Dancing with the Stars*, but do you know any of them? They are virtually real.

Still, this is not what most people think. This book will use the modern (2014+) interpretation of Virtual Reality as being something viewed through a VR headset or HMD of some type. Today, the term VR usually implies a headset or HMD, and is fairly often coupled with some form of hand controllers. Good, effective HMDs are all commercially available now to consumers. It is a great time to be interested in VR.

The nice thing about WebVR though, is that we can still see these VR worlds through the browser without an HMD; this is great for testing and for people without the hardware.

WebVR is very inclusive.

History of VR

Most people also think VR is fairly new, but it actually has been around for a long time, and I mean the traditional type of VR with a headset. The first HMD was created by Ivan Sutherland and Bob Sproull in 1968. Due to the technology of the time, it was large and heavy, and was thus suspended from the ceiling of the research room it was in. It also only showed wireframe images. Due to it's size, it was called the Sword of Damocles. It showed a simple wireframe world. Computers of the time were not fast enough to display anything more sophisticated than a handful of glowing lines.

In the late 90's, PCs began to be fast enough to display 3D worlds, and there was a new wave of VR. I participated in these efforts; I was working on a 3D environment for CompuServe, which was the place to be at the time.

You could go to malls and participate, with an expensive HMD, in a shared virtual world with up to four people online. This was called location-based entertainment as the systems were large and expensive. Today, you can also go to VR arcades and experiment with hardware, but the exciting thing about VR today is that many of these systems are very affordable for home enthusiasts.

User agency - interacting with the world through controllers

The HMD is not everything, although it is certainly the most important part. Being able to see a VR world is great, but at some point you want to be able to interact with it. If the world was static, you would feel like a disembodied ghost. It is Virtual Reality when you can interact with the world.

Eventually, something like full suit haptics (physical feedback) and body tracking, along with sophisticated software, will allow us to reach out and touch the virtual world. This is something to look forward to in the future.

For now, the way that we usually interact with the world is through various hand-held controllers. Different controllers have radically different capabilities and requirements. Controllers for high-end (but still consumer available) VR setups, like the Rift and Vive, work considerably differently from mobile VR controllers. We'll discuss the higher-end systems first, then discuss mobile VR controllers.

High-end controllers for PC, Mac, and Linux

With **PC VR**, such as the HTC Vive or Oculus Rift, controllers give a very important ability to interact with the VR world. These controllers are tracked in 3D space so that the software knows where they are. Developers can code these to look like hands, guns, and so on. This allows you to reach out and touch the world around you--very important to make the Virtual Reality you are interacting with actually something you can interact with.

To do this, both the Oculus and Vive controllers require external tracking hardware. With the Vive, these are lighthouses or VR base stations that are placed at the corners of the VR area. (There is a diagram here, and it is available at `http://bit.ly/VIVEManual`). These small unobtrusive cubes send out IR tracking signals that the controllers and headsets pick up and use to accurately position them in the real 3D world. With the Rift, there are two or three sensors that also track the devices to give them a real-world position:

The base stations and tracking hardware are really important for the HMD itself as well.

This tracking of your real world position (your actual head/hands) is what makes movement, turning your head, moving your hands/controllers seem real, because the position, orientation, and movement of the headsets and controllers is so precisely tracked in real 3D space, any head movement seems real once the software displays the VR world to the user.

In practice, this means that the PC controllers will seem right where you see them. My first experience with an HTC Vive at a tech demo was amazing--I'd put on the HTC Vive headset, and, in the virtual world, saw the controllers in front of me. I expected to sort of fumble around until the controllers were where I thought they would be. I reached out, and my fingers felt the controllers exactly where my eyes saw them--through the HMD.

I was hooked! The virtual world really was Virtual Reality! The phantom controllers I was looking at were *real* even though I knew I was looking at a small screen in front of my face.

How do they work?

HTC Vive

The HTC Vive uses two small square cubes, called **base stations** or **Lighthouses**, at opposite ends of the area they are covering. These send out beams of infrared light over 120 degrees; this means if they are in a corner, they can be a few inches away from the corner and still cover the walls (otherwise, you'd have to dig a hole in your wall to put the lighthouses at the right spot!)

Usually, you mount the two base stations at opposite sides of a room, up to about 16 feet or 5 meters apart, and above head height, around 2 meters or 6 feet 6 inches. It's okay if you're taller--mount them higher!

The base stations can also be mounted on microphone stands with the right adapters or with custom stands. Not everyone has a large living room, so these arrangements may help fit it in.

The Vive can also be used in a seated configuration, although the real point is what is called **Room Scale**.

Room Scale VR means that you can walk around in the VR world, as if you are walking around the real world. No teleporting or other tricks needed. Of course, the area needs to be clear of furniture, which is one of the issues with VR in general; not everyone has a big room they can clear.

The Vive will keep you safe by showing bounds or guards at the edges of your space, if you get too close.

Make your room bounds slightly less than the actual room, if it's a wall or other area. If it's a couch or chair, you can go right to the end of the chair.

We do this so you don't hit your arm on the walls. This is easy to do if you are standing up against the wall, but still in the virtual world and therefore can't see the wall, and you swing your arm, your hand won't go through the real wall!

Going to the edge of a sofa is nice, as your shins will run into the sofa before your hands hit the wall. In practice it's not that much of a problem, as you'll see the guards before you get close. Pay attention to the Vive/Steam VR tutorial!

The HTC Vive works by having some **Inertial Measurement Units** (IMUs), which detect where the HMD as well as the controllers are located. These IMUs drift, so the base stations have an infrared beam that sweeps over the room. When the controllers, trackers, or HMD detects these beams, they recenter themselves. This re-centering is completely undetectable. The advantage of such a system is that, even if a controller goes out of sight from one of the base stations or Lighthouses, the VR system still knows where that item is and where it is pointed.

The overall effect is precision and presence, although the main effect is stability. If you cross your hands and a controller briefly goes out of sight of the base station, the controller won't lose lock.

Try not to put your VR space in an area with a lot of windows or mirrors.

The Infrared beams can reflect off of them, leading to instability.

Oculus Rift

The **Rift** first came out just as a headset, without controllers. It's initial base stations are two cameras that you place on the left and right of a desk; they point at the HMD and are used to position it in the world.

Soon after, Rift added the capability of third camera; with three cameras, you can do room-scale VR. The positioning of them is slightly different than the Vive; take a look at the Rift documentation for the best positioning.

Be careful with cables. As I wrote this book, the Rift is cabled directly into the back of the PC. If you trip over the cables, you could yank them out of the PC fairly hard, leading to damage.

The Vive has a breakout box, so if you trip over a cable, you'll hopefully pull it out of the box.
Don't trip over the cables.

The purpose of this book is not to be an analysis of why the Vive or Rift is better or worse than another; both of them work roughly the same way with the base stations/cameras helping the controllers and HMD to keep track of their position and rotations. Here is a typical setup:

In it, the Vive base stations are mounted on the walls; we have a desktop PC and a VR user viewing a 3D model as if it was real. The VR user is holding two Vive controllers; the virtual image is holding a Xbox-style game controller.

This image also shows an Oculus Rift 3 camera tracker system. They are the light-gray items sitting to the left and right of the screen, and on the credenza on the back side of the couch (right in front of us).

That's right, the cybernetic robot is the user. She doesn't need an HMD; the system pumps in the video straight to her eyes. The virtual object is the human seeming to sit at the desk.

The preceding figure is the view that a third person in front of the couch might see of the scene.

What the lighthouses see is actually a little different, but interesting. They actually have a couple of infrared bars that sweep across the view and the controllers see these lines tracking across. When they do, the controllers (and HMD) will resync their inertially tracked positioning. This means that even if a controller is out of view of a base station, it still keeps tracking, although you don't want to hide a controller for very long. Inertially tracked systems will drift. The visual issue with drift is that your arm would seem to slowly move away from your body - which is obviously highly disconcerting. The Vive lighthouses and Rift cameras keep the drift from happening. The Vive angle of view that a lighthouse projects is around 120 degrees. This is what the rear, rightmost lighthouse would see if there were a camera with this field of view at the lighthouse:

You can see both controllers and the HMD through this Lighthouse. There is, however, an issue. Notice the red circles--the large mirror on the left is actually a gigantic TV, but it's shiny. As a result, the Lighthouse IR beams will bounce off of it and the controllers will sense two beams: one directly and one reflection.

This may cause the HMD and your point of view to jump or your controllers to move about inexplicably.

Avoid shiny objects, mirrors, and windows in your VR room.

You might need to draw drapes, or even throw sheets over TV's, glass china cabinets, and the like.

Art requires sacrifice!

From the other lighthouse, one of the controllers is blocked, but it is still tracked 100% through its internal inertial tracking and the other lighthouse.

Mobile VR

For **mobile VR**, there are also the Google Daydream and Samsung Gear VR controllers. Due to the simpler hardware used, which keeps the price more reasonable, these are not fully 3D tracked.

With mobile VR, due to the absence of room tracking external sensors, that the Vive and Oculus both have, the VR controllers are not so precisely tracked. In practice they will seem just as real, but will periodically drift. It's as if your hand slowly moved off to the right without your control. Mobile VR thus has a **reset controller** button that will move the controller to a predefined position, such as near your hip. Your hand might be held straight out, but if you hit the **Home** button the VR display will show your hand now at your hip.

This might take some getting used to. There are advantages to this setup; it's cheaper, requires less external hardware, and there are many more such systems out in the world. However, the PC hardware does give a better VR experience.

The other wrinkle with the mobile controllers is that there are only three **Degrees of Freedom (DOF)**. This means they track tilt, yaw, and roll, but not position; if you move the controller flat to your left, in the game your controller hasn't moved at all. This is why you can't grab things with a mobile controller. The Vive and Rift both have 6 DOF controllers, so you can move them around and grab things.

Rendering hardware

To avoid VR sickness, you need a **fast frame rate**. What is frame rate? This is how fast your computer can generate the images on the screen. A lot depends on the complexity of the scene, of course; showing a cube and a box is a lot faster than showing the city of Los Angeles with all of its buildings.

You can control this, of course, when you design the VR world you will implement.

Each image has to be generated, in real time. Most VR headsets try for 90 Hertz. Hertz refers to the frequency - in cycles per second, or in this case, frames per second.

The difficulty of VR is that nothing can slow down this frame rate. If something has to load, or a web page fetched, if you slow down the frame rate slightly, people get woozy.

There are two ways to speed up the frame rate. One is to have less scene complexity, the other is to have a fast computer.

A classic line in the Movie *Jaws* is when they discover that the shark is much bigger than they expect and it tears up their boat. Roy Scheider says, "*You're going to need a bigger boat.*"

To view VR, you're going to need a bigger computer.

Fortunately, computers keep get faster and faster. By computers, we also mean high-end smart cell phones. For the worlds we build here, a reasonably fast smart phone should be OK.

Scene complexity is a bit of a dilemma; you want a rich, detailed virtual world, but you also want that virtual world to render quickly. By render quickly, we mean 90 frames (updates) per second, as discussed previously. You also need to know your target audience in terms of hardware support. Are they all on high-end PCs with pairs of thousand dollar video cards? (somewhat an overkill; I'm making a point here.) Or are they on last year's cell phone models with a $10 cardboard box and some lenses? If you know your potential target audience, you can develop a VR application that works well with their system.

The United States Marine Corps has a saying: *"Train as you would fight."* During World War Two they practiced the combat operations of amphibious landings off the coast of Southern California. When they had to do this during the War in the Pacific, they hadn't planned for coral reefs. As a result, they developed a doctrine that you should train people in the same, or reasonably similar, environment that they were expected to fight in.

While a good VR experience is (hopefully) not life or death, this is still valuable advice. If you think most of your customers or consumers of your VR app will be on last year's cell phone, then test with last year's cell phone. If you think they will be on high-end PCs, test with a high-end PC.

Don't assume, if your VR app is slow, that customers will have much better computers and everything will be okay. Get something similar to what they use, and then you will suffer through the nausea and vertigo before your customers will, and then recode or simplify your scenes to be fast enough.

How much hardware is enough? For that, you should consult the minimum specifications of the headsets you plan to target. As this can change, I won't summarize it in this book, but the guidelines that different VR manufacturers give is good advice.

You may need a bigger PC (or cell phone); this is the price you pay to be an early adopter!

How to view VR?

To view VR, you need some type of headset or HMD. In the old days VR was also characterized by 3D images on 2D screens. In effect, VR back then meant any 3D program viewed with any device — basically sitting in front of your PC like normal, but this is not truly immersive. Today, VR means with an HMD/headset; so to view one, you need a headset.

Ironically, React VR works fine in a browser as a 3D world as well, and could be used to make parallax–capable web pages, although that's a bit overkill.

VR can be dangerous

You probably think, this is pretty safe. However, one VR headset came with 33 pages of warnings. *Read them.*

Most of the warnings are common sense, for example, don't wave your hands around if you are next to things or people. With what are essentially blinders on, you can really smack your hand. Philosophically, I don't believe in the nanny state, but you can really get hurt with VR. Imagine if someone gave you a blindfold, told you to put it on, and then wander around your house. You might be a little uncomfortable.

That's about what we're going to do in this book, except with the added wrinkle that you'll be wandering around in a state of wonder and excitement. There are plenty of YouTube videos where people smash walls, run into them, knock over lamps, and so on. They look silly, but when you have an HMD on, you are totally immersed in the virtual world and wouldn't think of pulling your punch. So, make sure you clear out of the room and warn friends not to come in.

This includes your furry friends. It's more difficult to keep out pets of your VR area, but a good idea as they won't understand that HMD has distracted you, and you can't see them. If you can find a way, it would be a good idea to prevent them from getting underfoot or you may step on them inadvertently.

VR is safe; use responsibly.

VR Headset options

With WebVR, there are a few options. I'll keep this to the simplest, most available headsets. You can certainly use **Open Source Virtual Reality (OSVR)**, which is actually a hardware platform, but you'll need to figure out what browser to use, and so on. Some of the terms, such as Gaze, will be covered later in the UI section. For now, Gaze movement means you need to stare at something for the UI to move you there or for you to select an object, typically.

Here are the various mainstream WebVR options (you can read about this at `https://webvr.info/`):

Type	Controls	Movement	Cost
Gear VR (Mobile)	1 handheld, HMD	Gaze/Touchpad	Medium
Daydream VR (Mobile)	1 handheld	Gaze/Touchpad	Medium
Cardboard/other headsets	None (click possible)	Gaze selection	Low
HTC Vive	Tracked, 2 controllers	Walk around	High
Oculus Rift 2 Camera	Keyboard/Joystick	Gaze Selection	High
Oculus Rift 3 Camera	Tracked, 2 controllers	Walk around	High

Types of headsets

Broadly characterized, they can be a PC-connected headset or a mobile headset. Some types of stand alone headsets, such as the Hololens or Vive stand–alone VR headset, include a fully working PC, so they are really more like a mobile headset, but don't require a PC.

Mobile headsets

Mobile headsets really just use your cell phone to display their data and put you into the VR world. As such, the performance is entirely based on what your cell phone can do.

This is a time when bigger really is better.

There is a limit though; there are some headsets that use tablets, but they are extremely heavy and don't really offer any advantages over a smaller mobile device.

While you use a mobile headset, you'll have battery life, weight, and control issues. There are various VR controllers in the market, as well as bundled options such as the Samsung Gear VR and Google Daydream, which include a controller as well as a case you put your phone into.

The nice thing about these bundles is that the phones are generally certified to work correctly and the software is easy to use. You can build your own VR headset/controller combination.

Mobile headsets can also be as simple as a box with some lenses in them, although there is actually a lot of math in the sizes and specifics of the optics. The most commonly referred to one is Google Cardboard; Google doesn't sell them directly but companies can implement Cardboard viewers. There is also the Unofficial Cardboard as well as a number of reasonably priced better built holders that you can put a cell phone into.

Generally speaking, most of them do not have sensors. Some have a small lever that will touch the screen, allowing some controls other than movement.

You can also purchase separate Bluetooth controllers, although they will most likely not have three–dimensional positioning. We cover different types of controllers in Chapter 11, *Take a Walk on the Wild Side.*

Some VR headsets work with glasses and some do not--a lot depends on your face size, the size of the glasses you use, and your exact vision issues. I have both a nearsighted eye and a farsighted eye, and do not need glasses (for either eye!), but your mileage may vary. I highly recommend trying out a headset before purchasing, or purchasing from a source that has a good return policy.

At the high end (of mobile headsets), there is the Samsung Gear VR and Google Daydream. These offer a well–constructed headset, which you again put a cell phone into, as well as a separate controller.

The controller is the most important part of this (although the headset is also worth it as they are much more comfortable than even the best Cardboard viewers). The controller in both the Daydream and Gear VR bundles are Bluetooth, meaning wireless, and are sort of tracked.

They have sensors in them that will detect movement, but are not precisely positioned in space. As a result, they have center buttons on them. This is because the type of three-dimensional positional sensors in these units will drift over time. In the VR world, it will seem as if your hand/control/gun (or whatever visual representation the controller has) will drift away from you or even move behind you! This can be very disconcerting. If/when this happens, merely use the appropriate button to recenter your controller.

Higher–end PC setups have different types of tracking, and re-centering is not usually required. However, note that they need initial calibration/setup and can have tracking issues as well.

Notes on GearVR

A few things with the GearVR I did a little wrong. There's an extra elastic strap that I thought was for slack or something; its not. They tell you to put the straps on, but neglect to mention this extra strap is to hold the controller. Flip ahead to the controller part before putting the straps on the headset.

The controller should actually be the part you fiddle with first. You need to pair it and carry out some downloads, and that can't really be done when the headset is on, so do this part first.

PC, Mac, and Linux headsets

Most people think choosing a PC headset will be between the HTC Vive or the Oculus Rift, but there are dozens or hundreds of PC type headsets.

All of them will perform based on how well your PC performs. Folks, this is where a Mac has a bit of a disadvantage; you need a fast video card, and Mac's typically are fast enough for graphics and some game play, but not for VR. However, Apple has introduced VR ready PCs. When you decide what platform to do React VR with, consider this.

As this is written, Mac support for the Oculus Rift or HTC Vive is experimental at best, so the steps and examples will assume you are using a PC. Linux support was promised for several of the headsets, but as this book is written it is experimental at best. If you are using Linux, you will need to check the documentation and/or follow along the Windows examples as best you can.

Most of the React VR demos have simpler geometry than a lot of VR worlds, so they will run on comparatively smaller hardware. Check with the manufacturer of your headset for minimums; don't think you can get by with less than the minimum. You'll get sick or have a less than comfortable experience.

Of the whole marketplace, there are really just two headsets we will cover in this book; the HTC Vive and the Oculus Rift. If you have a different headset, the samples should work OK, but you may need to fiddle with them slightly.

Generally speaking, PC, Mac, and Linux headsets will work with Firefox or an experimental browser, `Servo.org`. An experimental version of Chrome (Chromium) may also work to view WebVR. See the complete up to date list at `webvr.info`.

Summary

In this chapter, we've covered VR, why it works, and what it really is (pun intended). We've also covered how to get into a VR world with a brief overview of VR hardware and software.

Remember, even if you don't have an expensive HTC Vive or Oculus Rift, you can still view WebVR on your desktop PC.

Next, we will cover how to program VR at a very high level. There are many different ways to build VR software applications, and we will cover the different ways, and their advantages and disadvantages. You'll read an overview of the different software packages, and the advantage of WebVR. As this book is about WebVR, we will then cover installation of React VR, Node.js, and other tools to begin to make your own reality — really!

2
Flatland and Beyond: VR Programming

In the last chapter, you learned about what VR is and what it can be. How is it that programmers and developers (like you) create these virtual worlds? We found out that it is a difficult thing to do right. We have to maintain fast frame rates and proper stereoscopic rendering. How do we do that quickly and easily? Read on and find out how.

In this chapter, we'll cover the following topics:

- HTML and common programming methods, such as Node.js, JavaScript, and game engines
- The React Library
- Graphics libraries, for displaying 2D and 3D images
- How to install all of these software so that we can begin programming

HTML and ways to move beyond the 2D internet

While the web was developed, the early HTML language has evolved dramatically. A good web page experience typically involves more than just HTML. One of those ways to add more interactivity is via JavaScript. The combination of HTML, XML, and JavaScript is a large portion of what delivers the web, including applications, such as Google Documents or online Microsoft Word (also free).

These are, however, flat. To move into the third dimension has traditionally taken high–speed software, usually written in C++. As computers have gotten faster and faster and **Graphics Processing Units (GPU)** have taken over the bulk of the actual 3D generation, languages to describe 3D games have evolved.

There are currently quite a number of ways to program in VR. It is challenging to generate 90 frames per second at the resolution the Rift and Vive display at, so most VR programming is done in high-speed languages, that are direct to the metal or low level, such as C and C++. Game engines, such as Unity, Unreal, or Cryengine, however, do a lot of this for you.

At first, you may be thinking *why should I use a game engine? I'm not writing a game*. More generally, these engines are constructed for games, but do not have to build just games. Modern game engines handle rendering (what we need), physics (we need this to build realistic worlds), terrain (for outdoor scenes), lighting (for sophisticated rendering), Artificial Intelligence (to populate our world), networking (to build multi–user environments), and other code. None of this is necessarily game specific, although all of the various game engines do have nomenclature more suited for games than, say, enterprise data visualization. For example, in Unity a basic 3D object is referred to as a `GameObject`. So even if you aren't writing a game, you will have `GameObject`s.

Currently, the top contenders for VR software are:

- Unity (by Unity3D, more at `http://bit.ly/UnityForVR`)
- Unreal (by Epic games, makers of Unreal Tournament; more at `http://bit.ly/UnrealForVR`)
- Cryengine (by Crytek, makers of the game Crysis; more at `http://bit.ly/CrytekForVR`)
- Lumberyard (by Amazon; more at `http://bit.ly/LumberyardForVR`)

Many of these game engines also work on mobile platforms. The advantage of using a game engine is that you can *write once, run anywhere,* meaning that most of them have mobile support as well as PC support. Basically, you build a PC app, then change your build settings and build a mobile app. You now have two or more different apps for each platform.

There can be quite a steep learning curve with game engines, although it is still easier than writing your own rendering code. You do need to build an entire application, and that can be daunting.

Contrast this to the current state-of-the-art in web programming, people just want to describe what you want to see, not write the server-side code to send the web pages to your phone, nor write custom applications to download that information and display it.

So, why would VR require you to do that?

With React VR, you don't have to.

Instead of learning a game programming engine, you can build your worlds with JavaScript. You build a VR world and UI with declarative components, instead of building rendering code. In effect, you can operate at a higher level to describe what your VR world has in it, instead of building that world a pixel at a time. Doesn't that sound like more fun?

Background of Node.js and JavaScript

Say Node.js out loud. Gesundheit!

Node.js is an open source system for using JavaScript on the server side. It is, of course, the primary way that web browsers execute code. It was invented way back in the early days of the web for several reasons.

React and React VR make heavy use of JavaScript. To render React web pages to a browser requires server-side JavaScript, meaning that the web server doesn't just send the files to the browser, but rather executes code at the server side. Node.js allows you to program server-side code in the same language as the browser. For full-stack developers, this is ideal, as you can immerse yourself in one language.

Making servers React

React VR is based on React, a framework that allows web pages and interactive User Interfaces to built by declaration instead of programming. You build views for each state in the application, and then React will use the correct components to display that application.

Declarative views make your code easier, more robust, and easier to modify and debug.

Components use the Object-Oriented concept of encapsulation, meaning they are self-sufficient and manage their own state. You then take these components and use them to make complex UIs.

React allows developers to create applications that change over time, without having to constantly refresh a browser page. It uses the Model-View-Controller design pattern/template and can be used in combination with other JavaScript libraries, such as Angular.JS.

React was first used with Facebook's newsfeed in 2011. It was made open-source in March, 2015.

You can find more details about React at `https://facebook.github.io/react/`.

Graphics libraries — OpenGL and WebGL

This section covers general 3D programming, but some discussion of different things is in order.

OpenGL is a standard for displaying graphics. Without getting into PC versus Workstation politics (ancient history now), it was a standard that a workstation vendor (SGI) pioneered to standardize computer graphics and the ability for programs to display graphics.

There are other APIs, such as DirectX, which was backed by Microsoft and many PC game developers, CAD software, and other PC computer graphics.

OpenGL is not, strictly speaking, open source; yet the software can be used without royalty payments and is documented and freely available (to be fair, so is DirectX).

Basically, OpenGL is a way for software to display graphics. Software, in this case, usually means C++ (or other languages that can call native libraries and O/S utilities).

Vulkan is more or less an intended successor to OpenGL. It is on a lower level than OpenGL, and offers more ability to perform parallel tasking and directly utilize the power of the GPUs that are in most smart phones and PCs. As it is a low-level format, you'll hear more discussion of Vulkan with computer graphics, and less about Web graphics. As with OpenGL, it is usually used by a compiled native mode software (C++, and so forth).

WebGL is a JavaScript API for rendering 3D graphics within a web browser, without requiring plugins. As SGI, the creator of OpenGL, is no longer in business, both OpenGL and WebGL are now supported, defined, and marketed by the Khronos group, a non for profit, member funded consortium. WebGL is used via JavaScript or other browser supported languages.

The **three.js** is a series of JavaScript files that make WebGL easier to program in. It is, however, a fairly large download.

React VR is built on three.JS and React.

A-Frame is another WebGL frontend; it has a similar concept to Rea
declarative and high level and built on three.js. You don't have to (
them up to make a cube; you just declare a cube and give it a pos'
While this book primarily covers React VR, here are a few differences.

- React VR apps are written in **JSX**. It is a syntax that allows HTML-like ...
  mixed into JavaScript code. React VR is based on React and React Native. If you
  already know React, you can pick up React VR very quickly, and the underlying
  concepts are the same, so you will feel like a native.
- A-Frame apps use HTML, with custom HTML tags. It is a powerful framework,
  providing a declarative, composable, reusable entity-component structure for
  three.js. A-Frame can be used from HTML, although developers still have access
  to JavaScript, DOM APIs, three.js, WebVR, and WebGL.
- Both of them allow for custom JavaScript code and interfacing directly to three.js
  and WebGL.

But why make a decision? You don't have to. You can use both. Let's install React VR.

Installation of Node.js and React VR

Most desktop VR hardware currently available use Windows; because of this, the following
instructions, and indeed most of this book will be a mixture of Windows installations and
GearVR viewing. At the time of writing, Linux could be hacked to work with the HTC Vive
and Oculus Rift, but it's a difficult road and a bit beyond the scope of this book. Apple PCs
are just adding the capability to add an external video card for VR, as most of them simply
do not have the video processing capability to render VR at the resolutions used by the Vive
and Rift headsets.

React is, however, not PC specific. You could build all of the examples in this book with
Linux or a Mac, and follow alongside, and use a Google Daydream, Unofficial Cardboard,
or Samsung Gear VR to view all of the samples. In this case, some of the examples may use
slightly different syntax. I wrote the book so that the majority of users with a Vive and Rift
could follow along, and I apologize in advance for the platform restrictions for the rest of
you.

Why can't we all just get along?

Where possible, I will include links and information for other platforms.

stallation of Node.js

e will assume you know what platform you are on and have a computer (desktop PC) that is capable of having Node.js and React VR installed.

First, we will need to install Node.js. If you already have it installed, that's great, just make sure (at the time of the writing of the book) you have at least version 4.0. This book was constructed with the LTS Version: v6.11.0 and v8.5.0, which should be stable and out by the time you read this. (Includes npm 3.10.10)

1. You should be able to get Node.js from: `https://nodejs.org/en/download/`. Download the 64-bit `.msi` prebuilt installer file. Once it downloads, double-click on the file or run it, depending on your browser.
   We live in a nanny state, so it warns you that you are downloading native code. Then again, people get taken out all the time by spear phishing (virus emails that make you infect yourself). This one should be safe.

   These warnings only come up if the program you are downloading has not been digitally signed. A digital code signing certificate is not that hard to get; insist that companies and non-profit organizations sign their code.

   It will make the internet safer.

   Do this for any code you release.

2. Click **Next**.

3. I know, but you really should read the terms and conditions--agree and click on **Next**.

4. The default location is fine. Thank gosh we don't have to worry about Linux that can't handle spaces in filenames (just kidding with all of you Linux folks).

5. Most of the installation options are okay. They don't require a lot of space, so it's okay to install everything.

6. Click on **Install**.

7. You may (should) get an alert that a piece of software is installing; tell Windows it's okay.

8. You've finished! Time to install the rest of React VR. Click on **Finish**.

Node.js for Mac:

The Node.js organization recommends using Homebrew: https://brew.sh/.
But, you can also install Node.js via the Node.js download
page: https://nodejs.org/en/download/.
Installation should be straightforward.

Node.js for Linux:

While the source code is here: https://nodejs.org/en/download/, you
can download Node.js a little easier from the package manager;
instructions are here: https://nodejs.org/en/download/package-manager/.
Installation should be straightforward; this is Linux, so I'm sure you can
handle any wrinkles.

Post Node.js installation — installing React VR

The Node.js software includes a package manager called npm. Package managers install software, as well as that software's dependencies. You will use this to install React VR. It makes the installation very easy and up to date. Whatever your platform, you will need to get to a Command Prompt to work with most of the examples in this book. A Command Prompt is the window incorrectly referred to as DOS. In Windows, this is referred to as the Node.js **Command Line Interface (CLI)** tool, although the actual title is Node.js command prompt. The Node.js installer set this up when it installed. You should use the CLI from the installation, as it sets up certain environment variables and the like. After having said that, I use an alternative command-line tool called **Take Command Console (TCC)**, and after Node.js did the installation and registered path variables (part of the install), I can run npm and other commands from my TCC shell.

The installation steps are as follows:

1. Open up your preferred CLI (Start | `Node.js command prompt`)
2. Type the command:

```
npm install -g react-vr-cli
```

You can do this from any location (folder) and the package manager (npm command) will install the following:

If you run this program a second time, the nice thing is it will confirm what's already there (although like a lot of open source programs, it's a bit terse).

npm has a lot of other very useful options. For example, you can use `npm ls`, which will (just like `ls` in linux) give you a list of all objects installed. You can get exhaustive documentation by running the command `npm help npm`, which will open a web page.

3. Then, we want to use the same CLI to install the `WelcomeToVR` sample. First, go to a place (folder/directory) where you'd like to install your samples and code. I have a second, large hard drive installed as F: (your mileage, platform, and disk configuration will vary). So, before I started installing everything on my desktop, or my documents, I switched to my data drive:

```
f:
mkdir f:      2;reactVR
cd \reactVR
```

4. Then, I went ahead and used the ReactCLI to install the `WelcomeToVR` demo:

```
f:\reactVR>react-vr init WelcomeToVR
```

The process will start:

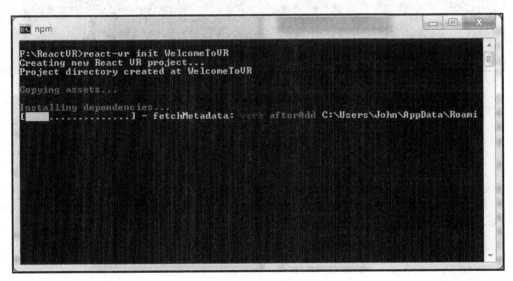

This will take quite a while. At the end of the process, it'll finish and tell you what to do next:

5. Then, go into your `WelcomeToVR` project directory that the tool just created, and initialize/start the local development server:

```
cd WelcomeToVR
npm start
```

This process will take a little while. While this runs, this command-line interface window will be busy running the program. It is not a service. If you close the window, it'll stop. So, don't close the window.

This window will also show helpful status information when you visit your various web pages:

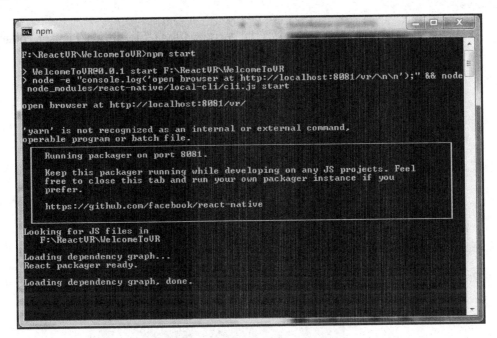

6. Then, from your desktop, open your browser to `http://localhost:8081/vr/index.html`, as the nice CLI tells you. You're done!

There is an easier way to go to this URL than opening your web browser, and typing the URL in the CLI window. You should turn on *quick edit mode*. Screenshots showing this are as follows:

1. Click on the little C:\ window in the corner of the CLI window. This is called the System Menu:

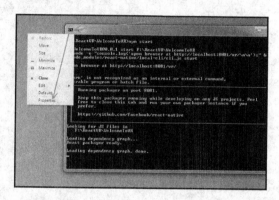

2. Once you've done that, click on **Properties**. Once in **Properties**, turn on **Quick Edit Mode:**

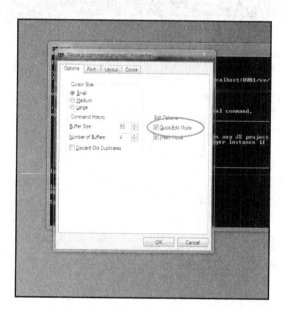

2. Click **OK**. Now, that **Quick Edit Mode** is turned on, you can highlight text in the window and press *Enter* to select. Then, you can paste the URL directly into your WebVR-enabled browser. Easy!

3. If, like me, you like to use a CLI different from COMMAND.COM (I use 4nt or TCC), assuming a default install as we discussed, you just have to add to your path the following, assuming you installed Node.js in the default location:

```
C:\Users\<user>\AppData\Roaming\npm;C:\Program Files\nodejs.
```

Installation of a WebVR browser

Now that you have the server-side software installed, you'll need to install a web browser that is capable of displaying WebGL, OpenGL, and WebVR. This changes constantly, so I highly recommend going to WebVR and checking their compatibility list.

Firefox, or the experimental Firefox Nightly is probably the easiest browser to use. For more information, refer to `http://bit.ly/WebVRInfo`.

The good news is that regular WebVR support is built into Firefox as of version 55, so just make sure you are up to date with Firefox and you can view WebVR. To view your new VR site that you just generated, you'll need to do the following steps:

1. Ensure your browser can run JavaScript. This is the default unless you've locked down your browser in a security conscious way (which is a good thing). WebVR uses JavaScript extensively. You can also add localhost to your white-list.
2. Once you bring up your WebVR-enabled browser (on PC, basically Chromium, Firefox Nightly, or IE), you will see **hello**. However, you are not in VR yet! You need to click on the **View in VR**. Your VR app should start. You can then put on your headset, and you will see a simple **hello**. No World? You're in a VR World!

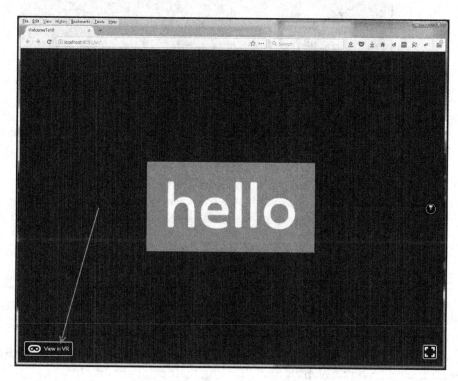

3. You will see a link that says **View in VR**. Until you click on this (on your regular desktop), your Vive/Oculus will not work.

4. Once you click on **View in VR**, and put on your headset, you will see the **hello** in your VR world!

Congratulations! You've built your first VR world. I bet that was a lot faster than learning Unity.

You can also view with a mobile VR, but you'll need to find out the IP address of your development machine, and go to that website from the mobile device, something like: `http://192.168.1.100/vr`.

In the URL `http://localhost:8081/vr/index.html`, you substitute `localhost` with the IP address of your server (your desktop development PC).

Note this is almost certainly not the correct IP address, you'll need to get the IP address from your development machine/server and enter that into the mobile VR headset. For Windows, go to the network properties, or from a CLI type `ipconfig`. If your desktop PC is 192.168.0.100, from the mobile headset, you type out (from the virtual keyboard) `http://192.168.0.100:8081/vr/index.html`.

Clean your mobile screen

If you don't, any specs, fingerprints, or crud on the screen will show up sharply in focus. These specs will be distracting as they will seem to hover in front of everything.

Congratulations! You've run and viewed your first React VR world!

Now, if you don't have a headset or get a little tired of taking the headset on and off and having to walk out of your room-scale bounds to get back to your PC, there is a quick way to preview the world. In Firefox Nightly, you can just click on the small radar display and what is on the screen will show you what one eye would see in the VR headset. This is really useful for developers like you!

Summary

In this chapter, we covered the basics of how to actually program VR worlds, and what software to use. We also went through installing the React VR system so that we could develop our own VR worlds! In the next chapter, we'll cover 3D basics and the math that we will need to build our VR worlds.

Don't worry about the math; there won't be a popup quiz.

Now to actually create an interesting world. But first, we need to understand what the world consists of. The next section will describe the React VR terminology to describe your virtual world.

3

3D or Reality in Dimensions Other than X and Y

We've decided to step into a virtually real world. To understand how to draw that world, we'll need to understand exactly how to describe it.

This chapter describes how we do that in a mathematical sense. Don't worry, this is not a return to high–school math! (Well, maybe geometry. OK, so maybe a little bit. OK, maybe a lot. I'll try to make it painless.)

There are many different ways to describe the world; it is still the same world no matter how we do so. As Shakespeare said in Romeo and Juliet:

"What's in a name? That which we call a rose by any other name would smell as sweet."

In our case, interestingly, this is not so: a box described incorrectly will look totally different. You need to learn the language. Not only that, you need to learn how React VR describes the world, as different 3D graphics programs all use different numbers (scaling), directions (vectors), and rotations.

With virtual worlds, the types of software and hardware all require different ways of describing the things you see. For example, coordinates can be left handed or right handed. If you mix them up, objects will move in a different direction than you had intended them to!

In particular, up has different meanings in 3D; more specifically, the up direction typically is not standard between different 3D programs. In React VR, Y is up. Why is Y up? Read on to learn about:

- Coordinates: These are fixing points in space
- Points: These are building blocks for polygons
- Vectors: These are directions
- Transforms: These are moving things to where you want them
- Rendering: This turns this discussion of points and transforms into something real

Beyond flatland - 3D concepts

To represent things in 3D, we have to translate what we see into things that the computer can use to generate images. These methods will involve files with 3D geometry, pictures, and code. First, let's discuss how we position things in 3D.

To represent objects in 3D, we need their locations. A spreadsheet such as Excel uses A-Z (across) and 1-66 down (actually, A-XFD and 1-1048576). Computer graphics use numbers for all three axes. However, there are different ways to code these coordinates.

This applies to both the scale (what is one, an inch? One mile?) and what direction they go (is it Y or Z that is up?). To figure this out, we need to talk about coordinate systems.

Coordinates

We're all used to graph paper, grids, glowing spreadsheets with X and Y grids, or, numbers and letters like A1 and B1 in whatever spreadsheet program you use. Moving into the third dimension can be confusing, even though that's where we live. This is why I called this section *Beyond flatland*.

Math operations we take for granted in two dimensions or general math turn out to be just different in three dimensions. For example, if you multiply X and Y, you get the same answer as if you multiplied Y and X. Yet in three dimensions, rotations do not behave that way. To see this in action, try taking both copies of this book. (I bought two copies, didn't you? Mom, aren't you reading it?)

OK, seriously, please pick up any two books, real books on paper. If you have two Kindles, you could use those.

1. With book number one:
   1. Physically flip it (while closed) a quarter turn left to right (toward your right hand).
   2. Then, flip the back edge toward you (flip it over).
   3. You are now looking at the back page, sideways.
2. With book number two, flip it in the opposite order:
   1. Flip the back edge toward you (flip it over).
   2. Then rotate it a quarter turn clockwise left to right (toward your right hand).

The two books are facing different directions, even though you rotated them the same way both times, just in a slightly different order.

Three-dimensional math can be confusing. Normally, if you multiply *A* and *B*, you get the same results as if you multiply *B* by *A*.

This concept is very important when it comes to translations, rotations, and scaling. Where your objects end up in the world and what they look like is dependent on the order you code it in.

We will use three numbers to designate a location for everything in 3D, specifically *X*, *Y*, and *Z*.

 This is called a **Cartesian coordinate system**. There are other types of coordinate systems, but nearly every computer system uses a Cartesian system for spatial locations. Rotations and vectors will sometimes use other systems. This is a **Euclidean space**.

To make 3D more confusing, some people use *X* and *Y*, with *Z* being the new dimension, while others say *Y* is up. Why is (it) up? When dealing with a screen, you're used to using *X* and *Y*. A sheet of paper is similar, although paper is usually horizontal and a screen is vertical.

This causes an interesting issue of conversion to 3D. In 3D, we use *X*, *Y*, and *Z*. If you're used to using *X* and *Y*, then the *Z* has to be the new third dimension, and it would be up. If, however, you're used to thinking of *X* and *Y* as a piece of graph paper, then *Y* is already up and so *Z* ends up being in and out. Each 3D system seems to be slightly different.

WebGL, which React VR is based on, uses the familiar X and Y as right/left and up/down; so Z has to be in/out. However, one difference is that in React VR, Y is up; in standard HTML, Y is down. In other words, HTML and React use a coordinate of (zero by zero) as the upper left-hand corner. Is Y is up? Most 3D programs use Y or Z as up, meaning in our case positive Y is up.

WebGL and HTML are different than React, and may take some getting used to. To put an object forward in front of you so you can see it, you'll need to give it a negative Z.

In 3D, coordinates can be left handed or right handed. As we've seen with X, Y, and Z, sometimes arrows don't go in the direction you'd expect. Why didn't React VR (really, it was OpenGL) decide to make Z go in the screen? Then the coordinates would be left handed. Instead, most graphics systems use a right handed coordinate system.

My brother is left handed.
Nothing wrong with a south paw.
(Actually, he's right handed, but why spoil a good story with the facts?)

What in the world does right versus left handed mean? It is a mnemonic that helps with the direction of the arrows and with rotations. If you take either hand and spread your first three digits out, they spell out the X, Y and Z directions. A diagram would help; your first three digits (thumb, index, middle finger) point in positive X, Y, and Z:

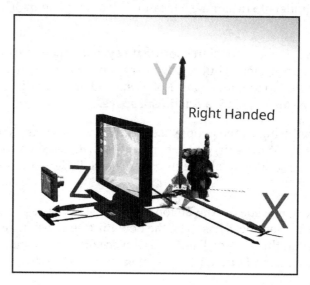

In this diagram, there are a few things to note. The camera represents us on the left, looking into the screen (depicted transparently). Because *Y* is up (why?) and *X* is to the right, the coordinate system that OpenGL uses isn't similar to HTML or to a piece of graph paper, but it is more or less a standard with the web.

This was chosen to map more easily to the way that 3D models, **Computer Aided Design (CAD)**, and modeling programs (such as Blender, Maya, 3DSMax) are constructed. It is backwards from the way that React works—*Y* is positive going down with React. This is a right handed system; if you try to do this with your left hand, you get a different order of the *X*, *Y* and *Z* axes.

What about rotations?

Rotations around any axis with React VR and OpenGL are also right handed. This means a positive rotation around any axis will go in the direction the thumb points and the fingers curl. For example:

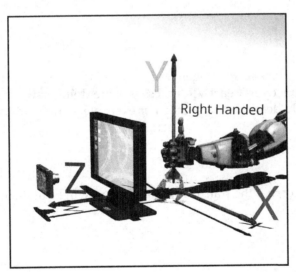

Are you looking at your right hand and curling your fingers? It's OK, it helps to visualize. Yes, those are arrows showing the positive direction along the respective axes.

Honestly, *Y* is up and *Z* is up seem to be pretty commonly mixed in the 3D CAD world. Your CAD system may work differently. It's OK, we can flip and invert it - just be aware that when importing models, you may find them on their side, or even inside out.

In particular, in Blender *Z* is up and *X* and *Y* are in the flat plane; however, it can substitute *Y* for up when you export. Why? Because it's on the up and up.

These numbers are dimensionless; a cube that is 1 x 1 x 1 can be thought of as 1 mile or 1 foot. However, in WebVR and React VR, the units are commonly thought of in meters.

Blender can use dimensionless units, metric, or imperial, so you'll need to fiddle with scaling when importing things.

The program Poser uses odd units—you will need to scale anything coming from it.

OBJ files, commonly used for importing models, have no unit information; they are dimensionless: 1 is 1, not 1 meter.

Points

Points refer to 3D locations in space, generally identified via *X*, *Y*, and *Z* locations. A point is rarely described directly in React VR, unless you are doing native rendering, but locations in space are frequently described as points. For example, a transform node may say:

```
transform: [{
        translate: [0, 400, 700]
        }]
```

The center of the object that the transform is applied to will be at the location *X*=0, *Y*=400, *Z*=700.

Vectors

Vectors refer to a direction. In Aviation, pilots talk about vectors. From the scene in the movie *Airplane*, Clarence Oveur, Roger Murdock, Victor Basta, and the control tower discuss heading: (http://bit.ly/WhatsOurVector)

> *"Roger Murdock: Flight 2-0-9'er, you are cleared for take-off.*
> *Captain Oveur: Roger!*
> *Roger Murdock: Huh?*
> *Tower voice: L.A. departure frequency, 123 point 9'er.*

Captain Oveur: Roger!
Roger Murdock: Huh?
Victor Basta: Request vector, over.
Captain Oveur: What?
Tower voice: Flight 2-0-9'er cleared for vector 324.
Roger Murdock: We have clearance, Clarence.
Captain Oveur: Roger, Roger. What's our vector, Victor?
Tower voice: Tower's radio clearance, over!
Captain Oveur: That's Clarence Oveur. Over."

From our standpoint as VR people, they really mean heading. In 3D space, you can also be aimed up or down. All three directions are very important to us.

Translations, properly speaking, use vectors; if you give a transform property to an object of [0, 2, 0], you are telling the object to move 2 units in the +Y direction, not necessarily to an absolute position of 0,2,0. However, note that if the object's origin is at 0,0,0, then it is the same. It is important to consider the origin of your 3D objects when translating them, and whether objects take absolute or relative positioning.

Transforms

This is not a book about bizarre foldable robots, so we are talking about transforms, not Transformers.

Transforms are ways to place, position, move, and scale objects, essentially, anything that transforms the X, Y, Z coordinates of an object, point, and so on.

In React VR, transforms are usually part of a style. For example:

```
style={{
    transform: [
        {rotateZ : this.state.rotation},
        {translate: [0, 2, 0]},
        {scale : 0.01 },
    ],
}
```

Transform order is very important. As we discussed earlier, in 3D, transforms are not transitive—if you translate, then rotate, you end up in a different spot than if you rotate, then translate. Remember the book example?

In React VR, the Transform is a standard props node for most objects that have a physical presence. (See Appendix and `Chapter 4`, *The React VR Library*.)

Transforms take really three main arguments (and a number of deprecated props); a transform, or matrix arguments.

Yes, I said the matrix.

A matrix has always been a mathematical concept for quite some time. It also made a great movie. Due to copyright restrictions, I can't include a picture of the matrix here, but above is my representation of our VR controller scene viewed in the matrix. In any event, I don't mean the movie. We will use the matrix to create 3D scenes of our own.

A matrix is a mathematical way to describe translation (vectors), rotations, scaling, and skewing. Some of my friends get skewed on the weekends, but skewing is a mathematical term meaning to shift, say, the top of an object more than the bottom. You might think of it as tilted.

To fully understand matrices, let's talk about the non-Keanu Reeves way of doing it.

Anytime there is a physical object, such as a box, a model, a light, or a VR button, you have various style props, one of which is a transform. A transform node can use matrices, or, a little easier sometimes, direct translation properties. For example, if you define a `Cylinder` in React VR, you might transform it like this:

```
<Cylinder
        radiusTop={0}
        radiusBottom={2.20}
        dimHeight={2.8}
        segments={10}
        style={{
                transform: [
                {rotateX: -45},
                {translate: [0,1, -4]}
                {scale: .4}
                ]
            }}
        />
```

Transform order is important. Here is an example of three cylinders, identical except for their color and transforms:

```
<Cylinder
    radiusTop={2}
    radiusBottom={2.20}
    dimHeight={5}
    segments={10}
    lit = {true }
    style={{
      color: 'red',
      transform: [
        {translate: [1,.5, -6]},
        {rotateZ: -90},
        {scale: .2}
      ]
    }}
/>
<Cylinder
    radiusTop={2}
    radiusBottom={2.20}
    dimHeight={5}
    segments={10}
    lit = {true }
    style={{
      color: 'blue',
      transform: [
        {rotateZ: -90},
```

```
            {translate: [1,.5, -6]},
            {scale: .2}
        ]
    }}
/>
<Cylinder
    radiusTop={2}
    radiusBottom={2.20}
    dimHeight={5}
    segments={10}
    lit = {true }
    style={{
        color: 'green',
        transform: [
            {scale: .2},
            {rotateZ: -90},
            {translate: [1,.5, -6]}
        ]
    }}
/>
```

This is the resulting React VR world:

What about the matrix?

A matrix is a four column by four row series (array) of numbers.

You can use a matrix in the transform node as well. A complete discussion of matrix math is beyond the scope of this book. There are plenty of reference materials on the web. The basic concept is fairly straightforward, but rotations can be a bit difficult (although deterministic) to program free-hand.

Translations are stored as:

```
[1, 0, 0, 0,
 0, 1, 0, 0,
 0, 0, 1, 0,
 Tx,Ty,Tz,1].
```

Scaling is represented by:

```
[Sx,0, 0, 0,
 0, Sy,0, 0,
 0, 0, Sz,0,
 0, 0, 0, 1].
```

Rotations can be represented by the R values in:

```
[R00,R01,R02,0,
 R10,R11,R12,0,
 R20,R21,R22,0,
 0, 0, 0, 1].
```

Rotations via matrix math are very precise, but also very complicated. As we saw earlier, the order of rotations will change the location of the resulting object. A matrix does not have these problems as the order is baked into the matrix itself. Calculating the rotations can be messy. Generally speaking, you'll want to use the transform styles instead of the matrix math, when moving an object by hand (manual coding).

You'll want to use matrices when copying an object's position and orientation or programmatically moving it.

A `matrix` that scales all axes by one tenth and translates by [3, 2, 1] can be applied as a `matrix` as such:

```
style={{
    transform: [
        {matrix : [0.1,0,0,0, 0,0.1,0,0, 0,0,0.1,0, 3,2,1,1]},
    ],
}}
```

You cannot use a transform matrix and a transform style (separate translate, rotate, scale) at the same time. There is really no need to, as you can do everything with a matrix you would do by specifying individual transformations. If you do use a matrix, you're pretty hardcore! In any event, any transforms that you create will be converted to a matrix behind the scenes.

Welcome to the matrix - now you can create it.

Rendering

Bing defines rendering as:

rend·er·ing

[ˈrend(ə)riNG] ◀))

NOUN

1. a performance of a piece of music or drama:
    "her fine rendering of "Che farò senza Eurydice" was enough to win her strong commendation"

2. the action of applying plaster to a wall.

3. the action of giving, yielding, or surrendering something:
    "the rendering of dues"

Well, that was fun, but is obviously not what we mean. Rendering refers to taking all of the mathematical description we've been discussing and making something visual out of it.

The rendering engine used with React VR is three.js (http://bit.ly/2wHI8S9), which normally uses WebGL for rendering (http://bit.ly/2wKoKCe). WebGL is a robust JavaScript API for generating high performance graphics. It will use any high performance graphics hardware (GPU) in your system, and is native in most browsers, allowing 3D graphics without requiring plugins.

Usually, however, the web can be a wild place. You would think browser manufacturers would have learned from the compatibility problems of 20 years ago, but sadly this is not the case. There may be wrinkles or issues with some browsers, especially on mobile.

Can't we all just get along?

This will affect how well React VR works. If you want to see whether your browser and hardware support WebGL, go to the WebGL test page at `http://bit.ly/WebGLTestPage`. The page will display a spinning cube; it may also display some warnings if you use a browser that is not one hundred percent compatible. The WebGL Wikipedia page (`http://bit.ly/2wKoKCe`) has a good description of which browsers do what, but things change.

You need to test.

Testing how it looks

In World War II, the Marines tested amphibious landings extensively before the War in the Pacific. They had tactics and strategy down.

The first landing they did, they hit coral reefs. There are no coral reefs in San Diego/Camp Pendleton. As a result, although it was a successful landing, it was a bit more calamitous than they thought it would be. As a result, the Marine Corps has a saying:

"Train as you would fight."

This has apparently been a long–standing saying. The Roman Legion used to say:

"Training should be a bloodless battle, so that in battle, it will be just like bloody training."

-Roman Legion Training Maxim

If you get used to using Firefox, send your React VR solution out into the world, and your Aunt Petunia uses the Orchestra browser to view your world, it may not work, and Aunt Petunia will still think you're that shiftless spawn of her aimless sibling. Note that Orchestra isn't a real browser as far as I know, although I use Opera.

If this is an internal company-only app, and you have a standard (and can enforce it!) of only one browser, then you can test and develop with that browser.

If, however, you want a wide number of people to use your React VR app, you really should test with a variety of browsers. If you have a Mac, a PC, and a Linux machine, so much the better. These can be virtual machines (especially Windows, with the appropriate license, and Linux), otherwise you need beta testers.

You need to test it like you expect people to use it, otherwise you'll think it works fine but people will not be happy with your virtual world. You'll need to test with as many browsers and hardware platforms as you can. Of course, this is not really practical, but it is necessary. This is where beta testers can come in handy.

How rendering works

We were talking about rendering. This is the process of taking the mathematical model, with the attributes expressed, and turning it into something you can see on your screen.

To render your models in VR, React VR uses WebGL, which is based on OpenGL. WebGL is a JavaScript implementation and should, generally, look the same on most platforms if they have a fairly functional implementation in the browser. If you describe an upright red arrow, then in all browsers it will look like an arrow pointing up. The advice about testing is generally to make sure that it works at all, not so much to make sure an up arrow will not suddenly point to the right.

In the game industry, people usually have to make a decision between DirectX and OpenGL. WebVR uses neither, although WebGL is based on the design of OpenGL. Unlike OpenGL, it also includes HTML elements such as HTML5 canvas and DOM (Document Object Model). If you are using WebVR, you are using WebGL.

If a browser you are testing doesn't show your scene right, but does in other browsers, *please* file a bug report. Many of these applications are, like most cool things on the internet, bleeding edge.

You want these bugs fixed — so tell people. Programmers can't fix what they don't know about. You'll be contributing to a saner, cleaner, more effective web.

Be part of the solution!

WebGL will generally use your high performance GPU, through either OpenGL or through DirectX. You don't need to worry about, nor are you able to control, what React VR uses (unless going native), although this is an advantage. The web browser will generally do the right thing and use any hardware available on either mobile (phones, tablets), laptop, or desktop machine.

What if you want to control rendering more precisely? That is possible with React VR Native, which we will cover in more detail in a later chapter.

Summary

In this chapter, we learned the important ways to describe our VR world. If you want to think about it this way, we're learning the language of the matrix, and it even involves matrices. We learned about 3D coordinates, points, vectors, right-and left-handed worlds, and transforms.

We learned how all of these concepts come together and are rendered, and how the different web pages take that information and create a visual space out of it. We also learned to test!

To be able to test, we need something in the browser. To do that, we need to know not only how to describe the world in terms of numbers and rotations, but also how these numbers are used in building blocks. The next section will cover the keywords, components, and objects that React VR uses to describe the world.

4

The React VR Library

This chapter is about the layout of the React VR library; the objects and components in it. Many of the concepts in this chapter will be referenced in later chapters, so if you are reading an electronic version of this book, it will be heavily hyperlinked for your enjoyment and pleasure.

React VR has six basic elements within it and is coded with a new, yet familiar, paradigm called JSX (JavaScript eXtension). If you already know React, you are already familiar with React VR, although there are important differences. We will cover the following:

- JSX, the language and syntax of React VR:
    - Differences between React VR and React
- Components and VR components:
    - Props
    - State
    - Events
    - Layout
    - Style
- Details of all components and keywords:
    - Objects-visible and invisible
    - Lights
    - Multimedia - sound and video
    - Cameras and viewing

I have not covered all of the APIs available, as that is mostly a long, dictionary-like recitation, and it would be better if you used the documentation on the website to explore the APIs. We will, in later chapters, use critical APIs to add life to our world and navigate in it. For a full, up-to-date list of APIs, check the documentation (`https://facebook.github.io/react-vr/docs/getting-started.html`).

JSX - the syntax of React VR

React VR will look familiar to HTML; this makes it easy to read, edit, and deploy. Behind the scenes, the UI syntactical glue that React and React VR use will be compiled into JSX or JavaScript eXtension. JSX is a React grammar extension to allow coding in a blend of HTML and JavaScript. You can also code JSX directly.

An example of React JSX is as follows:

```
const element = <h1>My title!</h1>;
```

This is not a string, as it's not in quotes, and it's also not JavaScript. It's much more readable and easier to use than coding in JavaScript directly. JSX makes programming faster and more declarative.

It is useful, but all of this readability and easy-to-program nature comes with a few pitfalls. One of them is that semicolons will automatically get entered. Just like with HTML, you can include extra lines, but your code may get extra semicolons that you didn't intend.

Put parentheses around your code to avoid this--I also highly recommend reading up on the JavaScript syntax. A few of the things in this book took me longer than they should have, as I'm a C++ programmer, not a native JavaScript programmer.

After your React VR is compiled, JSX is converted automatically into JavaScript. An implication of this is that you can include JSX anywhere you would use JavaScript.

Differences between React VR and React

In React, most of your thinking is around the **Document Object Model** (**DOM**) that has both captivated and infuriated us since the beginning of JavaScript. With React VR, you need to forget about the DOM; in this way, React VR is more similar to React Native. Even then, there are concepts that you need to forget about.

Forget about pixels as a dimension; the concept is meaningless with VR.

You can have a huge photo spread across so much of the world that it looks grainy, and a small photo on the side of a small physical object that looks very sharp. You can move closer or further away from objects (assuming you've programmed movement), which will dramatically change how many "pixels" wide something is. Instead, everything is referred to in real-world units of meters (if you are from a country that clings to outmoded units of "feet," you can pretend the units are in Yards. Close enough for VR work).

Another concept that might seem slightly strange with React VR is the speed of rendering. With React, your page is loaded, then displayed, then elements of the page can be interacted with (clicked on), but the whole page is rarely re-rendered unless someone clicks on *Refresh*. The `render` method of an object is called when the properties change. This does not mean you have to have a timer to "tickle" the rendering of your page in VR.

With React VR, the entire page is rendered in less (hopefully) than 16 milliseconds to make the 60 frames per second that is now consider essential for VR. The entire page is not reparsed. This is, sort of, the opposite of regular HTML. In particular, with active, alive web pages, individual VR components will be rendered (displayed) at 60 frames per second, and when their properties change, they are rendered (to the three.js code) to update that representation.

Rendering the object is not the same thing as page rendering. This may be slightly confusing. Your page will be rendered as soon as it starts loading, even if the `render()` method for various objects, to turn them into three.js code, has not run yet.

The net result is that without any extra programming, when properties update in your world, the objects will display as appropriate for those property changes. This is a cornerstone of how React works, and it is just as applicable with React VR. This adds multiple frame rates per second rendering.

Now that we've covered what React VR is not, let's cover what React VR is.

Core Components

React VR has reusable UI elements that you can use in a variety of places. These are called **components**. There are two built-in components:

- Text
- Image

You can also build your own components by extending `React.Component`.

Components are real things, not just labels or placeholders, as they have been built in ways to present themselves through the world via a `render()` function. This is not just a function; like everything with React VR, `render()` generally has a set of child components that render or describe it's contents. An example of a component could be as follows:

```
<Greeting/>
```

This would be a text component, a built-in type.

VR Components

VR objects, what you would commonly think of components, are covered later. The React VR documentation doesn't mention them under the section Core Components, which is a bit confusing. You're probably thinking *"just text and images? What about objects?"* VR components are my terminology for the following things:

- **VR physical components**: These are objects that you can "see" in the world:
  - 3D primitives, including boxes, cylinders, planes, spheres, and imported objects (which can be very detailed)
  - UI elements, such as panels and buttons
- **Lights**: These illuminate the preceding objects and can be of several types. Note that in React VR, currently lighting does not cast shadows for real-time speed.
- **Multimedia**: This includes video and sound. In this way, you can both create moving backgrounds for 360 video as well as have "TVs" inside the the world you are creating.
- **Cameras and scenes**: Cameras control the rendering and the scene contains all of the objects you are placing in it.

We will cover each of these keywords later in the *The next level - the details* section.

Props

Components would be boring if they didn't have properties. An example of a property for our salutation might be the following:

```
<Greeting name='Hello React VR Dude!'/>
```

name and other values such as this are referred to as **props**. The prop is name and has a value, which I set to a humorous string. They can be programmatically accessed, for example, {this.props.name}.

Many of the 3D objects also have properties; these vary from object to object.

State

Perhaps we're in a state of confusion, but React VR state is very important as it affects the display of all components, and thus, the various props of those components. If a component's props (external) or state (internal) changes, the component will re-render itself.

 Rendering does not necessarily refer to "creating an image for the eyeball", although it can. Rendering, in this case, can refer to building code through the React VR/JSX compilation process.

React VR is encapsulated, per object orientation philosophy/coding paradigm, so that the modifiable state is inside a this.state object within the component. It should only be modified through a "set" function, specifically as follows:
this.setState({myStateVariableBeers: 99 })

Note that while at first this might seem like it's stretching the HTML/JSX format, this is what makes React VR so powerful and easy.

Events

Events aren't just fun things to go to in your neighborhood, they are also ways to make your VR world really come alive. Events are generated when the user does certain things through the **user interface (UI)**. A View component sends onEnter and onExit events when you move the cursor in and out of the view area.

The astute reader should be confused--we are talking about VR and I just mentioned area. Why is a 2D concept being discussed as a fundamental component of a 3D language?

Events and layout (covered next) follow the 2D paradigm and are one example of an easy bridge between what you're used to working with (HTML, CSS, and JavaScript, and the VR world). There are differences, however, and the one that states "pixels" are not considered at all in any of the props and keywords may seem fundamentally weird. This is because with a true 3D world, the idea of using pixels as a unit of measurement is essentially useless. An object one meter in front of you is going to have a much wider screen representation than one ten meters behind you. Dimensions are therefore given in units of world space; one is a meter (a bit more than a yard).

The point of React VR is to quickly and declaratively build great 3D worlds. It is a declarative programming approach. If you want to build worlds with more complexity, the power of React VR is that you can use React Native and other Node.js programming methods to add to React VR.

Layout and style

Aspects of WebVR and React VR still follow the browser paradigm. Cursors are viewed as 2D interactions, and UI elements are generally described in terms of 2D flex boxes and layout rules to lay those components out in 2D. This does not mean we are not developing a VR environment; although most of the UI is in a 2D format, these are fully present within a VR environment.

Layout and style naturally move into 3D. Instead of having to describe what your 3D objects are for every item (inline), you can set up something similar to a style sheet or CSS. It's not actually similar to a style sheet, it is a style sheet, so all of your skills will transfer over.

Style sheets can be messy, so React VR makes it even easier to lay out UI elements. It uses Flexbox, via YogaLayout (at `https://github.com/facebook/yoga`). React VR is all about creating reality quickly. React is all about user interfaces, so it's natural that the UI elements in React VR are so powerful.

The next level - the details

Although the React VR library is simple, to really learn what it's all about, you need to learn a lot of syntax. You could skim it, but there is a danger to knowing a little bit without being somewhat familiar with everything.

> *"A little Learning is a dang'rous Thing;*
> *Drink deep, or taste not the Pierian Spring:*
> *There shallow Draughts intoxicate the Brain,*
> *And drinking largely sobers us again."*

> *-An Essay on Criticism, by Alexander Pope.*

You may be thinking *"OK, but where's all the VR stuff? You know, tables, chairs, lamps, people ... and so forth."* These are going to be a deep drink indeed--there are quite a number of components.

The best reference is the online documentation, although they can be a tad sparse at times. Remember that the online documentation is *live*, meaning you can file an issue or even modify it, if you see a typo or need clarification.

I highly recommend that you view the next section as a reference section. Of course, you could need help going to sleep at night, in which case read on! After having said that, this section is very important as you'll need to use many or all of these components to actually build your VR world. I will attempt to make this section funny. It is a good thing I am writing a book, and not trying to make a living on stage.

Stuff (objects, whether visible or not)

Most of the interesting things in the world are visible objects or objects that you can interact with. Roughly, in the order of complexity, these are as follows:

- Box
- Cylinder
- Plane
- Sphere
- CylindricalPanel
- Model
- Pano

- VideoControl
- VrButton

Primitives

The Box, Cylinder, Plane, and Sphere are 3D primitives. They have `lit`, `texture`, and `wireframe` props. Lit objects will be affected by the lights in the scene. If texture is specified (usually an image file), your browser will look up (fetch or render) this image and use it to wrap around the 3D primitive. UV mapping we will discuss in Chapter 6, *Working with Poly and the Gon family* and Chapter 7, *Sitting Down with a (Virtual) Teapot*, but most of the 3D primitives are mapped the way you would expect.

Note that the texture can be a `string` (referring to an image file), an `asset()` call, or a `require()`.

Box

A `Box` is a basic cube. It's dimensions will default to one (unit) if not specified.

```
<Box
 dimWidth={4}
 dimDepth={1}
 dimHeight={9}
 lit
/>
```

This would be the Monolith from 2001, a Space Odyssey; the dimensions being the squares of the first three primes. For more information, see `https://facebook.github.io/react-vr/docs/box.html`.

Cylinder

A `Cylinder` is a basic capped cylinder. It can also be used to make cones by making the top a radius of zero (or bottom for a closed funnel).

 The `Cylinder` uses radius, not diameter. Don't make your cylinders twice as large as they need to be!

```
// Round cylinder
//Doric order column
<Cylinder
    radiusTop={.825}
    radiusBottom={1}
    dimHeight={8}
    segments={20} />

// Great Pyramid
<Cylinder
    radiusTop={0}
    radiusBottom={2.20}
    dimHeight={2.8}
    segments={4}
/>
```

Note the creative use of the number of sides to make the cone a pyramid. For more information, see `https://facebook.github.io/react-vr/docs/cylinder.html`.

As with all 3D primitives, the `Cylinder` has `lit`, `texture`, and `wireframe` props.

Plane

This is not an Airbus, but rather a flat surface. While it is called a **plane**, it is more like a flat, square 2D slab. It is not a cubic slab, that would be a `Box`:

```
//concrete slab using industry norms for size
<Plane
    dimWidth={2.4}
    dimHeight={2.4}
/>
```

One thing about a plane that can be tough to work with; they are visible only from their primary side. They are quick, lightweight objects, but can only have one texture map on them so may look repetitious if you use a large plane. If you rotate a plane the wrong way, you may see nothing at all; you could be looking at the back side. Be careful with transforms or use a `Box` instead of a `Plane`.

For more information, see `https://facebook.github.io/react-vr/docs/plane.html`.

As with all 3D primitives, the `Cylinder` has `lit`, `texture`, and `wireframe` props.

Sphere

Follow the bouncing ball, although animation is covered later. As with the `Cylinder`, the `Sphere` has a prop that will change its resolution:

```
<Sphere
  radius={0.5}
  widthSegments={20}
  heightSegments={12}
/>
```

Similar to the way we did the pyramid, putting in a really low number of segments for the width and height could make the `Sphere` look like different types of solids. For more information, see `https://facebook.github.io/react-vr/docs/sphere.html`

As with all 3D primitives, the `Sphere` has `lit`, `texture`, and `wireframe` props.

Model

The `Model` component allows us to do really interesting things. Until now, the VR objects have been fairly simple, but Model allows you to import CAD models of arbitrary complexity.

Be careful with `Model`:

You can easily import objects that are more complex than your platform can handle. Remember, you still maintain the smooth frame rates that are required for Virtual Reality to seem real.

In `Chapter 6`, *Working with Poly and the Gon Family*, we will explore the details of using `Model` effectively. The basic method of showing `Model` is as follows:

`Model` with a material file:

```
<Model
source={{
obj: asset('sculpture.obj'),
mtl: asset('sculpture.mtl'),
}}
/>
```

`Model` without a material file:

```
<Model
  source={{
  obj: asset('standalone.obj'),
  }}
/>
```

As of the time of writing this book, `Model` imports the Wavefront OBJ file format, as well as **GL Transmission Format (glTF)**. OBJ is the most common 3D model format. One would wonder why React doesn't import X3D, which is the WebVR format of choice. This is one of the things that frustrated me into putting so much effort, way back when, into VRML and X3D.

In any event, OBJ files consist generally of two files; the `filename.obj` contains the geometry of the object, and a companion `.MTL` file (material) contains the colors, materials, and references to external textures (image files). Note that the implication is that you may need far more than just these two files, if the OBJ file has many textures loaded in the material file.

We will cover this in more depth in `Chapter 6`, *Working with Poly and the the Gon Family*.

Note that `Model` has `lit`, `texture`, and `wireframe` props. The texture prop applies to the whole model, which could have multiple UV mappings. It is usually better to assign textures through the `.MTL` file, which may be done automatically from your modeling program.

Don't plan on the texture keyword to apply to a `Model` that you have imported. It's far better to texture and map the model in the CAD program you are using, than to try to override it in React VR.

Secondly, you may need to hand edit the `.MTL` file; my experience is that most exporters can't handle all of the complexity of a nodal-based shader that even real-time engines make dramatic use of; as a result, your `.MTL` file is almost certainly not going to have all of the different baked-in maps.

CylindricalPanel

`CylindricalPanel` is a bit of a transitional object. It is intended to have child objects and provides an ability to draw these on an invisible cylinder centered on the current viewpoint. Its main purpose is to allow familiar 2D elements to be placed in a 3D world. To be able to do this requires a few anachronistic elements.

When you work with HTML, to do precise layouts of HTML elements, you may have to think and code with pixels; for example, a certain element may be 200 pixels wide. This allows you to precisely lay out graphics.

In 3D, none of this is applicable. Is the moon one, two, or 10 pixels wide? The world does not have *dots per inch*. As a result, most of the VR primitives established their actual size, well, their *virtual* size, in meters. Your VR display method will then show the right amount of pixels. If you move your head right up to that cube, it could be 2,000 pixels; if you see it at the end of a hallway, it might be 10 pixels wide. So you normally do not use pixels for sizes with React VR.

The CylindricalPanel object, however, *does* need a property for the amount of pixels. This is not for the object itself (well, sort of), it's for an off-screen buffer to hold the visible rendering of any child objects. Like many things in the web, it has reasonable defaults. The defaults are quite large, but that is to make it look less grainy if you get up close.

I highly recommend not using CylindricalPanel, but rather recode your UI into actual 3D objects. The resolution and system resource use (RAM mainly) could actually be lower this way.

For example:

```
<CylindricalPanel
 layer={{
 width: bufferWidthPx,
 height: bufferHeightPx,
 density: numberOfPxForACompleteTurn,
 radius: distanceFromTheViewer
 }}>
 ... Child components ...
</CylindricalPanel>
```

The Child components line is very important--here is where you put the actual 2D objects that will show up spread across CylindricalPanel. It is not literal code.

VideoControl

VideoControl is a physical object with the normal VideoPlayer functions, in other words, start, pause, and so forth. As it is intended to be used in playing videos, the example here (straight from the documentation) will show it embedded with an animation object:

```
class VideoPlayer extends React.Component {
constructor(props) {
    super(props);
    this.state = {
    // init with muted, autoPlay
    playerState: new MediaPlayerState({autoPlay: true, muted: true}),
  };
}
render() {
    return (
    <View>
        <Video
        style={{height: 2.25, width: 4}}
        source={{uri: 'assets/1.webm'}}
        playerState={this.state.playerState} />
    <VideoControl
        style={{height: 0.2, width: 4}}
        playerState={this.state.playerState} />
    </View>
    );
}
}
```

Don't feel limited to its intended use. You can also experiment with it--maybe it's a good train controller!

VrButton

The VrButton isn't actually a real button (well, it's all virtual, right?), meaning it doesn't have any geometry, but is an object that you may, nay, will, find very useful to include in the world.

The VrButton is mainly used for gaze detection. We discuss this and other VR movement (locomotion) techniques in Chapter 11, *Take a Walk on the Wild Side*. For now, let's just discuss what the VrButton is:

```
<VrButton
  style={{width: 0.7}}
    onClickSound={{
        ogg: asset('click.ogg'),
        mp3: asset('click.mp3'),    }}
  onClick={()=>this._onViewClicked()}>
  <Image style={{width:1, height:1}}
  source={{uri:'../../Assets/Images/gaze_cursor_cross_hi.png'}}
  inset={[0.2,0.2,0.2,0.2]}
  insetSize={[0.05,0.45,0.55,0.15]} >
  </Image>
</VrButton>
```

This VrButton wraps an image and plays a sound. We'll discuss sound further on in Chapter 8, *Breath Life in Your World*, but briefly here, the file format allows the browser to decide which sound will play in your chosen browser.

Lights

The world would be a pretty dark place and full of vampires if we didn't have lights. Let's chase those undead things away. There are four principal lights:

- AmbientLight
- DirectionalLight
- PointLight
- SpotLight

Common light properties

All lights have two common properties:

- `intensity`: This is how bright the light is in the scene. The default is `{1.0}`, but you can go higher. In practice, higher settings make the shadows on the curved edge of objects (spheres for example) more sharp and look brighter (washed out), but can't actually get whiter than white (RGB 255, 255, 255) on the most lit faces.
- `color`: Color is not listed under light properties, but it is a style prop that all lights have. This is an RGB property. You can even have colored ambient lights, which could be used for sepia tones and the like, as well as simulating background illumination from brightly colored environments. In a forest, for example, maybe a light green ambient color. The default is white.

Other lights have properties specific for the type of illumination they represent.

AmbientLight

`AmbientLight` is the simplest way to make your scene visible. It isn't actually a light, really, but it does light up everything in the scene.

Lighting in the real world is very complex. Photons bounce all around, reflect off of objects, penetrate into them, and even make some objects glow (fluorescence and luminescence). A useful trick is to make objects light up even if there are no lights or to add a light fill to the room that can help simulate background light scattering, without the overhead of calculating this.

This is called ambient light. Many CAD systems have ambient as a value in materials. `AmbientLight` lets you light up the whole room. For you disco, festival-loving people, it even lets you change the color from white to whatever color you want. Now, you can make a scene that looks like the hallways at the W hotel chain.

Oddly, not a single sample in the React VR download shows how to use `AmbientLight`; although it's not that hard, it's important.

Here is a screenshot of a sphere with an ambient of .2:

The code is as follows:

```
<AmbientLight
intensity={.2}
/>
```

Notice a few things--we also have a directional light in the last photo, so you can see the differences. The sphere is white from the directional light, yet the underside is dark, but not pitch dark. AmbientLight can fake a little global illumination or radiosity in real time. GI is the amount of light that bounces off other objects and creates "fill light" in the real, non-virtual world. Three.js also has a THREE.HemisphereLight for this, and you can add it to React VR through the Native Views or Native Bridge.

DirectionalLight

From `AmbientLight` to `DirectionalLight`, we are moving from the abstract to the slightly less abstract. A `DirectionalLight` is really there to take the place of the Sun. The sun's rays are always parallel to each other; in the same way, the `DirectionalLight` doesn't spread out like a light that's located closer would.

Here is a `DirectionalLight` and no `AmbientLight`:

The code is as follows:

```
<DirectionalLight
  intensity={.9}
  style={{ transform: [{ rotateZ: 35 }] }}
/>
```

 In the picture, we've rotated the `DirectionalLight` to the side slightly; the sphere looks interesting, but not quite right compared to the rest of the scene. This is because the lighting for the Pano background is substantially different than the scene. You would want to try to match the two up with the appropriate transform statement for your `<DirectionalLight>`.

PointLight

A `PointLight` is like an old-school light bulb; light spreads out in every direction from the point. One interesting thing about Point and Spot lights is again a simplification to make our VR look real. To avoid very slow rendering, the atmosphere is not strictly modeled. This means that a light that would normally fade out due to the atmosphere would instead shine for miles (atmospheric effects might be more of an issue where I live than where you live, unless you live on the moon. If you do, give me a ticket, and I'll come and personally read this book out loud to you).

To avoid modeling atmospheric effects such as extinction (fading), fog, clouds, and so forth, `PointLight` and `SpotLight` both take decay and distance props.

`distance` is how far the light shines. If it is non-zero, the light intensity will be zero at that distance.

`decay` is how often if fades away. It's sort of a generic (dimensionless) number; 2 is physically realistic light falloff. 0.1 makes a much sharper fade and is useful for artistic effects.

For example:

```
<PointLight
  intensity={1}
  style={{ transform: [ { translate: [0, 0, -5] }]}}
  distance={10}
  decay={2}
/>
```

To better visualize the preceding, I've constructed a demo scene three times; the first with a distance of 10, the second with a distance of four, and the third with a distance of four and a decay of 0.1 instead of 2. You can see the third scene looks very unnatural. Note that all three scenes have an intensity of exactly one.

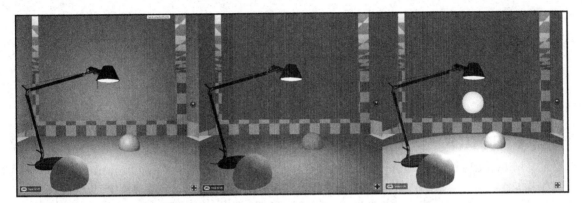

If your point lights seem dim, check the distance parameter. I recommend leaving decay at two.

SpotLight

A SpotLight is like those lampshade things they shine in a bad guys faces in bad film noir or a flashlight. Like PointLight, it also has decay and distance props (as seen earlier).

The distance and decay props are the same as the PointLight. The SpotLight also has a penumbra and angle props; the two are how far the light spreads out. Angle is the maximum outside angle,while penumbra is a number from one to 100 that defines how soft the SpotLight is.

```
<SpotLight
    intensity={1}
    style={{ transform: [{ translate: [0, 2, -5] }] }}
    distance={25}
    decay={.1}
    penumbra={1}
    angle={40}
/>
```

Currently, the position of the SpotLight defines where the light is shining "from." The target of the light, in other words what it is pointed at, is currently not exposed in React VR. At the time of the writing of this book, this issue is not resolved.

Using a View to wrap the SpotLight doesn't seem to change the target either.

I recommend not using SpotLight, unless you can arrange your scene to have the object of interest located at [0,0,0].

Multimedia - sound and video

The world would be a boring place if you couldn't hear anything. Video is normally part of dynamic web pages, although in VR, we have a bit of a challenge — video itself might not be engaging unless it's 360 video, which some people call VR (it can't give you more than disembodied ghost feeling, so from my viewpoint, it's not really VR as you can't be totally immersed, but other people may feel it is VR. At this point in VR/AR/XR, we really need to all just get along!).

Video in a VR world can be an important part of providing atmosphere. If you walk into a room and a video is playing, it's going to seem more like most homes.

Sound

Sound in VR is much more complicated than it initially sounds (pun intended). The Sound node allows an audio source to be placed into your VR world. Sound will make your world come alive.

From the React VR manual, consider the example of a waterfall:

```
<Image style={{height: 2.0, width: 2.0}}
    source={uri: 'images/waterfall.jpg'}>
    <Sound source={uri: 'sounds/waterfall.wav'} />
</Image>
```

This example shows how easy it is to add things by declaring them in React VR. The waterfall sound is simply attached to the location of the image of the waterfall. If you are walking around inside the 3D world, you will *hear* the waterfall as if it is located where the image is; this is all done by simply adding the Sound component as a leaf node (child of image in this case). The Sound node should not have any child components itself.

If the `Sound` node is not attached to an object with a position, it will default to being at position absolute, for example of position: absolute.

The `Sound` node has a number of props. They are as follows:

- `autoPlay`: Boolean
  When the audio starts playing automatically when a component is loaded. The default is `true`.

- `loop`: Boolean
  When the audio repeats automatically when finished playing. The default is `false`.

- `muted`: Boolean
  When the audio is muted. The default is `false`.

- `onDurationChange`: (callback function)
  This function is called when the sound duration changed, with a parameter for the duration of the sound.

- `onEnded`: (callback function)
  The function `onEnded` is called when audio is done playing.

- `onPlayStatusChange`: (callback function)
  This function is called when the play status changed.
  `event.nativeEvent.playStatus`: This is the play status of the sound; one of the strings `'closed'`, `'loading'`, `'error'`, `'ended'`, `'paused'`, `'playing'`, or `'ready'`.

- `onTimeUpdate`: (callback function)
  This function is called when `currentTime` of sound is changed.

- `event.nativeEvent.currentTime`: The `currentTime` of the sound file.

- `playControl`: *play*, *pause*, or *stop*.
  This variable controls the playback status. If not set, the value of `autoPlay` determines whether the audio plays when the component is loaded.

- `playerState`: (object)

    `playerState` is a `MediaPlayerState` that controls video playback with its inner state. When `playerState` is set, the value of `autoPlay`, muted volume and `playControl` properties are ignored as they will be set by `playerState` instead. See `MediaPlayerState`.

- source: (object)

  The object source audio in the form of {uri: http}.

- volume: 0-1.0 (not actually limited)
  Value of the audio volume. The minimum is zero, which mutes the sound, and the suggested maximum is 1.0, which is also the default value. Values greater than one are allowed; this may cause clipping/distortion, depending on the audio hardware.
  An example: To lower the volume by 50% set volume={0.5}. As different platforms may have differing audio capabilities (sigh), the source can be of several different file formats, and the browser will pick the appropriate format that it can read.

It appears that mono files work best; not all browsers seem to support stereo sound files. This is because the browser will convert the sound to a stereo sound and try to replicate 3D audio (which can be done with only two speakers through a Head Related Transfer Function).

Use mono files for the best compatibility.

Video

As a Video is only a two dimensional (2D) object, it takes a width and height. This is not, as you are probably used to, in pixels, but instead in world units for the reasons discussed earlier. If people move their point of view closer or further away from your 2D video, it will change resolution from a dots per inch standpoint. You may need to experiment with sizes and video compression/storage to find the ideal balance of quality, download speed, and resolution (graininess).

Video is best when used with the VideoControl (described earlier in this chapter).

This example showing a Video as well as a VideoController:

```
<Video
    style={{height: 3, width: 4}}
    source={{uri: 'assets/Video1.webm'}}
    playerState={this.state.playerState}
/>
<VideoControl
    style={{height: 0.2, width: 4}}
    playerState= {this.state.playerState}
/>
```

Note that the VideoControl is not a child of Video; it is an independent object with its own location. In this example, presumably playing a 4:3 ratio video, it coordinates their stop/start/pause activity through this.state.playerState. In effect, you could think of the VideoControl's playerState as being an output and the Video's playerState as being an input.

Cameras and viewing

There is a camera object, called LiveEnvCamera, although it is not what you would normally expect.

In most CAD systems, the camera sets up basic statistics such as focal length, focus, what direction the camera is looking at, and the like.

With React VR, instead, we have a <View> at the top level in the index.vr.js; this is what constructs the VR view.

The parameters of visibility of the view are really controlled by your physical viewing device. If your HMD has a 110 degree horizontal field of view, you will be seeing a 110 degree horizontal field of view.

This is something that traditional 3D artists have to get used to--VR is different.

 Along the same lines, lens flares and other effects, although they look great in movies, look terrible in VR. Your eyes don't have lens flares.

Don't try to add them with React Native.

You might wonder, how do we move the camera? The answer is that you transform the <View>. If you want to move say five meters forward, you transform the view five meters backwards, and the point of view will move into the scene. Note that this does not work for the SpotLight.

LiveEnvCamera

This object displays the environment–facing camera. This may or may not be part of your viewer's hardware. GearVR, for example, may have an environment–facing camera; the Vive does, a Google Cardboard probably does not.

By default, the camera is position: absolute `<LiveEnvCamera />`. The camera image is displayed on geometry that is 1000m away from the viewer.

 The LiveEnvCamera is probably intended for **Augmented Reality (AR)** applications; its use in React VR is experimental at best.

View

A `View` object is both the initial scene or camera in the world; it is also useful to aggregate objects in the world. In this way, it is very similar to a group node in traditional CAD programs. It really is essential to effective React VR software as a grouping node, not just the main rendering loop.

The reason we mention that view is a camera is that it has layout props and transforms. If, in your main `render()` loop, you transform the `<View>` you are essentially moving where the camera, your current point of view, is looking.

If you are using `<View>` as a grouping node, then the transforms apply to all of its children. You could build articulated models in this way, by properly exposing their properties and transforms, although it's more likely to do this through a glTF file.

Summary

In this chapter, we covered the basics of the React VR library, what components are in it, and the APIs and coding techniques they will be using to build your app. Enough background! Now that we have done this, in the next chapter, let's create an actual VR app.

5
Your First VR App

Well, four chapters of background. Hopefully you just skimmed the last chapter, although I expect you'll be looking at it quite a bit, or the online documentation, as you build each of your worlds. Now that you have this background, we are well prepared to build the first React VR app. We will start by diving deep into React VR components, props, and states.

You'll learn the following topics:

- Initial world creation/laying down the React VR framework
- Setting up a good background image
- How to fix background images so they are truly equirectangular
- Adding VR components
- Creating new VR keywords (class construction)

Moving beyond hello world - our first VR world

This actually isn't out first VR app, although we didn't really make the first app, the npm installer did. In Chapter 2, *Flatland and Beyond – VR Programming*, in the *Post Node.JS installation - installing React VR* section, we installed a simple Hello World example.

We will start by creating a new application (directory). But first, let's talk about what we are creating, and for that, you get a special prize!

VR world design - or, congrats, you are the new Astronomy Museum curator!

Any project should start, even if informally, with a design. In this case, you've received an email telling you *"Congratulations, you have been chosen as the new European Space Agency outdoor Museum Curator!"* For your prize, you don't worry, no astronomer's night vision will be harmed during this visit. As the museum curator, you may pick different art items than I will; in fact, you could go about creating a completely new location as well.

If we do a good job at that, we will then move into outer space, and be able to be the first art museum in orbit. As we're the first, we'll be the best museum in orbit.

Creating the base React VR components

React VR has a number of base components and code that has to be installed. Nearly 19,987 files and 8,111 directories. You don't have to install all of those by hand (and the browser won't download all of them, much of this is framework that may or may not be packaged). So, how do we install all this?

To install everything takes only one step. We will open a Node.js command prompt, navigate to whatever directory you want to place your application in, and create a new React VR template. Type the following code once you are in the correct directory:

```
react-vr init SpaceGallery
```

This will install a fresh application called `SpaceGallery`. It'll start installing things:

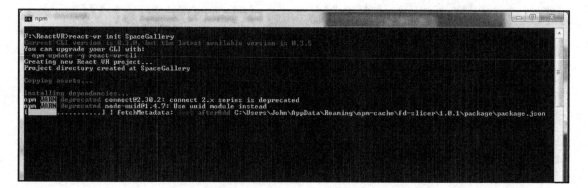

Note the line:

```
Current CLI version is 0.3.0, but the latest available version is 0.3.5
You can upgrade your CLI with:
    npm update -g react-vr-cli
```

These commands frequently take a long time to run, but some of the information they show is important.

In this case, while I was writing the book some of the tools upgraded, and the system told me. I generally recommend upgrading as soon as you get one of these notices; if you don't, any bugs you submit won't get quite the attention you would like, and new features and bug fixes are frequently added.

Sometimes, however, you'll get warnings about stuff you don't really have control over, like the note about `connect@2.30.2`.

The React VR init command will process through everything it needs to install, including dependencies (and there's a bunch) and then get it all installed. When it's done, it'll list out everything and then exit. Don't worry, not all of this code will be delivered to the client. The actual download is fairly small, compared to a VR game engine such as Unity or Unreal.

```
Administrator: Node.js command prompt                                     _ □ x
  +-- yargs@6.6.0
  | +-- camelcase@3.0.0
  | +-- cliui@3.2.0
  | | `-- wrap-ansi@2.1.0
  | +-- decamelize@1.2.0
  | +-- get-caller-file@1.0.2
  | +-- os-locale@1.4.0
  | | `-- lcid@1.0.0
  | |   `-- invert-kv@1.0.0
  | +-- read-pkg-up@1.0.1
  | | +-- find-up@1.1.2
  | | `-- read-pkg@1.1.0
  | |   +-- load-json-file@1.1.0
  | |   | +-- parse-json@2.2.0
  | |   | | `-- error-ex@1.3.1
  | |   | |   `-- is-arrayish@0.2.1
  | |   | +-- strip-bom@2.0.0
  | |   | `-- is-utf8@0.2.1
  | |   +-- normalize-package-data@2.4.0
  | |   | +-- hosted-git-info@2.5.0
  | |   | +-- is-builtin-module@1.0.0
  | |   | | `-- builtin-modules@1.1.1
  | |   | `-- validate-npm-package-license@3.0.1
  | |   |   +-- spdx-correct@1.0.2
  | |   |   | `-- spdx-license-ids@1.2.2
  | |   |   `-- spdx-expression-parse@1.0.4
  | |   `-- path-type@1.1.0
  | +-- require-directory@2.1.1
  | +-- require-main-filename@1.0.1
  | +-- set-blocking@2.0.0
  | +-- which-module@1.0.0
  | +-- y18n@3.2.1
  | `-- yargs-parser@4.2.1
  |   `-- camelcase@3.0.0
  +-- react-test-renderer@15.4.2
  +-- react-vr@1.0.0
  +-- react-vr-web@1.0.0
  +-- three@0.80.1
  `-- xopen@1.0.0

Done!
  Now enter the new project directory by running 'cd SpaceGallery'
  Run 'npm start' to initialize the development server
  From there, browse to http://localhost:8081/vr/
  Open 'index.vr.js' to begin editing your app.

F:\ReactVR>
```

The React VR init command will even tell you what to do to start your world. If we start this up, we will see essentially the same *hello world* app that we saw in Chapter 2, *Flatland and Beyond – VR Programming*.

First, make sure you've stopped the hello world app that was already running--use *Ctrl+C*, then Y to stop the batch file. Then, using the cd command (change directory) go into the new SpaceGallery directory you created.

If nothing you do seems to change your application, no matter what you try, it's quite possible you left an npm package running in some other directory. Kill all npm sessions and restart it.

Go ahead and start it up:

If you get the error yarn is not recognized as an internal or external command, operable program or batch file, you can ignore this error; Yarn is similar to npm. Advanced users can use either one you want; as npm is used in the React VR examples, I'll use that in the course of this book.

Welcome to open source, sometimes the land of too many options. DuckDuckGo is your friend.

Let's change the background to get us in the mood.

Creating the larger world - background image

This is a *do it* chapter - the previous chapters covered the general background of VR. However, now we're actually going to change the background (image).

The *chess world* you see in the hello world app is actually a panoramic image used in the Pano statement (in the index.vr.js file). When I first installed React VR, for a second I thought it was some of the geometry included in the default world. Here is our view of the SpaceGallery app (2D browser view):

Everything except the **hello** textbox comes from the <Pano> object:

```
<Pano source={asset('chess-world.jpg')}/>
```

This is a specially constructed **spherical panorama** or **equirectangular projection**. It is warped to display properly in 360 degrees left/right and 180 degrees top/bottom (just like latitude and longitude covers +/- 90 and +/- 180, a 360x180 spherical image covers an entire sphere).

Here is `chess-world.jpg`, which is the file that is included as the background every time you make a VR world:

A few things to note:

- This is a very large file. It is 4096x2048 in pixels. Even so, when you look around in 3D it will occasionally look grainy. This is because when you look at an item on say a fifteen-inch laptop, let's say about 35 centimeters wide, at roughly a half a meter distance from your eyes, you are looking at a 1920 pixel image and it looks sharp. When you spread that image 360 around you, that equates to over 17,000 pixels (2*pi*.5m * 1920 / .35m).
- Large files will make for slow downloads, even in today's world.
- Now imagine if that background was a video. VR has very high bandwidth requirements. It's the price of admission.
- The file looks warped, but when it is displayed in the browser and in your favorite HMD, it will look straight.
- This particular image is great for testing due to the straight lines; if you look straight down or straight up, everything will match up.

You can find 360 degree panoramic photos all over the web, but make sure they are spherical 360 by 180 panoramic photos. If they were made by a camera, typically things will get weird at the very top and very bottom of the image; many people assume you won't look straight down or straight up.

Map projections are also equirectangular images, so you are probably familiar with them and how stretched out things are at the poles. If you use a map projection as your background it will look like you are inside a globe.

That might be a little weird.

> It is a good idea to put some geometry that is part of your world directly underneath the viewpoint to cover any discontinuities or aberrations in your spherical panoramas.

> It also helps avoid a floating feeling; because the Pano is 2D and infinitely far away, stereoscopic depth perception wouldn't show how far away the Pano is. Objects will seem to move oddly against the floor if you move your point of view around in the VR world. Physical geometry through the primitives or model statements underneath the point of view may help avoid this and make your world look more virtually real.

As we're talking about a gallery in space, before we get into orbit let's investigate a few new panoramic photos, and use them to prepare our background. Feel free to search the web with your favorite search engine for more panoramic photos. Here are the steps I followed:

1. Let's go to the **European Space Agency (ESO)** and copy a fantastic space panoramic image from `http://bit.ly/PanoESO`. If you want to experiment with different resolutions, they have a range of resolutions on this download page. This image is great:

2. Download this to the `static_assets` folder underneath where we created the new application, and then open up `index.vr.js`. In that file, make the change to the Pano statement:

```
<Pano source={asset('uhd_vlt_circular_cc_eq.jpg')}/>
```

3. Now refresh your browser and we're already seeing space:

4. You'll notice the buildings look a little weird. If we continue to look down, the background image looks even stranger:

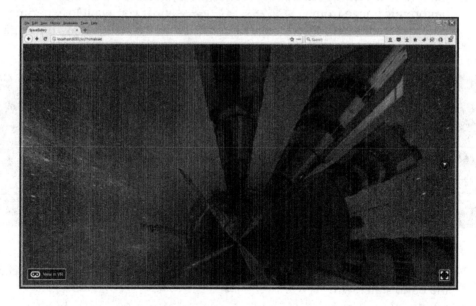

5. This is because, if you look closely at the original background image, it's actually not 360x180 degrees, but more like 360x90. This is very common with cell phones taking panoramic images; very few people capture the top and bottom to make it a true 360x180. A true panoramic picture looks just as warped at the bottom as at the top. For example, look at the flat chess world image we saw previously.

6. This is fixable. The fix is to just add a black strip (or background color) to the bottom of the original 360x90 panormaic photo, like this:

Using this technique, you can more or less fix any panoramic image, as long as it's at least 360x90; these are fairly common even if not marked as such. Now if we put this panoramic image in our `Pano` statement, or VR app looks much better:

5. To do this, I used a freeware image viewing/editing program called **Irfanview**, although you can use Photoshop or any other image editing software. I would highly recommend Inkscape or Gimp; they are full featured and free/open source.

6. When we view this in VR and examine the console, we can see an error:

5. `THREE.WebGLRenderer: image is not power of two (2000x2000). Resized to 2048x2048`

Let's fix that by resizing. Irfanview has a nice fairly fast resize that will preserve most of the detail. Just resize (*Ctrl+R*) and make it be 2048x2048 or 2048x1024. As we added the black stripe to the bottom, we can resize the image without stretching it. If you have to, you should clip or extend the bottom of the image; it's hard to tell with these 360 projections, but if you alter the aspect ratio of the image, the world will look squished when you view it.

 If you get a blank or incorrect background, check the image format and size.

Cluttering up the world - adding our first VR components

Okay, now let's start adding our objects.

In our description at the beginning of the chapter, we mentioned moving to orbit. You might wonder why we didn't start with a space background. We will, after we create a world on the ground. I found space images as backgrounds can be disorienting, without a floor, and we needed to discuss equirectangular images before we float about in orbit and up and down become meaningless. So, for now, you've got to do a great job at the earth bound gallery before we end up in space.

This brings up an important point. The <Pano> statement is usually described as a background. A better way to think of the <Pano> statement and background images are of the *rest of the world* or the part of the world you can't reach out and touch. Whatever your background image is, without any VR objects, it will place you *there*. The <Pano> really isn't just a background, it's really the whole world except for the objects you place.

This is why your choice of background is important for a sense of presence. If you have a weird, or disorienting background, people will feel disoriented. This may or may not be what you want; it can also spoil the sense of immersion. Also, they can never touch what is in the Pano, so if there are objects that are close, it may be disorienting.

So, let's add a Plane for the outdoor gallery floor so that we're not floating against our background. After the first <View> statement generated by the code generator in index.vr.js, add the following Plane and Box elements:

```
export default class SpaceGallery extends React.Component {
    render() {
        return (
            <View>
//the above code is generated automatically, add your code below
//or after the <Pano> statement
<Plane
    dimWidth={5}
    dimHeight={5}
    texture={asset('DeckPlate.jpg')}
    lit
    style={{
        transform: [
            {translate: [0,-1.8, -5]},
            {rotateX: -90}
        ] }}
/>
<Box
        dimWidth={5}
        dimDepth={5}
        dimHeight={.1}
        texture={asset('DeckPlate.jpg')}
        lit={true}
        style={{
        transform: [{
          translate: [5.2,-1.8,.1],
        }]
        }}
```

```
/>
```

Before we save and view the world, we'll need the `DeckPlate.jpg` file. You'll need to download this file from `http://bit.ly/VR_Chap5` inside the `static_assets` folder and copy it to the `static_assets` folder inside of `SpaceGallery`. I created the `DeckPlate.JPG` file with a program called *Substance Designer*, by Allegorithmic, located at `http://bit.ly/AllegSub` via their material sharing site. I found this material `http://bit.ly/MatSciFi01`. As you may not have substance player, I exported this image for you as `DeckPlate.jpg`. Later on, we will build more complicated models and use other textures to build an actual material. You can also use Quixel.se for good effect, if you use Photoshop. See the site at `http://bit.ly/QuixelSuite`.

After we've done this, what happens? We hit refresh and we get a blank screen. Open up your web developer console. If you're in Firefox, click on **Tools** | **Web Developer** | **Toggle Tools** (or *Ctrl+Shift+I* on a PC).

The console will open and we see lots of errors, followed by:

```
Expected a component class, got [object Object]
```

This is a clue that we forgot to add to the `import` directive. When we generated the object, it put all the React VR JSX imports that we needed for the **hello** world. Whenever we add a new object or API, we need to make sure React VR knows about it. Insert the following lines in bold:

```
import {
 AppRegistry,
 asset,
 Box,
 Pano,
 Plane,
 Text,
 View,
} from 'react-vr';
```

In a large project, you may forget this on occasion. Check the console in your browser if your scene doesn't change. I also recommend using some code organization by adding your `import` declarations either in alphabetical order, or in the order you use them. Alphabetical order is easier to quickly scan. You could just import everything, but that may add some overhead you don't need.

Lighting up the world

Once we add the import statement, we'll notice the world is somewhat dark; it may be hard to see the box and plane we added. To light things up, we'll add both an AmbientLight and a DirectionalLight (sun or moon light) to the image. We're going a little unreal in this app as we've got an obviously night time image background, but our objects will be lit. Adding an AmbientLight as well as a DirectionalLight is an easy way to fake the natural world. In the real world, objects take on light from light reflected off of objects near them. An AmbientLight can simulate this gentle glow (this is often referred to as global illumination on other rendering systems). The direction light simulates either overhead room lighting (many lights, like in a classroom) or the light of the sun or moon.

Put your lighting statements at the top of the render() statement in your app, so that you can easily find them. I would make them the first statements after the top level <View>.

If lighting is part of an object, such as a desk lamp, keep that light near the object (or as a child of the object).

This will allow you to quickly modify scene lighting.

Our AmbientLight statement is simple; the DirectionalLight takes a little more thought but is also pretty straightforward. Code them this way:

```
<AmbientLight
intensity = {.3}
/>

<DirectionalLight
intensity = {.7}
style={{
  transform:[{
    rotateZ: 45
  }]
}}
/>
```

You should be able to see the platforms now, although they look small.

Don't forget the import statements!

Why did I have you paste in both a Plane and a Box?

They both become the floor of our world, so why did we do both? If you look to the right in the VR View, you'll see that the Box has a funny looking edge. The texture map is equally applied to all six sides, and may look funny when stretched for boxes that aren't close in overall dimension. That is one disadvantage to the Box. The Plane doesn't have this problem, but if you get the Plane tilted the wrong way, you may not see it; the Plane is one sided so will be invisible if tilted away from the current camera. The Plane is also infinitely thin. I included both so you could see how they look.

In the section on transforms, I mentioned how important the order of transforms are. This is particularly important with the Plane object; if you rotate, then translate, the image may be oriented completely wrong, and in the case of a Plane, invisible.

To build the entire gallery, we'll need to include several squares for the platforms. Add a little bit of a gap between them. Now, we could do this by copying and pasting each Box or Plane (use whichever one you like!) and updating the translate statement:

```
{translate: [0,-1.8,-5.1]},
...
{translate: [0,-1.8,.1]},
...
{translate: [5.1,-1.8,.1]}
```

There is a better way though; React VR is not just a hardcoded geometry file, but rather an actual object-oriented JSX file, and we can make use of that.

Let's define a new object that is one of our deck plates. We will put everything but the position in as components of that object. First (and I pounded my head against the table for a while on this), change the first line of your code from:

```
import React from 'react';
```

To:

```
import React, {Component } from 'react';
```

Note that this is a different import statement than what we're using on the second line (and easy to overlook).

 If you don't see an object you created, or get an error that a keyword that you know is valid isn't recognized, don't forget the import directive at the top of the file!

Got Class - consolidating objects as new keywords

Once we've importing the React Component, we can define an object as a `class`. For this version, we'll use individual numbers as props (like parameters) and then instantiate them as often as we need to. We can paste this code anywhere; for now, you can put it in the `index.vr.js` file above the the `export default class SpaceGallery extends React.Component` line. Your new `class` is:

```
class Platform extends Component {
    render() {
      return (
      <Box
         dimWidth={5}
         dimDepth={5}
         dimHeight={.1}
         texture={asset('DeckPlate.jpg')}
         style={{
            transform: [
                 {
                 translate: [ this.props.MyX, -1.8, this.props.MyZ]
                 }
                 ]
            }}
      />

      );
    }
}
```

To instantiate copies of this, inside your `<View>` use this code (in your `SpaceGallery` class):

```
<View>
...
<Platform MyX='0' MyZ='-5.1'/>
<Platform MyX='0' MyZ='0'/>
<Platform MyX='0' MyZ='5.1'/>
<Platform MyX='5.1' MyZ='-5.1'/>
<Platform MyX='5.1' MyZ='0'/>
<Platform MyX='5.1' MyZ='5.1'/>
<Platform MyX='-5.1' MyZ='-5.1'/>
<Platform MyX='-5.1' MyZ='0'/>
```

This is the most direct way to make prefabs or classes so that you don't have to cut and paste endless declarations of `Box` components to make your floor.

If you're familiar with the React concept of state, don't use state at this time. You should use state for values that change over time; we will discuss this more in Chapter 7, *Breathe Life in Your World,* and especially Chapter 11, *Take a Walk on the Wild Side.* Since this is a static version of the app, you don't need it. We will build the platform in the right place with props.

You might think instead of two named parameters, you could make a vector, but JavaScript doesn't have the concept of a vector. You can, with the { } operators, paste in the appropriate code, however. An alternative way of creating our slab floor segments is as follows:

```
class VecPlat extends Component {
  render() {
    return (
    <Box
      dimWidth={5}
      dimDepth={5}
      dimHeight={.1}
      texture={asset('DeckPlate.jpg')}
      style={{
        transform: [
            {
            translate: this.props.MyPos
            }
            ]
          }}
    />

    );
  }
}
```

Notice that the translate statement does not have square brackets around this.props.MyPos as it would have with a literal. You then instantiate it like this:

```
<VecPlat MyPos={[-5.1, -1.8, -5.1]}/>
```

Note the extra { } braces and the missing braces in the translate statement as mentioned. In this case, you need it to create the vector (array).

Putting it all together

We now have a basic platform to put our art on, you've learned how to create objects that we can instantiate, we've put basic lighting into the scene--now let's add some objects.

You find out from the powers that be, that you have done a fantastic job and can now move the Space Gallery into space. From the link to GitHub, you can download a few new files, including `BabbageStation_v6_r5.jpg`. Once we change the `Pano` statement with this file, we'll blip right into orbit--none of that shaking in your acceleration chair stuff. Nice and quiet.

Let's get back to building the gallery. First, let's consolidate and use the `Platform`; your new `index.vr.js` file should be the following once you've downloaded the new `static_assets`:

```
import React, {Component } from 'react';

import {
  AppRegistry,
  asset,
  AmbientLight,
  Box,
  DirectionalLight,
  Div,
  Pano,
  Plane,
  Text,
  Vector,
  View,
  } from 'react-vr';

class Platform extends Component {
    render() {
      return (
        <Box
          dimWidth={5}
          dimDepth={5}
          dimHeight={.1}
          texture={asset('DeckPlate.jpg')}
          style={{
            transform: [{ translate: [ this.props.MyX, -1.8,
this.props.MyZ] } ]
            }}
        />
      );
    }
```

```
        }


export default class SpaceGallery extends React.Component {
    render() {
        return (
          <View>
            <Pano source={asset('BabbageStation_v6_r5.jpg')}/>
            <AmbientLight

    intensity = {.3}


    />
    <DirectionalLight
    intensity = {.7}
    style={{
        transform:[{
            rotateZ: 45
        }]
    }}
        />
        <Platform MyX='0' MyZ='-5.1'/>
        <Platform MyX='0' MyZ='0'/>
        <Platform MyX='0' MyZ='5.1'/>
        <Platform MyX='5.1' MyZ='-5.1'/>
        <Platform MyX='5.1' MyZ='0'/>
        <Platform MyX='5.1' MyZ='5.1'/>
        <Platform MyX='-5.1' MyZ='-5.1'/>
        <Platform MyX='-5.1' MyZ='0'/>
        <Platform MyX='-5.1' MyZ='5.1'/>

        <Text
        style={{
            backgroundColor: '#777879',
            fontSize: 0.8,
            fontWeight: '400',
            layoutOrigin: [0.5, 0.5],
            paddingLeft: 0.2,
            paddingRight: 0.2,
            textAlign: 'center',
            textAlignVertical: 'center',
            transform: [{
                translate: [0, 0, -4]}]
        }}>
    Hello
  </Text>
</View>
);
```

```
        }
    };

    AppRegistry.registerComponent('SpaceGallery', () => SpaceGallery);
```

Note that your code will be considerably shorter if you used either `Platform` or `VecPlat` as your object.

 Note that I used `MyX='-5.1'` instead of `MyX={5.1}`. This works, but it is really incorrect. `{}` is used to insert JS into the code. Basically, if you want `MyX` to be a number, use `{`'s in the initialization list. JavaScript will covert, but sometimes lead to weird behaviors if you don't pass a number as a number.

You may have noticed that the basic primitives that React VR includes are a bit sparse. Without constructive solid geometry, often called Boolean operations, or native three.js, there's a limit on what you can create.

Fortunately, you can import files from other CAD programs. We will cover this more in `Chapter 6`, *Working with Poly and the Gon Family* but for now, you can import a few models that I've included in the files for the book at `http://bit.ly/VR_Chap5`.

Adding the pedestals

Before we put the art in the world, we need to build a pedestal. To make it easier to line up, we can create an object as we did before. Let's make a square pedestal and put a cap on the top and bottom.

If you broke for the day in triumph, go ahead and restart the React VR server; to make it easy on ourselves we can copy the URL so that we can paste it into our web browser:

```
Select npm

F:\ReactVR\SpaceGallery>npm start

> SpaceGallery@0.0.1 start F:\ReactVR\SpaceGallery
> node -e "console.log('open browser at http://localhost:808

open browser at http://localhost:8081/vr/
```

If you have selected the preceding text to paste into your browser, you are going to be waiting a long time. Notice in the address bar where it says **Select npm**.

 When you are using the console to start your app, if you "select" any text, and keep it selected, it may block the web browser from serving up the content.

So, instead of a simple cube we used for the floor, we'll create a square `Pedestal` with a top and bottom:

```
class Pedestal extends Component {
    render() {
        return (
            <Box
            dimWidth={.4}
            dimDepth={.4}
            dimHeight={.5}
            lit
texture={asset('travertine_striata_vein_cut_honed_filled_Base_Color.jpg')}
            style={{
                transform: [ { translate: [ this.props.MyX, -1.4,
this.props.MyZ] } ]
                }}
            />
            <Box
            dimWidth={.5}
            dimDepth={.5}
            dimHeight={.1}
            lit
texture={asset('travertine_striata_vein_cut_honed_filled_Base_Color.jpg')}
            style={{
                transform: [ { translate: [ this.props.MyX, -1.1,
this.props.MyZ] } ]
                }}
            />
            <Box
            dimWidth={.5}
            dimDepth={.5}
            dimHeight={.1}
            lit
texture={asset('travertine_striata_vein_cut_honed_filled_Base_Color.jpg')}
            style={{
                transform: [ { translate: [ this.props.MyX, -1.7,
this.props.MyZ] } ]
                }}
            />
```

```
    )
  }
}
```

Now, when you try this, you will get an error:

Adjacent JSX elements must be wrapped in an enclosing tag (31:10)

Remember, this is React VR; with regular React, you would enclose any multiple tags in a `<div>` statement. This won't work here as we are are not dealing with HTML; the closest thing is React-Native. So, for VR, we want to wrap multiple elements/objects in a `<View>` statement. The correct code is thus:

```
class Pedestal extends Component {
    render() {
        return (
          <View>
              <box etc='...'/>
              <snipped for='brevity'/>
          </View>
        }
    }
}
```

 If you got the error `Expected a component class, got [object Object]` in your web console, you may have accidentally typed view instead of `View`

Now that we've set up the `Pedestal` object, paste it into your `index.vr.js`, underneath all the platforms:

```
<Platform MyX={ 0.0} MyZ={-5.1}/>
<Platform MyX={ 0.0} MyZ={ 0.0}/>
<Platform MyX={ 0.0} MyZ={ 5.1}/>
<Platform MyX={ 5.1} MyZ={-5.1}/>
<Platform MyX={ 5.1} MyZ={ 0.0}/>
<Platform MyX={ 5.1} MyZ={ 5.1}/>
<Platform MyX={-5.1} MyZ={-5.1}/>
<Platform MyX={-5.1} MyZ={ 0.0}/>
<Platform MyX={-5.1} MyZ={ 5.1}/>

<Pedestal MyX={ 0.0} MyZ={-5.1}/>
<Pedestal MyX={ 0.0} MyZ={ 0.0}/>
<Pedestal MyX={ 0.0} MyZ={ 5.1}/>
<Pedestal MyX={ 5.1} MyZ={-5.1}/>
<Pedestal MyX={ 5.1} MyZ={ 0.0}/>
<Pedestal MyX={ 5.1} MyZ={ 5.1}/>
```

```
<Pedestal MyX={-5.1} MyZ={-5.1}/>
<Pedestal MyX={-5.1} MyZ={ 0.0}/>
<Pedestal MyX={-5.1} MyZ={ 5.1}/>
```

Now, we have a nice series of `Pedestals`. The other thing we did was, by careful scaling, every object is at the same location, [5.1 ... 0 ... -5.1], in two dimensions. This will make it easier to import the various art objects.

As we've seen with creating additional classes or components, item composition is a bit difficult in React VR. It is not intended to be a full blown 3D modeler; it is a VR presentation system. Therefore, any really complicated object should be created in a CAD system. There, you will have some type of visual modeling that is a lot easier than trying to estimate what the `<Box>` offset will be when stacking them.

We will use the Model statement. In `Chapter 4`, *The React VR Library*, we detailed the Model keyword. Time to use it! Add the following lines inside the `<View>` statement in the main code, underneath the `Pedestal` it'll be on. Don't forget to change the `import` line!

```
<Model
  source={{
      obj: asset('teapot2.obj'),
      mtl: asset('teapot2.mtl'),
      }}
      lit
      style={{
        transform: [{ translate: [ -5.1, -1, -5.1 ] }]
        }}
  />
```

I've created a version of the Utah teapot from internet sources and some of my own UV editing in Blender; this is the `'teapot2.obj'` object. Creating objects in Blender could be the subject of a whole book, and probably is, so for now, you can just download the teapot from the files from the book. They are at `http://bit.ly/VR_Chap5`, in the `static_assets` folder.

This one is a little different as it has a rubber handle, blue enamel, and a copper spigot. For now, the material file (the .mtl file) has just simple colors, but in the next chapter, we will find out how to make these be richly detailed with texture maps.

 If you get `Model is not defined` it means you forgot to add `Model` to your `import` line at the top of your file.

Go ahead and save that, and you'll see we've added a teapot! However, there are a few issues - the deckplates look a bit boring and weird on the edges, and we'd like to see the teapot looking a little different. We can do this by creating our own models, in the next chapter.

Summary

Congrats! Your gallery is now finished, with one simple object. You've learned how to modify our world, change the background to make it look like we're anywhere we want, and you've learned how to create groups of objects and instantiate them. Next, you will learn how to populate it with more models; read the next chapter to find out how!

6

Working with Poly and the Gon Family

When people that are just getting used to computer graphics see some of the first VR graphics, their first reaction is "*Oh no, not polygons!*" A friend of mine said this in exasperation, when looking at her first massively multiplayer online role play game. It wasn't as low poly as *Money for Nothing*, but it was pretty close. *Money for Nothing* was one of the first music videos that used computer graphics and looked something like this:

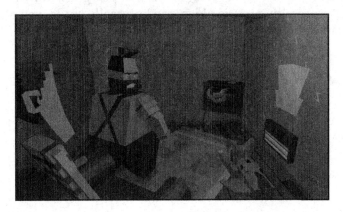

Polygons are the best way to present real-time graphics. In this section, we will have to make a few of them! You may already be familiar with **Computer Aided (Design/Drafting/Drawing) (CAD)** software or Computer Modeling software; or you might be a complete newcomer. There are so many different CAD systems, we are going to use Blender, a freely available/open source CAD system to illustrate some of the important ways to bring interesting objects into Virtual Reality.

In this chapter, you will learn:

- How to perform basic polygon modeling
- How to export a model in OBJ form from Blender
- How to apply basic UV texture mapping
- How to export texture maps
- How to create an MTL file to properly show real-time OBJ texturing and materials

Polygons and why we like them

I think the confusion with *"Oh no, not polygons"* is that polygons, unless they are elevated to an art form, as in the preceding music video, can be a really crude way of creating something. For example, this does not look much like an apple:

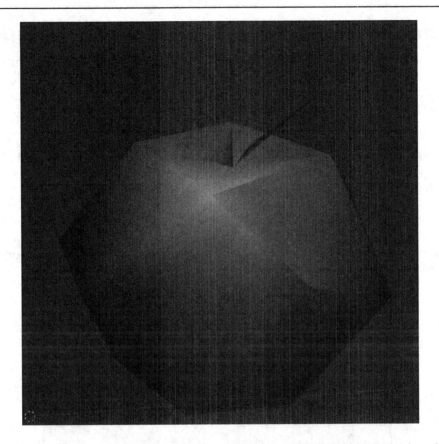

Many CAD systems do have other representations such as **Non-Uniform Rational B-Spline (NURBS)**, which is a type of curve, or primitives that essentially have no polygons but are what they represent. A sphere, for example, may be arbitrarily smooth with no facets or flat areas.

The world would be boring if everything was just cubes and spheres. Unless it was Minecraft, then it would be pretty cool. Aside from Minecraft, many CAD systems build up more interesting objects via **Constructive Solid Geometry (CSG)** to drill out and add the basic primitives to other primitives to make more complex objects.

Why doesn't VR use some of these techniques?

Generally speaking, they are slow. Something has to convert the precise, accurate mathematical models into something that video hardware can display. Some video cards and advanced APIs can build objects out of things other than polygons, calculate smooth curves, and the like, but by far the most common workflow in the VR and game industry revolves around polygons and textures.

We can, therefore, take polygons as a given. Modern video cards, and high-end cell phones have quite a lot of capability when it comes to rendering objects, although to maintain frame rates for VR, we do have to pay attention to the number of polygons.

The good news is that, you can make very good looking VR objects for a reasonable low number of polygons. For example, take a look at our apple. The low resolution version just shown has just 44 faces (polygons) and 24 vertices (points). If we increase the number of polygons to just **492**, it looks significantly better:

In these examples, I'm using Blender version, v2.79. You can use any CAD program that will read and write to OBJ files, which is nearly all of them. I use Blender because it is free, so anyone reading this book can follow along without worrying about purchasing an expensive CAD program.

Blender is very full featured and can certainly be used for production work, although describing every possible CAD system and recommending one is out of the scope of this book (and I never like to discuss religion publicly!). From the preceding model though, you can see the limits of Blender; this model had rather strange **texture mapping** and reducing the resolution too much created some weird stripping on the texture map.

Of course, we could just throw polygons at the system like we are running on a PC from 2030, nearly 512 times faster than what we have now, if Moore's law holds out. Our apple would look like this:

It is really not that much different to the medium resolution apple, although those weird texture lines have disappeared. It looks pretty good (and this is not a full detail render). To make the lower resolution polygons, I did a quick decimation in Blender. Decimate is Blender's way of taking a model with a lot of polygons and reducing it to fewer, and is a very handy way to take very complicated models and make them Virtual Reality ready. Performing a decimate by hand, and applying new textures to the model, would probably get rid of the seams.

For advanced modelers, you can use a low polygon version of your model, in conjunction with a high polygon version, to make a normal map, which unlike a bump map, allows the model to look like it has more polygons than it really does.

You may need to experiment some with normal mapping; it really depends on the browser and model.

Now, you might be thinking you'd prefer to use the apple with 25,206 faces. It might work, but this is a fairly large model. Many people ask *"How many polygons can I use?"* although this is a difficult question to answer. It would be like asking your mother how many groceries can she fit in the car? A lot of it depends on what groceries. If she is bringing back a 24 pack of that nice comfy toilet tissue, I can tell you from personal experience that only one or two will fit in a 2-seater sports car. (Relax, I'm not bragging, my sports car is 12 years old.)

A better way to think of your polygon budget is in comparison to the other objects you could have. That high resolution apple? For the same speed (very roughly), you could have over 48 of the medium resolution apples.

If you are going to offer refreshments to your Space Gallery patrons, would you rather give out 1 or 48?

Keep your objects as low resolution as possible, and still maintain the visual look you need. You may need access to low poly objects or a good CAD system that can reduce polygons.

After having said that, I was getting somewhat reasonable frame rates from the previous one. My goal isn't to give you an absolute number, but to show how important a vertex budget is.

What is a polygon? discussion of vertices, polygons, and edges

If you use a modeling program, you will not have to deal with the intricacies of the definitions of these objects much. However, from time to time you may need to get into the details, so some background is in order. If you are an old hand at computer graphics, you may already know a lot of this. I do include some practical advice on how best to get them into React VR, so it would be good to review.

A polygon is an *n*-sided object composed of vertices (points), edges, and faces. A face can face in or out or be double sided. For most real-time VR, we use single–sided polygons; we noticed this when we first placed a plane in the world and, depending on the orientation, you may not see it.

To really show how this all works, I'm going to show the internal format of an OBJ file. Normally, you won't hand edit these — we are beyond the days of VR constructed with a few thousand polygons (my first VR world had a train that represented downloads, and it had six polygons, each point lovingly crafted by hand), so hand editing things isn't necessary, but you may need to edit the OBJ files to include the proper paths or make changes your modeler may not do natively–so let's dive in!

Polygons are constructed by creating points in 3D space, and connecting them with faces. You can consider that the vertices are connected by lines (most modelers work this way), but in the native WebGL that React VR is based on, it's really just faces. The points don't really exist by themselves, but more or less "anchor" the corners of the polygon.

For example, here is a simple triangle, modeled in Blender:

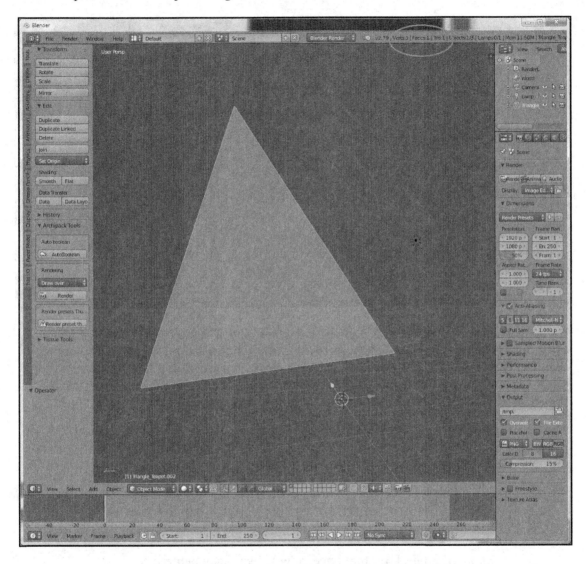

In this case, I have constructed a triangle with three vertices and one face (with just a flat color, in this case green; if you are reading a physical book or an eInk electronic reader (Kindle), it'll be a shade of gray of course). The edges, shown in yellow or lighter shade, are there for the convenience of the modeler and won't be explicitly rendered.

Here is what the triangle looks like inside our gallery:

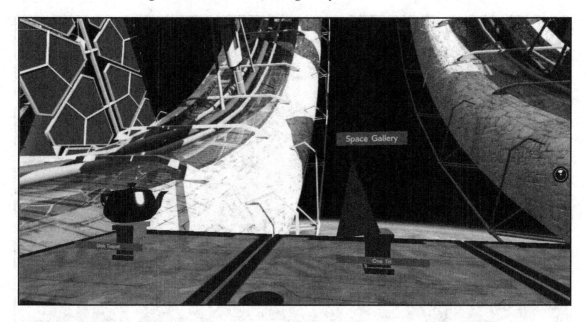

If you look closely in the Blender photograph, you'll notice that the object is not centered in the world. When it exports, it will export with the translations that you have applied in Blender. This is why the triangle is slightly off center on the pedestal. The good news is that we are in outer space, floating in orbit, and therefore do not have to worry about gravity. (React VR does not have a physics engine, although it is straightforward to add one.)

The second thing you may notice is that the yellow lines (lighter gray lines in print) around the triangle in Blender do not persist in the VR world. This is because the file is exported as one face, which connects three vertices.

 The plural of vertex is vertices, not vertexes. If someone asks you about vertexes, you can laugh at them almost as much as when someone pronouncing Bézier curve as "bez ee er."

Ok, to be fair, I did that once, now I always say Beh zee a.

Okay, all levity aside, now let's make it look more interesting than a flat green triangle. This is done through something usually called texture mapping.

Honestly, the phrase "textures" and "materials" often get swapped around interchangeably, although lately they have sort of settled down to materials meaning anything about an object's physical appearance except its shape; a material could be how shiny it is, how transparent it is, and so on. A **texture** is usually just the colors of the object — tile is red, skin may have freckles — and is therefore usually called a texture map which is represented with a JPG, TGA, or other image format.

There is no real cross software file format for materials or **shaders** (which are usually computer code that represents the material). When it comes time to render, there are some shader languages that are standard, although these are not always used in CAD programs.

You will need to learn what your CAD program uses, and become proficient in how it handles materials (and texture maps). This is far beyond the scope of this book.

The OBJ file format (which is what React VR usually uses) allows the use of several different texture maps to properly construct the material. It also can indicate the material itself via parameters coded in the file. First, let's take a look at what the triangle consists of. We imported OBJ files via the `Model` keyword:

```
<Model
    source={{
        obj: asset('OneTri.obj'),
        mtl: asset('OneTri.mtl'),
        }}
    style={{
            transform: [
                { translate: [ -0, -1, -5. ] },
                { scale: .1 },
            ]
        }}
/>
```

First, let's open the `MTL` (material) file (as the .obj file uses the .mtl file). The OBJ file format was developed by Wavefront:

```
# Blender MTL File: 'OneTri.blend'
# Material Count: 1

newmtl BaseMat
```

```
Ns 96.078431
Ka 1.000000 1.000000 1.000000
Kd 0.040445 0.300599 0.066583
Ks 0.500000 0.500000 0.500000
Ke 0.000000 0.000000 0.000000
Ni 1.000000
d 1.000000
illum 2
```

A lot of this is housekeeping, but the important things are the following parameters:

- Ka : Ambient color, in RGB format
- Kd : Diffuse color, in RGB format
- Ks : Specular color, in RGB format
- Ns : Specular exponent, from 0 to 1,000
- d : Transparency (d meant *dissolved*). Note that WebGL cannot normally show refractive materials, or display real volumetric materials and raytracing, so d is simply the percentage of how much light is blocked. 1 (the default) is fully opaque. Note that d in the .obj specification works for illum mode 2.

Transparent materials, at the time of writing this book, are not supported by React VR. This is currently under development, however, so perhaps soon they will be.

- Tr : Alternate representation of transparency; 0 is fully opaque.
- illum <#> (a number from 0 to 10). Not all illumination models are supported by WebGL. The current list is:
    1. Color on and Ambient off.
    2. Color on and Ambient on.
    3. Highlight on (and colors) <= this is the normal setting.
    4. There are other illumination modes, but are currently not used by WebGL. This of course, could change.
- Ni is optical density. This is important for CAD systems, but the chances of it being supported in VR without a lot of tricks are pretty low. Computers and video cards get faster and faster all the time though, so maybe optical density and real time raytracing will be supported in VR eventually, thanks to Moore's law (statistically, computing power roughly doubles every two years or so).

Very important:
Make sure you include the "lit" keyword with all of your model declarations, otherwise the loader will assume you have only an emissive (glowing) object and will ignore most of the parameters in the material file!

YOU HAVE BEEN WARNED. It'll look very weird and you'll be completely confused. Don't ask me why I know!

The OBJ file itself has a description of the geometry. These are not usually something you can hand edit, but it's useful to see the overall structure. For the simple object, shown before, it's quite manageable:

```
# Blender v2.79 (sub 0) OBJ File: 'OneTri.blend'
# www.blender.org
mtllib OneTri.mtl
o Triangle
v -7.615456 0.218278 -1.874056
v -4.384528 15.177612 -6.276536
v 4.801097 2.745610 3.762014
vn -0.445200 0.339900 0.828400
usemtl BaseMat
s off
f 3//1 2//1 1//1
```

First, you see a comment (marked with #) that tells you what software made it, and the name of the original file. This can vary. The `mtllib` is a call out to a particular material file, that we already looked at. The `o` lines (and `g` line is if there a group) define the name of the object and group; although React VR doesn't really use these (currently), in most modeling packages this will be listed in the hierarchy of objects. The `v` and `vn` keywords are where it gets interesting, although these are still not something visible. The `v` keyword creates a vertex in x, y, z space. The vertices built will later be connected into polygons. The `vn` establishes the normal for those objects, and `vt` will create the texture coordinates of the same points. More on texture coordinates in a bit.

The `usemtl BaseMat` establishes what material, specified in your .mtl file, that will be used for the following faces.

The `s off` means smoothing is turned off. Smoothing and vertex normals can make objects look smooth, even if they are made with very few polygons. For example, take a look at these two teapots; the first is without smoothing.

Looks pretty computer graphics like, right? Now, have a look at the same teapot with the "s 1" parameter specified throughout, and normals included in the file. This is pretty normal (pun intended), what I mean is most CAD software will compute normals for you. You can make normals; smooth, sharp, and add edges where needed. This adds detail without excess polygons and is fast to render.

The smooth teapot looks much more real, right? Well, we haven't seen anything yet! Let's discuss texture.

I didn't used to like Sushi because of the texture. We're not talking about that kind of texture.

Texture mapping is a lot like taking a piece of Christmas wrapping paper and putting it around an odd shaped object. Just like when you get that weird looking present at Christmas and don't know quite what to do, sometimes doing the wrapping doesn't have a clear right way to do it. Boxes are easy, but most interesting objects aren't always a box. I found this picture online with the caption *"I hope it's an X-Box."*

The "wrapping" is done via U, V coordinates in the CAD system. Let's take a look at a triangle, with proper UV coordinates. We then go get our wrapping paper, that is to say, we take an image file we are going to use as the texture, like this:

We then wrap that in our CAD program by specifying this as a texture map. We'll then export the triangle, and put it in our world.

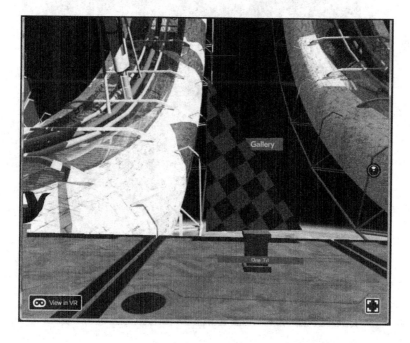

You would probably have expected to see "left and bottom" on the texture map. Taking a closer look in our modeling package (Blender still) we see that the default UV mapping (using Blender's standard tools) tries to use as much of the texture map as possible, but from an artistic standpoint, may not be what we want.

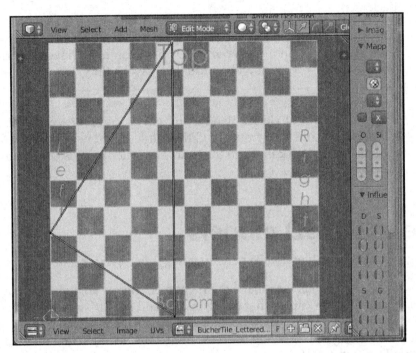

This is not to show that Blender is "yer doin' it wrong" but to make the point that you've got to check the texture mapping before you export. Also, if you are attempting to import objects without U,V coordinates, double-check them!

 If you are hand editing an .mtl file, and your textures are not showing up, double–check your .obj file and make sure you have vt lines; if you don't, the texture will not show up. This means the U,V coordinates for the texture mapping were not set.

Texture mapping is non-trivial; there is quite an art about it and even entire books written about texturing and lighting. After having said that, you can get pretty far with Blender and any OBJ file if you've downloaded something from the internet and want to make it look a little better. We'll show you how to fix it. The end goal is to get a UV map that is more usable and efficient. Not all OBJ file exporters export proper texture maps, and frequently .obj files you may find online may or may not have UVs set.

You can use Blender to fix the unwrapping of your model. While this is not a Blender tutorial, I'll show you enough here that with a book on Blender (Packt has several good Blender books) you can get a head start. You can also use your favorite CAD modeling program, such as Max, Maya, Lightwave, Houdini, and so on. (and forgive me if I missed your favorite package!).

This is important, so I'll mention it again in an info box. If you already use a different polygon modeler or CAD page, you don't have to learn Blender; your program will undoubtedly work fine. You can skim this section.

If you don't want to learn Blender anyway, you can download all of the files that we construct from the Github link. You'll need some of the image files if you do work through the examples. Files for this chapter are at: http://bit.ly/VR_Chap7.

Where to get 3D models

Which brings us to a brief diversion. Where do you get these models in the first place?

The best way to get 3D models is to make them yourself. If you do, you are probably not reading this, as you already know what polygons are and how to texture them. However, more likely you will go to a paid or free model site and download something you find appealing for the world you are trying to create. It just saves time. Here's a brief mention of a few sites that I've found useful over the years. Some of these sites can have very expensive models, as they often cater to high–end graphics companies (television, architecture, movies, designers), as well as high quality, but expensive, game art. Game art is about what you're looking for, to do good VR; some sites now have "low poly" or VR/AR categories. Some of them, especially ShareCG and Renderosity, tend to be very amateur in places. The site itself is great, but the uploaded files frequently have no editorial control; as a result, you may be able to find things that violate copyrights (Star Wars and Star Trek models) that you won't find on other sites for obvious reasons (lawyers!). Then again, you may find your own content on these sites that people are making money off of, and thus want to find your own lawyers.

Speaking of lawyers, you need to check the license for any files you do download. You may have the right to use these models for rendering, for example, but not distribution. This may or may not allow you to ship a game with these models in it, or that may require an additional (more expensive) license.

A few websites (by no means exclusive) where you can download models are at:

- `Turbosquid.com`
- `CGStudio.com`
- `creativemarket.com/3d`
- `CGTrader.com`
- `Grabcad.com`
- `ShareCG.com` (several of the models for this book came from here)
- `3dwarehouse.sketchup.com`

Why do you find such good models on these sites? Why do some of the models look so — odd, artistically? Many artists have contracts that do not require exclusivity, or people are working on a game that disbands and never ships. They can upload these unused or lesser used models and let other people use them, and even profit off of their sales.

 You can spend days searching all of these sites for that perfect content for your site.

You've been warned!

There are also a large number of 3D model sites intended for 3D printing. These models may be very dense (high polygon), but might have some content you could use.

I like to use a program called "Poser" to do human modeling, although many CGI artists would prefer to roll their own. DAZ3D sells human models as well, and many of them work with Poser. Both of these are good resource sites for inexpensive, reasonable quality rendering (depending on your skill setting up a scene). The Poser program has many sites dedicated to objects, scenes, models, and textures usable for it. Poser human models won't display terribly well in VR due to high polygon counts and very dense textures, but these sites may still have objects and add-on tools, usually at a very reasonable price.

A few web sites that have good Poser models, as well as a lot of other free objects are:

- `my.smithmicro.com/poser-3d-animation-software.html`
- `DAZ3D.com`
- `Contentparadise.com`
- `Renderosity.com`

Several images in this book were done with Poser and DAZ Studio.

Summary

In this chapter, you learned the basics of polygon modeling with Blender. You've learned the importance of polygon budgets, how to export those models, and details about the OBJ/MTL file formats. You've also learned where we can get 3D models for our worlds.

These objects can look plain; however, in the next section, you will learn how to wrap a paper around a teapot. This is not just a skill for giving gifts to people, it'll be vital for making our virtual worlds look real.

7
Sitting Down with a (Virtual) Teapot

In the last chapter, we found out a lot about polygons and how to use them in real-time graphics. We will continue the work with polygons, and learn more about texturing them.

In this chapter, we will learn the following:

- Basics of how to use Blender
- How to apply basic UV texture mapping
- How to export texture maps
- How to create an MTL file to properly show real-time OBJ texturing and materials
- Pulling it all together for our teapot gallery

Blender is just one of many polygon modelers that you can use to make virtual objects for use with WebVR. If you are already familiar with the concepts of polygon modeling, and creating and editing UV maps, you wouldn't really need most of this chapter. Once we do the UV mapping, we import the model into the world. I've also placed the static files for this chapter at: http://bit.ly/VR_Chap7 so you can download them instead of building them.

UV modeling can be tedious. You won't hurt my feelings if you just download the files. Please skim through the following though, as we build these models we will put them in the virtual world.

The teapot in Blender

To learn how to UV map, let's put a teapot in Blender. Today, this will work pretty well, but normally a teapot wouldn't fit in a Blender.

You can download Blender at blender.org. While there, I highly recommend the tutorials on the site at bit.ly/BlendToots. Packt also has quite a few good books on Blender. You can find these at: http://bit.ly/BlenderBooks. You might be a little confused or frustrated with basic cursor movements, and selecting if you haven't been through these tutorials; seeing an animation of the cursor moving helps more than writing about it would. In particular, please watch the cursor selection tutorials under *Getting Started* at: http://bit.ly/BlendStart.

To start texturing, we will use the venerable Utah teapot by Martin Newell. It is one of the more famous "test models" for computer graphics. This is the original Utah teapot, currently on display at the Computer History Museum in Mountain View, California (courtesy of Marshall Astor):

The computer graphics version was *squished* in a demo and the squish stuck. You can read more about this at: http://bit.ly/DrBlinn.

Here's the teapot in Blender. You can get here by turning on extra shapes in the preferences:

1. Click on the menu File, then User Preferences (**File->User Preferences**), and then click on **Extra Objects**:

2. Don't forget to then click the button at the bottom of the screen, **Save User Settings**, or the objects won't be there the next time you go in. Once you save, close the Blender User Preferences window.

3. Then, on the menu at the bottom of the 3D window, click on **Add->Mesh->Extras->Teapot+**:

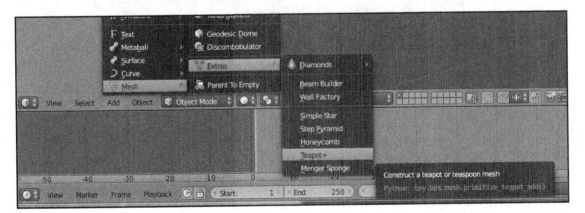

4. Once you do that, for instructional purposes only, choose a resolution of 3 on the pane on the bottom left hand side as shown here.

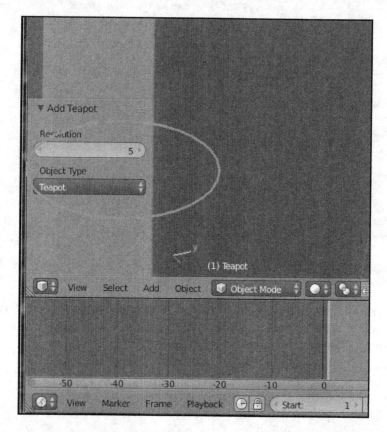

It is pretty neat that you can increase the resolution of the teapot; this would have saved me an hour of poking around on the internet while writing this chapter, had I noticed that earlier. We change it to 3 to make the polygons bigger, which will be a lot easier to click on while doing this tutorial.

5. Then, you want to click on the teapot (left-click) in the 3D window to select it; the teapot will then have an orange outline. Then get back to Edit Mode by clicking on the word **Object Mode** next to the menu item Object, then select **Edit Mode:**

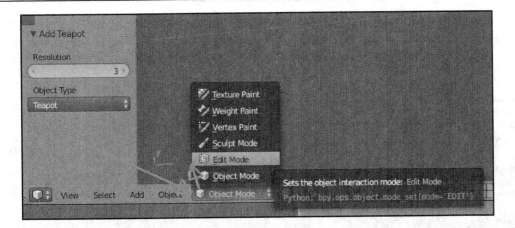

Once you are in **Edit Mode**, we'll need to be able to see the UV map while we select polygons on the teapot. Initially, there won't be a UV map though; keep following and we'll create one.

6. With your mouse over the slight line above the timeline window, the bottom window of the screen (the area circled in red in the following screenshot), drag the window *up*. This will make enough room for the window.

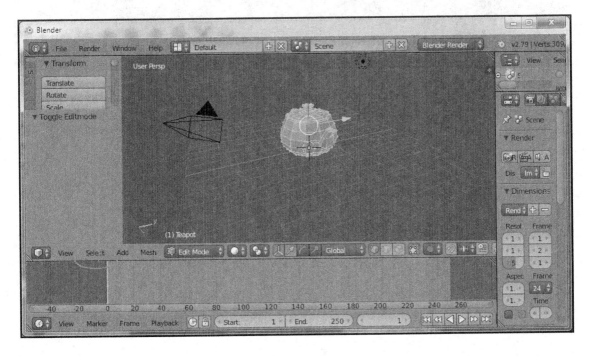

7. We aren't doing animations, so we don't need that window, we'll change it to a UV display. To do this, change the timeline display to show UV map information by clicking (red arrow) on the small icon of a clock face (wow, remember analog clocks?), and choose **UV/Image Editor**:

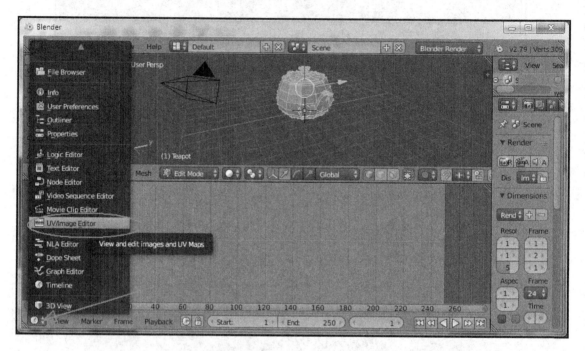

This is just one way of changing your window layouts. One of the confusing things with Blender is that you can really mess up your UI by accidentally clicking on a few things, but one of the great things is that you can make windows, subwindows, pull outs, shelves, and much more with a few clicks of the mouse. The way I just showed you is the most straightforward way for teaching, but for real work, you should customize the windows the way you want to.

Once you have changed this view, note that you can zoom in, pan, and move the window around just like any other Blender window. For how to zoom, pan, and so on. you should watch the tutorial video files located at: `http://bit.ly/BlendStart`

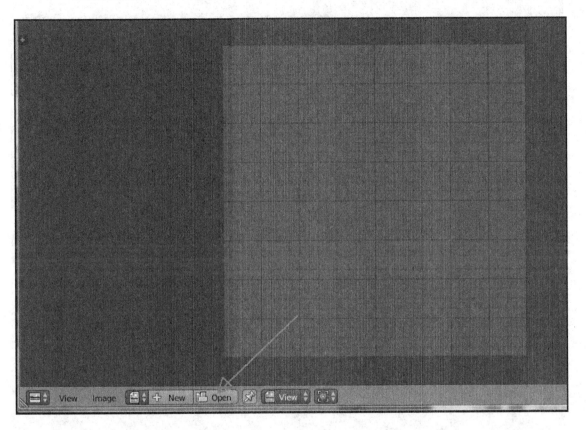

8. So, we can see what our texture looks like with our model; click on **Open** and find a texture file you want to map onto your teapot (or model). I'm using `ButcherTile_Lettered.jpg`.

9. Once you've done that, do the first UV unwrapping! In the upper window's menu, click on **Mesh->UV Unwrap->Unwrap**, like so:

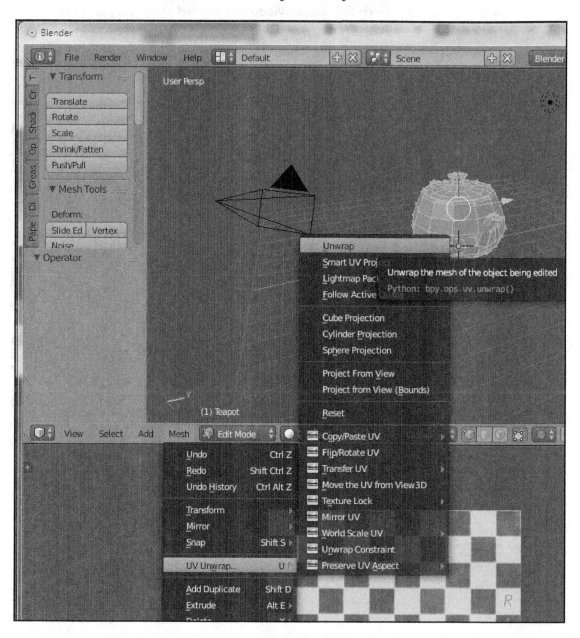

In the bottom window, it'll show you how it has unwrapped the texture.

It looks terrible. Your results may vary with different models.

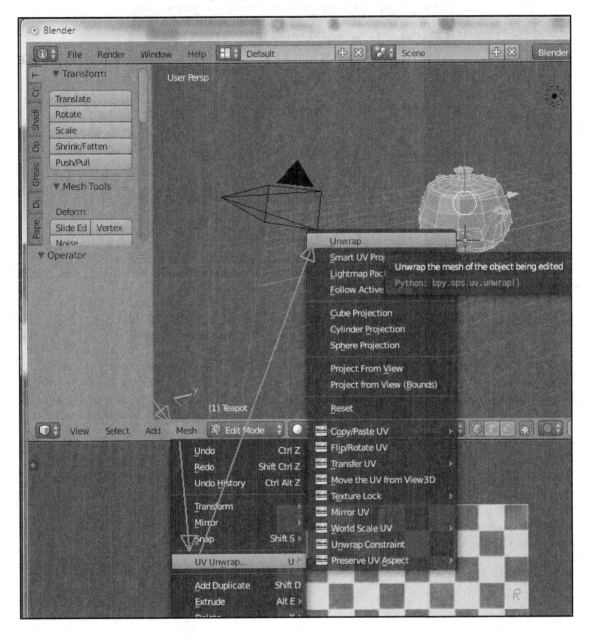

Why is this UV map terrible? From a real-time graphics' standpoint, it's not bad; it packs all the polygons onto just one texture map, which will help with video card RAM:

For some objects, it may be fine. If you look at the upper-right and lower-right, we see the spout and handle, and they look odd. It may look a little funny rendered; let's take a look at what it looks like. To do that, we have to assign some textures and then export the teapot. (We will cover exporting in a bit; for now, we just need to see that we have additional work to do in Blender.)

Note that you can get a quick look by rendering inside Blender, but this may disappoint you, as Blender will almost certainly render your model totally differently. The overall colors and textures will be the same, but the more subtle (and important) texture details that React VR, and WebGL are capable of will be lost (or better, with an offline, non real-time renderer); conversely, if you really work with Blender or look better, rendering can produce phenomenal work.

For example, in Blender, using the cycles renderer, it took me 11.03 seconds to render our teapot.

In React VR, to maintain at least 60 frames per second, this has to happen in less than .016 seconds. Blender took over 600 times longer to generate the same image; shouldn't it look better? The teapot doesn't look bad, but the UV mapping is just weird.

We can see that the squares are stretched a little oddly over the teapot. (If you stop and think about what we're doing, we just put a tile pattern on a teapot; these are the wonders of computer graphics. I'm using the checkerboard pattern, so we can see stretching on the pot. Later on, I'll have a better texture that I made with Substance Designer.)

You can experiment in Blender by clicking on a polygon (in **Edit Mode**) and see where that polygon is in the UV map. In Blender's defense, the map isn't terrible, it's just not what we want. Sometimes (nearly all the time), a human is required to really make art.

Fixing the UV maps for the teapot

To texture the pot a little easier, first let's create separate materials for the spout, handle, and lid. This will make our texture maps larger and less "stretched". You can also do this by packing textures together in one larger bitmap, which honestly is sometimes a little better for VR; the overall approach is the same, just more packed into a smaller area.

Let's create four materials for the pot, handle, spout, and lid (you should still be in Edit Mode).

1. Click on the little icon that sort of looks like a shiny globe. Then, click on the "+" key four times, as shown, and then on the new key:

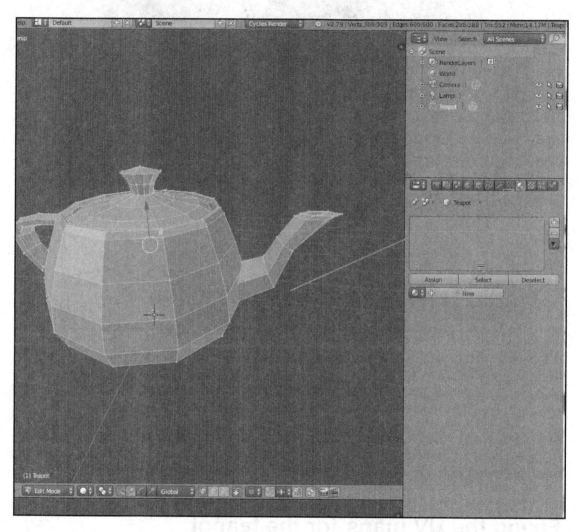

2. Once you've clicked on the **+** key four times, you'll have four slots for the materials we are creating. You then click on **New** to actually add a material. It seems slightly clunky, but that's how Blender works:

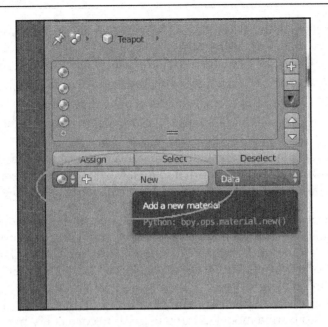

3. When you click on **New**, you will get a **Material.001**:

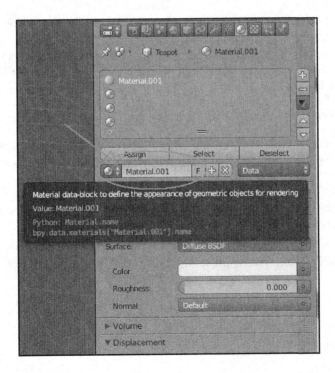

4. You can click on the area in the red circle and change the name. In this way, create four materials, as follows:
    1. Create a Pot material (will be a ceramic coated metal).
    2. Create a Lid material (the same texture as the pot).
    3. Create a Spout material (let's make that copper).
    4. Create a Handle material (let's make that worn rubber).

We don't really need to create these materials; you can overlay the same texture map on several UVs, but I wanted to do a fresh take on the teapot (which, as we can see, was a solid piece of ceramic), and it's instructive to see different materials.

Now that these extra materials are created, you can move the UVs to map the object better. UV mapping is a large subject, and it takes a certain technical and artistic skill to do well, or the PC could do it automatically. This is a little beyond the scope of this book, but I'll show you a quick and dirty method to UV map some common objects. Many of the files you find on the web may not have good UV maps applied, so you may find yourself in a situation where you think you don't need to learn a modeler, but will use it to correct UV maps (which is a pretty high-end activity when it comes to polygon modeling!).

Once you have created the four materials, you can map each section independently to its own UV maps; when it is time to present this in our VR world, we will use different texture maps for each piece. You can use the same texture map if you want to make a single ceramic pot, but our battered metal one may look better.

It's art; beauty is in the eye of the beholder.

Once you've established the four materials as we did above, select the polygons in each major area and click on **Assign** to make them part of this material:

5. Press the "A" key on the keyboard (or Select->(De)select All | A) to deselect all the polygons. We will then select the ones in each of the areas, the lid, handle, spout, and pot (main body).
6. Switch to 'Poly Selection'. Blender has different selection modes–point, line, polygon. For this, you want to switch to selecting polygons, by clicking on this icon:

7. Click on the main pot polygons by using *Shift + click* to select multiple polygons. Blender has a wealth of selection tools like box select, and others, per the tutorials at: http://bit.ly/BlendStart

8. Once you've selected the polygons in the main body, you click on the **Assign** button to assign that polygon to a material, in this case the 'Pot' material.

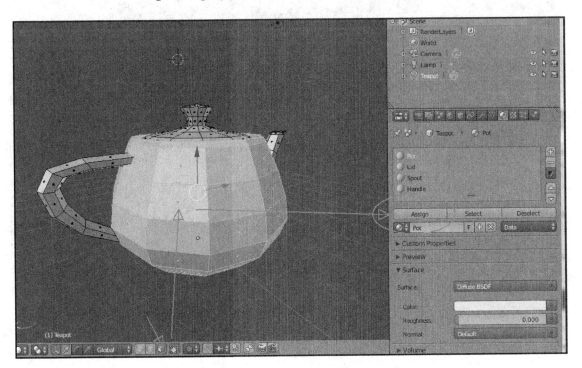

9. Once you have the polygons assigned, click on **View->Front** then click on **Mesh->UV Unwrap->Cylinder Projection.** You will then have a UV map in our image editor we set up earlier, although it stretches off of the image you could assign.

10. To fix this, in the menu on the lower half of the screen, select **UVs->Pack Islands:**

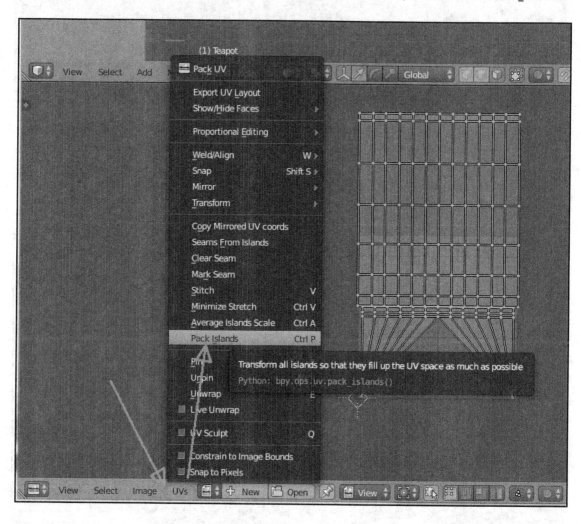

That's a basic texture mapping. You can fiddle with this a lot (and it can be frustrating). Blender has a number of useful automatic UV assignment tools; in the 3D (modeling) window, as we saw earlier, **Mesh->UV Un<u>w</u>rap->**(options) offers a lot of ways to do the unwrapping. I found that Project from View as well as Cylinder Projection, both from a strict top/bottom/left/right view can unwrap UVs pretty well. After having said that, some artistry comes into play. The spout, lid, and handle are smaller than the body, so you may want to waste some UV space and make these smaller if you want your texture to line up more or less with the main, pot, and texture.

Or you can download the `teapot2.obj` and `teapot2_Mats.mtl` from the GitHub files at: `http://bit.ly/VR_Chap7` and save yourself some sanity.

These four UV mappings would not be bad (but feel free to learn, study, and do better! I'm not an artist!). The UV mapping for the main body, the Pot material is shown here:

The UV Mapping for the Lid material:

The UV mapping for the Handle material (intentionally made smaller, to make the squares line up, more or less, with the main pot):

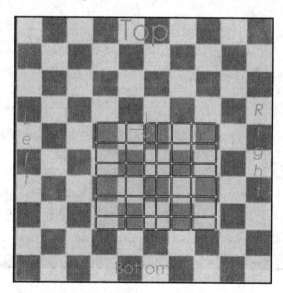

The UV mapping for the Spout material (intentionally made smaller, to make the squares line up, more or less, with the main pot):

With these UV assignments, our teapot, displayed twice, rotated slightly between each one, looks much better:

You can fiddle with UVs a lot. In the preceding screenshot, if we were mapping a texture that was mostly tile squares over the pot, we can see that although the handle and the spout match the main body pretty well, the lid, although it doesn't look stretched as our first picture did, still looks a little smaller than the other squares. The fix for this is to go into the 3D panel, select just the lid polygons (first hit "a" until nothing is selected), go to the material in the properties tab and click on the Lid material, "select" to select all polygons, and then go to the UV window and scale the UV mapped polygons down a little smaller.

However, in our case, we want to make totally different materials for these items anyway, so getting too worried about UVs at this point may be misdirected.

Your mileage may vary.

Importing materials

At the same time, we can use all the capabilities that React VR offers with regard to materials. The MTL file, unfortunately, doesn't always have the values possible. If you are using a modern material, that has base color, bump map or normal map, height, specular (shinyness), or metallic (similar to shinyness) maps, I've found that you may need to just hand edit the MTL file.

You would think with the wealth of computer graphics programs out there, that we wouldn't be at this point. Unfortunately, different rendering systems, especially nodal based ones, are too sophisticated for an OBJ exporter to really understand; as a result, typically most MTL files (materials) that go along with an OBJ file have only the base color as a texture map.

If you are using a program such as Quixel or Substance Designer, most **Physically Based Rendering (PBR)** materials consist of most of the following texture maps (images), which are also supported by the OBJ file format:

- **Base color**: This is what the material usually looks like, almost always exported with most CAD systems to OBJ (MTL) files as `map_Ka`.
- **Diffuse map**: Usually the same thing as the base color, it is the "diffuse" color of the object. You would implement this as `map_Ka` as well.
- **Bump map**: Bump maps are "height" information, but do not physically deform the polygons. They will look like they are carved, but if you look closely, the polygons will not actually displace. *This may cause an issue in VR*. One of your eyes will say *this is dented*, but your stereoscopic depth perception will say *no it's not*. Bumps can, however, make things look really good in the right circumstances. This is written as *bump* in the MTL file.

- **Height map**: Very similar to bump maps, the height map will usually physically displace polygons off of the surface. However, in most web rendering, it will displace only the modeled polygons, so it's far less useful than with offline renderers. (Game engines can do microdisplacements, however.)

- **Normal map**: A normal map is an RGB representation for something similar, but more complex than the height or bump maps, which are gray scale. A normal map is an RGB map, and can displace polygons to the *left* or *right* in addition to up or down. Modern game engines calculate the normal map from a high resolution (hundreds of thousands to millions) model to a lower resolution model. It allows for an object with simple polygons to look like it is built out of millions of polygons. It may or may not physically deform the model (depending on the shader). It is not directly supported by the OBJ/MTL file format, but *is* supported by WebGL, and thus three.js, although implementation is left as an exercise for the reader.

- **Specular map**: This controls (use glTF) how shiny or dull an object is. Usually a gray map (no color information). More specifically, a specular map controls "if" an area of a texture is shiny or not. This is map_Ns. Map_Ks is also a specular map, but controls what color the highlights are. This can be used for "ghost paint" on cars, for example.

- **Glossiness**: Not quite the same thing as specular, but is often confused. Glossiness is how tight the specular highlight is; it could be broad but shiny, like dull rubber, or tight and shiny, like a candy apple, or Chrome. It is basically the *value* that is applied to the specular map. Often used with PBR, it is not used by the OBJ/MTL file format.

- **Roughness**: Very similar to the specular and glossiness maps, it's often included instead or along with the preceding. Often used with PBR, it is not used by the OBJ/MTL file format.

- **Reflectivity**: Generally speaking, the OBJ file format is used for offline rendering, which does raytracing reflections that approximate the way the real world works. WebGL, for performance reasons, doesn't ray trace everything, but can simulate reflectivity with a reflection map. In the OBJ file, the amount of reflection is static; you can't directly make patchy reflection. This map is coded as *refl* in the OBJ file, but is not simulated by React VR in the OBJ/MTL file format.

- **Transparency**: Mapped as *d* and *map_d*. (d stood for "density" in the original MTL file.) This is not refractive transparency; light will either go through or not. It's useful for things like glass bottles and is not used by React VR.

- **Decal**: This applies a stencil on top of objects, and is very useful for avoiding the repeating texture look, and adding words on top. In the MTL, the file is coded as *decal*. This can be very useful, and decal is supported in React VR. However, I find that most modelers will not export it, so you may need to hand edit a material file to include a decal. This is not so bad, as typically you'll have different decals (such as signs, stains, and more) with different models in your world.

Fixing the deck plates

Now that we have learned how to UV map, let's fix those cubes that we use to represent the deck plates. We found out, while doing textures on top of the basic React VR objects, that the cube represented the same texture on all six sides of the cube. As a result, when we make a thin cube, like we did for the top and bottom of the pedestals, or with the deck plates, the texture map looks "squished" on the sides. The red arrow shows the squished texture; it's because we have a box that's only .1 high and 5 wide, with a texture that's square (the double red arrows), so it looks squished.

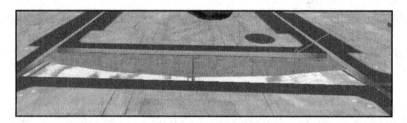

We can fix that with a cube in Blender. We'll also add the additional texture maps that we downloaded.

I have Substance Designer, which is a fantastic texturing tool; there are many others, such as Quixel. It will output different texture maps depending on how you set it up. You can also use any of a variety of packages that will allow you to bake textures. WebGL will allow you to use shaders, but this is somewhat complex. It is supported through React Native, but this is a bit difficult at this point, so let's cover the case of individual texture maps for the different material values. It will all break down to that in the .obj file usually anyway (.obj doesn't have the concept of modern GPU shaders):

1. Create a cube in Blender, and resize it (in Edit Mode) so that it is much shorter than it is wide or high. This will make our deck plate. In our VR world, we made it 5x5x.1, so let's make the Blender cube 5x5x.1.

2. Then, we texture map it roughly, as follows:

3. Export it to OBJ and choose the following parameters; the important ones are -Z forward, Y up (Y is up!) and Strip Path (otherwise, it'll include your physical disk location, which the Asset call from a web server obviously can't serve up):

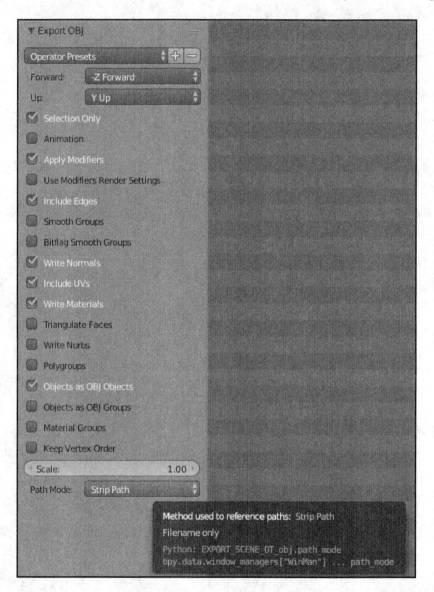

Once this is done, we'll do it the hard but direct way, which is to modify the deck plate's MTL file to directly include the textures we want:

```
# Blender MTL File: 'DeckPlate_v1.blend'
# Material Count: 1 newmtl Deck_Plate

Ns 96.078431
Ka 1.000000 1.000000 1.000000
Kd 0.640000 0.640000 0.640000
Ks 0.500000 0.500000 0.500000
Ke 0.000000 0.000000 0.000000
Ni 1.000000
d 1.000000
illum 2
map_Kd 1_New_Graph_Base_Color.jpg
bump -bm 0.01 1_New_Graph_Height.jpg
# disp will be mostly ignored, unless you have a high-polygon cube
# disp -mm .1 5 1_New_Graph_Height.png
map_Ks 1_New_Graph_Metallic.jpg
```

Displacement textures are somewhat useless; the current rendering engines will apply a displacement map, but will not automatically subdivide any polygons to achieve microdisplacement. So you've got to generate geometry with as many polygons to whatever you want to displace.

If you are generating that many polygons, a better way is to just bake in the displacement in your modeling program, and export the polygons already displaced. It's the same number of polygons anyway, and you have more control. You can selectively decimate (reduce polygon count) with this method as well and still preserve your surface detail.

Baking displacement will dramatically increase the number of vertices and polygons in your scene, of course, so it is a tradeoff. Using displacement maps in offline renderers (non–Virtual Reality rendering) is often done to reduce polygon counts, but doesn't always work for VR. It is possible that VR shaders will do microdisplacement and adaptive subdivision, as the state of the art constantly moves forward.

If you get a blindingly white texture, or something doesn't look like you expect, double-check the node.js console and look for a 404, like this:

```
Transforming modules 100.0% (557/557), done.
::1 - - [20/Sep/2017:21:57:12 +0000] "GET
/static_assets/1_New_Graph_Metallic_Color.jpg
HTTP/1.1" 404 57 "http://localhost:8081/vr
/?hotreload" "Mozilla/5.0 (Windows NT 6.1; Win64; x64;
rv:57.0) Gecko/20100101 Firefox/57.0"
```

This means you misspelled the texture name.

Then, we'll use object-oriented design coding to modify the class we created, which will update all the deck plates! Make the change to the platform call to the new deck plates OBJ file instead of a box.

The finished VR world

Your complete code should look like this:

```
import React, {Component } from 'react';

import {
  AppRegistry,
  asset,
  AmbientLight,
  Box,
  DirectionalLight,
  Div,
  Model,
  Pano,
  Plane,
  Text,
  Vector,
  View,
  } from 'react-vr';


class Pedestal extends Component {
    render() {
        return (
          <View>
          <Box
          dimWidth={.4}
          dimDepth={.4}
```

```
                    dimHeight={.5}
                    lit
texture={asset('travertine_striata_vein_cut_honed_filled_Base_Color.jpg')}
                    style={{
                        transform: [ { translate: [ this.props.MyX, -1.4,
this.props.MyZ] } ]
                    }}
            />
                <Box
                dimWidth={.5}
                dimDepth={.5}
                dimHeight={.1}
                lit
texture={asset('travertine_striata_vein_cut_honed_filled_Base_Color.jpg')}
                    style={{
                        transform: [ { translate: [ this.props.MyX, -1.1,
this.props.MyZ] } ]
                    }}
            />
                <Box
                dimWidth={.5}
                dimDepth={.5}
                dimHeight={.1}
                lit
texture={asset('travertine_striata_vein_cut_honed_filled_Base_Color.jpg')}
                    style={{
                        transform: [ { translate: [ this.props.MyX, -1.7,
this.props.MyZ] } ]
                    }}
                />
        </View>
    )
    }
    }


        class Platform extends Component {
            render() {
                return (
                    <Model
                    source={{
                        obj: asset('DeckPlate_v1.obj'),
                        mtl: asset('DeckPlate_v1_AllMats.mtl'),
                        }}
                        lit
                        style={{
                            transform: [ {
                            translate: [ this.props.MyX, -1.8,
this.props.MyZ]
```

```
                                }]  }}
                          />


                );
                  }
                  }


    export default class SpaceGallery extends React.Component {
        render() {
            return (
              <View>
                <Pano source={asset('BabbageStation_v6_r5.jpg')}/>
                <AmbientLight

    intensity = {.3}

    />
    <DirectionalLight
    intensity = {.7}
    style={{
        transform:[{
            rotateZ: -45
        }]
    }}
        />
        <Platform MyX={ 0.0} MyZ={-5.1}/>
        <Platform MyX={ 0.0} MyZ={ 0.0}/>
        <Platform MyX={ 0.0} MyZ={ 5.1}/>
        <Platform MyX={ 5.1} MyZ={-5.1}/>
        <Platform MyX={ 5.1} MyZ={ 0.0}/>
        <Platform MyX={ 5.1} MyZ={ 5.1}/>
        <Platform MyX={-5.1} MyZ={-5.1}/>
        <Platform MyX={-5.1} MyZ={ 0.0}/>
        <Platform MyX={-5.1} MyZ={ 5.1}/>

        <Pedestal MyX={ 0.0} MyZ={-5.1}/>
        <Pedestal MyX={ 0.0} MyZ={ 0.0}/>
        <Pedestal MyX={ 0.0} MyZ={ 5.1}/>
        <Pedestal MyX={ 5.1} MyZ={-5.1}/>
        <Pedestal MyX={ 5.1} MyZ={ 0.0}/>
        <Pedestal MyX={ 5.1} MyZ={ 5.1}/>
        <Pedestal MyX={-5.1} MyZ={-5.1}/>
        <Pedestal MyX={-5.1} MyZ={ 0.0}/>
        <Pedestal MyX={-5.1} MyZ={ 5.1}/>

        <Model
          source={{
```

```
        obj: asset('teapot2.obj'),
        mtl: asset('teapot2.mtl'),
        }}
        lit
        style={{
            transform: [{ translate: [ -5.1, -1, -5.1 ] }]
            }}
    />
    <Model
    source={{
        obj: asset('Teapot2_NotSmooth.obj'),
        mtl: asset('teapot2.mtl'),
        }}
        lit
        style={{
            transform: [{ translate: [ -5.1, -1, 0 ] },
            { rotateY: -30 },
            { scale: 0.5} ]
            }}
    />

    <Model
    source={{
        obj: asset('Chap6_Teapot_V2.obj'),
        mtl: asset('Chap6_Teapot_V2.mtl'),
        }}
        lit
        style={{
            transform: [{ translate: [ -5.1, -1, 5.2 ] },
            { rotateY: -30 },
            { scale: 0.5} ]
        }}
    />
    <Model
    source={{
        obj: asset('Chap6_Teapot_V5_SpoutDone.obj'),
        mtl: asset('Chap6_Teapot_V5_SpoutDone.mtl'),
        }}
        lit
        style={{
            transform: [{ translate: [ 5.1, -1, 0 ] },
            { rotateY: -30 },
            { rotateX: 45 },
            { scale: 0.5} ]
            }}
    />

    <Model
```

```
            source={{
                obj: asset('Chap6_Teapot_V5_SpoutDone.obj'),
                mtl: asset('Chap6_Teapot_V5_SpoutDone.mtl'),
                }}
            lit
            style={{
                transform: [{ translate: [ 5.1, -1, 5.1 ] },
                { rotateY: 46 },
                { scale: 0.5} ]
                }}
        />
    <Text
        style={{
            backgroundColor: '#777879',
            fontSize: 0.1,
            fontWeight: '400',
            layoutOrigin: [0.0, 0.5],
            paddingLeft: 0.2,
            paddingRight: 0.2,
            textAlign: 'center',
            textAlignVertical: 'center',
            transform: [
                {translate: [-5.2, -1.4, -4.6] }]
                }}>
        Utah teapot
    </Text>
    <Text
        style={{
            backgroundColor: '#777879',
            fontSize: 0.1,
            fontWeight: '400',
            layoutOrigin: [0.0, 0.5],
            paddingLeft: 0.2,
            paddingRight: 0.2,
            textAlign: 'center',
            textAlignVertical: 'center',
            transform: [
                {translate: [0, -1.3, -4.6] }]
                }}>
        One Tri
    </Text>
    &amp;amp;lt;Model
    lit
    source={{
        obj: asset('OneTriSkinnyWUVTexture_1.obj'),
        mtl: asset('OneTriSkinnyWUVTexture_1.mtl'),
        }}
        style={{
```

```
                    transform: [
                        { translate: [ -0, -.8, -5.2 ] },
                        { rotateY: 10 },
                        { scale: .2 },
]
                    }}
        />
          <Text
          style={{
              backgroundColor: '#777879',
              fontSize: 0.2,
              fontWeight: '400',
              layoutOrigin: [0.0, 0.5],
              paddingLeft: 0.2,
              paddingRight: 0.2,
              textAlign: 'center',
              textAlignVertical: 'center',
              transform: [
                  {translate: [0, 1, -6] }]
          }}>
      Space Gallery
    </Text>
</View>
);
    }
};

AppRegistry.registerComponent('SpaceGallery', () => SpaceGallery);
```

That's a lot to type, and a lot of UV modeling. You can download all of these files at: `http:/` `/bit.ly/VR_Chap7`

In the preceding code, I make use of this:

```
<Platform MyX='0' MyZ='-5.1'/>
```

This will work, but it is more correct to do this:

```
<Platform MyX={0} MyZ={-5.1}/>
```

If you know JSX and React, this will be an obvious goof, but not everyone will pick up on it (honestly, as a C++ programmer I missed it at first). Anything inside { } braces is *code* and anything that is quoted is text. The documentation says this:

> *Props - Components can take arguments such as a name in* `<Greeting name='Rexxar'/>`. *Such arguments are known as properties or props and are accessed through the this.props variable. Name, from this example, is accessible as* `{this.props.name}`. *You can read more about this interaction under Components, Props, and State.*

The mention about the argument is only true for text props. For numeric props, using the quoted syntax like `'0.5'` will seem to work, but have weird consequences. We'll see more in `Chapter 11`, *Take a Walk on the Wild Side*, but basically, for numeric variables, you *should* use `{0.5}` (braces).

Summary

In this chapter, we learned how to do polygon modeling with Blender, and how to override texture assignments and wrap textures around models. We learned to make textures that can make your world seem more real.

However, the world is still static. In the next chapter, you will learn how to make things move to really bring your worlds to life.

8
Breath Life in Your World

In the last chapter, with materials, we made objects look more real. We know that is not totally necessary for VR to work as we discussed in Chapter 1, *What is Virtual Reality, Really*, but it certainly helps. Now, we will learn how to really make things seem real by making them move. This does two things: things that move look more alive, and it also helps parallax depth perception.

React VR has a number of APIs that will make it very easy to include animations that are fluid and natural. In most traditional CGI, making animation fluid is not so easy; you've got to start a motion out slow, ramp up to speed, and slow it down gently as well, otherwise the movement looks fake.

We will cover these topics in this chapter:

- The Animated API that is used to animate objects
- A one-shot animation
- Continuous animation
- Life cycle events such as componentDidMount()
- How to inject sound into the world

Movement and sound go a long way in making a world look alive. Let's do that!

The Animated API

React and React VR make this easy as the animation API has a number of animation types that make this straightforward, without having to do math or have key frames, as you would with traditional animation. Instead of keyframing, you can ramp up things slowly, bounce, and pause declaratively. These props are spring, decay, and timing; more detail on these is in the online documentation at http://bit.ly/ReactAnims.

It's fine to animate, but we need to know where we are going. To do this, the Animation API has two value types: value for scalar (single values), and ValueXY for vectors. You might wonder why in this case a vector is only *X* and *Y*—ValueXY is intended for UI elements, that by their nature, are flat. If you need to animate an X, Y, and Z location, you would use three scalars.

First, we'll create an animated teapot that spins. This will be especially helpful to see how our texture mapping works. If you've been following along the code, your `SpaceGallery` app should already have most of what we need to start writing this chapter. If not, you can download the source files to start with at: `http://bit.ly/VR_Chap7`. If you really don't want to type all of this, I put the final files at: `http://bit.ly/VR_Chap8`.

Assuming you either downloaded or finished the last chapter, take the `index.vr.js`, from `Chapter` 7, *Sitting Down with a (Virtual) Teapot,* start and enter the following new class, `TurningPot()` at the top of the file but under the `import` statements (note that we are still in the `SpaceGallery` app).

```
class TurningPot extends React.Component {
    constructor(props) {
      super(props);
      this.state = {
        yRotation: new Animated.Value(0),
      };
    }
}
```

This sets up our animated value/variable—`yRotation`. We've created it as a scalar, which is OK, as we'll be mapping that to `rotateY`.

Don't forget to `import` the animated keyword.

Next, we'll use a life cycle override called `componentDidMount`. Life cycle overrides are events that are called at specific times during the loading and creation (rendering) of the VR world; in this case, the `componentDidMount` function is called after mounting (as per the "Did" fragment in the name of the event). Mounting means that the object is loaded, available, and created inside three.js; in other words, it's in the world. The function `componentWillMount` is called when that component is about to be mounted but doesn't exist yet; we don't use this one as we want the object to move when it's actually a visible object, although it's really useful for loading objects, initializing state, and the like.

Note that we haven't finished the declaration yet, so the final closing { brace isn't there:

```
componentDidMount() {
    Animated.timing(
        this.state.yRotation, // Animate variable `yRotation`
        {
            duration: 10000,   // Time
            toValue: 360,      // Spin around a full circle
        }
    ).start();                 // Start the animation
}
```

The `componentDidMount()` is an important object life cycle API call that is used to do things like what we're doing; starting the animation.

> This event will most likely happen before the browser finishes loading everything, so you may miss the actual start. If this is a concern, you can overload some other methods to ensure that it fires at the right time, or introduces a small delay.

Flying teapots

Now for the important thing, the rendering itself. Write the following method using the `Animated.View` keyword:

```
render() {
    return (
        <Animated.View // Base: Image, Text, View
            style={{
                flex: 1,
                width: 1,
                height: 1,
                transform: [
                    {rotateY: this.state.yRotation}, // Map yRotation to rotateY
                ]
            }}
        >
        <Model
        source={{
            obj: asset('teapot2.obj'),
            mtl: asset('teapot2_Mats.mtl'),
            }}
            lit
            style={{
                transform: [{ translate: [0, -0.7, -5.1 ] }]
```

```
                    }}
            />
        </Animated.View>
        );
    }

}
```

Now, save this file. If you used `?hotreload` in the URL `http://localhost:8081/vr/?hotreload` when bringing up your world, and typed everything correctly, you'll see the teapot spinning in front of you automatically. Otherwise, hit the 'refresh' button in your browser.

Wait, what? What just happened? Why is the pot flying!

The teapot revolved around *us,* the center of the `<view>`, not about its own axis. Why was that? Remember that translation order is important. In this case, we had a separate translation and rotation:

```
render() {
    return (
      <Animated.View
...
        {rotateY: this.state.yRotation}, // Map yRotation to rotateY
...
      <Model
...
            transform: [{ translate: [0, -0.7, -5.1 ] }]
...
      </Animated.View>
    );
```

What is happening here is that the view is rotating, and then the model is transforming. We want to do it in the opposite order. One solution is to leave the model where it is and change the `render()` loop to this (note the bold part):

```
render() {
    return (
      <Animated.View // Base: Image, Text, View
        style={{
          transform: [
            {translate: [0, -0.7, -5.1 ] },
            {rotateY: this.state.yRotation}, // Map `yRotation' to
rotateY
          ]
        }}
      >
        <Model
        source={{
            obj: asset('teapot2.obj'),
            mtl: asset('teapot2_Mats.mtl'),
          }}
          lit
          // we comment this out because we translate the view above
          // style={{
          // transform: [{ translate: [0, -0.7, -5.1 ] }]
          // }}
        />
      </Animated.View>
    );
  }
```

Spinning once and forever

When we save this file and view it again in our VR browser, we will see the pot turn once. Note that we may not see the startup, and also note that when the pot finishes turning, it does so gracefully instead of being a computer animated 'smash stop':

This is fantastic, but the pot turns and then stops. We might want it to continue to turn. So let's do that!

Modify the component creation to do the following (yes, we sort of get rid of all the cool Animate keywords):

```
class TurningPot extends React.Component {
  constructor(props) {
    super(props);
    this.state = {yRotation: 0};
    this.lastUpdate = Date.now();
    this.rotate = this.rotate.bind(this);
  }
```

Okay, in this part, make note of a few things. The variable we are using is called `yRotation`; we also use the word `rotate`, which is actually a new function:

```
rotate() { //custom function, called when it is time to rotate
    const now = Date.now();
    const delta = now - this.lastUpdate;
    this.lastUpdate = now;
    console.log("Spinning the pot");
    //note: the 20 is the rotation speed; bad form to
    //hard code it- this is for instructional purposes only
    this.setState({yRotation: this.state.yRotation + delta / 20} );
    //requestAnimationFrame calls the routine specified, not a variable
    this.frameHandle = requestAnimationFrame(this.rotate);
}
```

We also need to change the object loading/unloading routines, to both start up the rotation as well as to end the timer callback:

```
componentDidMount() { //do the first rotation
    this.rotate();
}
componentWillUnmount() { //Important clean up functions
    if (this.frameHandle) {
        cancelAnimationFrame(this.frameHandle);
        this.frameHandle = null;
    }
}
```

The `<View>` itself doesn't change; it's merely rotating the object as the driving function does; this time, we're driving it with a custom function called on every `render()` loop.

It's very important to check the time lapsed, as different platforms will have different frame rates, depending on hardware, GPU, and many other factors. To ensure that all types of computers and mobile devices see the pot spin at the same speed, we take the `now` variable and calculating the difference between `now` and `this.lastUpdate` giving us a delta time. We use the delta for the actual spin speed.

The final code

Now that we have all that fixed, we have a well rendered spinning teapot. While doing the coding, we also fixed a bad piece of programming; the pot speed was hard coded to be 20 or so. This is better if it's a `const` from a programming maxim, "never embed constants in the body of your program":

```
import React, {Component } from 'react';

import {
  Animated,
  AppRegistry,
  asset,
  AmbientLight,
  Box,
  DirectionalLight,
  Div,
  Model,
  Pano,
  Plane,
  Text,
  Vector,
  View,
} from 'react-vr';

class TurningPot extends React.Component {
  constructor(props) {
    super(props);
    this.state = {yRotation: 0};
    this.lastUpdate = Date.now();
    this.rotate = this.rotate.bind(this);
  }
  rotate() { //custom function, called when it is time to rotate
    const now = Date.now();
    const delta = now - this.lastUpdate;
    const potSpeed = 20;
    this.lastUpdate = now;
    this.setState({yRotation: this.state.yRotation + delta / potSpeed}
);

    //requestAnimationFrame calls the routine specified, not a variable
    this.frameHandle = requestAnimationFrame(this.rotate);
  }
  componentDidMount() { //do the first rotation
    this.rotate();
  }
  componentWillUnmount() { //Important clean up functions
    if (this.frameHandle) {
```

```
                cancelAnimationFrame(this.frameHandle);
                this.frameHandle = null;
            }
        }
    render() {
        return (
            <Animated.View // Base: Image, Text, View
                style={{
                    transform: [ // `transform` is an ordered array
                        {translate: [0, -0.5, -5.1 ] },
                        {rotateY: this.state.yRotation}, // Map `yRotation' to
rotateY
                    ]
                }}
            >
                <Model
                source={{
                    obj: asset('teapot2.obj'),
                    mtl: asset('teapot2_Mats.mtl'),
                }}
                lit
                //style={{
                // transform: [{ translate: [0, -0.7, -5.1 ] }]
                // }}
                />
            </Animated.View>
        );
    }

}


class Pedestal extends Component {
    render() {
        return (
            <View>
            <Box
            dimWidth={.4}
            dimDepth={.4}
            dimHeight={.5}
            lit
texture={asset('travertine_striata_vein_cut_honed_filled_Base_Color.jpg')}
            style={{
                transform: [ { translate: [ this.props.MyX, -1.4,
this.props.MyZ] } ]
            }}
            />
            <Box
```

```
                dimWidth={.5}
                dimDepth={.5}
                dimHeight={.1}
                lit
    texture={asset('travertine_striata_vein_cut_honed_filled_Base_Color.jpg')}
                style={{
                    transform: [ { translate: [ this.props.MyX, -1.1,
    this.props.MyZ] } ]
                    }}
            />
                <Box
                dimWidth={.5}
                dimDepth={.5}
                dimHeight={.1}
                lit
    texture={asset('travertine_striata_vein_cut_honed_filled_Base_Color.jpg')}
                style={{
                    transform: [ { translate: [ this.props.MyX, -1.7,
    this.props.MyZ] } ]
                    }}
            />
        </View>
        )
        }
        }


        class Platform extends Component {
            render() {
                return (
                    <Model
                    source={{
                        obj: asset('DeckPlate_v1.obj'),
                        mtl: asset('DeckPlate_v1_AllMats.mtl'),
                        }}
                        lit
                        style={{
                            transform: [ {
                            translate: [ this.props.MyX, -1.8,
    this.props.MyZ]
                        }] }}
                    />

        );
            }
            }


    export default class SpaceGallery extends React.Component {
```

```
render() {
    return (
      <View>
        <Pano source={asset('BabbageStation_v6_r5.jpg')}/>
        <AmbientLight

intensity = {.3}

/>
<DirectionalLight
intensity = {.7}
style={{
    transform:[{
        rotateZ: -45
    }]
}}
    />
    <Platform MyX='0' MyZ='-5.1'/>
    <Platform MyX='0' MyZ='0'/>
    <Platform MyX='0' MyZ='5.1'/>
    <Platform MyX='5.1' MyZ='-5.1'/>
    <Platform MyX='5.1' MyZ='0'/>
    <Platform MyX='5.1' MyZ='5.1'/>
    <Platform MyX='-5.1' MyZ='-5.1'/>
    <Platform MyX='-5.1' MyZ='0'/>
    <Platform MyX='-5.1' MyZ='5.1'/>

    <Pedestal MyX='0' MyZ='-5.1'/>
    <Pedestal MyX='0' MyZ='5.1'/>
    <Pedestal MyX='5.1' MyZ='-5.1'/>

    <Pedestal MyX='5.1' MyZ='5.1'/>
    <Pedestal MyX='-5.1' MyZ='-5.1'/>
    <Pedestal MyX='-5.1' MyZ='0'/>
    <Pedestal MyX='-5.1' MyZ='5.1'/>

    <Model
        source={{
            obj: asset('teapot2.obj'),
            mtl: asset('teapot2_Mats.mtl'),
            }}
            lit
            style={{
                transform: [{ translate: [ -5.1, -1, -5.1 ] }]
                }}
        />
    <Text
        style={{
```

```
                        backgroundColor: '#777879',
                        fontSize: 0.1,
                        fontWeight: '400',
                        layoutOrigin: [0.0, 0.5],
                        paddingLeft: 0.2,
                        paddingRight: 0.2,
                        textAlign: 'center',
                        textAlignVertical: 'center',
                        transform: [
                            {translate: [-5.2, -1.4, -4.6] }]
                            }}>
                Utah Teapot
            </Text>
            <Text
                style={{
                    backgroundColor: '#777879',
                    fontSize: 0.1,
                    fontWeight: '400',
                    layoutOrigin: [0.0, 0.5],
                    paddingLeft: 0.2,
                    paddingRight: 0.2,
                    textAlign: 'center',
                    textAlignVertical: 'center',
                    transform: [
                        {translate: [0, -1.3, -4.6] }]
                        }}>
                Spinning Pot
            </Text>


            <Text
            style={{
                backgroundColor: '#777879',
                fontSize: 0.2,
                fontWeight: '400',
                layoutOrigin: [0.0, 0.5],
                paddingLeft: 0.2,
                paddingRight: 0.2,
                textAlign: 'center',
                textAlignVertical: 'center',
                transform: [
                    {translate: [0, 1, -6] }]
                }}>
        Space Gallery
    </Text>
    <TurningPot/>
</View>
);
```

```
    }
};

AppRegistry.registerComponent('SpaceGallery', () => SpaceGallery);
```

Sound

Sound in VR is actually pretty complicated. Our ears hear things differently to someone else's ear. Many VR systems do a simple "if it's on the right, it's louder to my right ear" stereo pan (stereo panning), but this isn't really the way that actual sound works. For VR, and the high frame rates that they require, just like our lighting effects skip doing full raytracing, this sound panning is okay.

More sophisticated VR systems would use something called a **Head Related Transfer Function** (**HRTF**). An HRTF is how sound changes when you tilt your head. In other words, how does sound "transfer" based on *your* head? Each person has their own HRTF; it takes into account the shape of their ears, the bone density in their heads, and the size and shape of their nose and mouth cavities. Our ears, coupled with the way we are raised, during which we train our brain, allows us to do amazing things with an HRTF. For example, humans can locate something in three dimensions by only hearing it from two points. That would be like being able to see in stereo with only one eye! HRTF gives us what vision doesn't; it gives us spatial awareness of what is happening all around us, even if we don't see it.

To use HRTFs for Virtual Reality will require every person hearing a sound in a virtual world to have their HRTF loaded into the VR world's sound system. Further, that HRTF has to be measured in an anechoic chamber (a chamber with foam lining on the walls to eliminate echo). This is obviously not very common.

Most VR sound, thus, just does a left/right panning.

This is an area where VR can have significant breakthroughs. Sound is very important, and allows us to perceive things in 3D space; it is an important aspect of immersion. Many people think Stereo Panning is 3D; this is where a sound is simply louder in one ear than the other. In an audio system, this is the *balance* knob. In headphones, it'll sound weird, but it's not actually localizing the sound. In the real world, your right ear will hear a sound just a split second before (or after) the left ear, and as you tilt your head, the curves in your ear change that delay and your brain says "Ah, the sound is right *there*."

Stereo panning is about all that can be done without the HRTF measuring, but an HRTF is significantly better. The good news is that audio hardware and computing power is so great now that with an HRTF or reasonable software to simulate an average HRTF, much more complicated sound processing is possible. Look to this area for future enhancements.

The power of React VR again comes to our rescue. We don't have to worry about all that; we just have to put the sound in our world.

Seriously, don't get too discouraged with all that talk, just be aware that sound is difficult (as important as graphics rendering), but at this point, all you really need to do is to get a good mono (not stereo) sound and describe it in the scene file.

That's the whole point of React VR. Describe what you want; you don't need to tell people how to do it. Still, you need to know what is going on behind the scenes.

Putting sound in our world

Now, let's actually make some noise. Freesound.com is a good place to go for free game sounds. Most of the sounds there require attribution. Giving credit to the people who help build your world is the right thing to do. Go to the site and download several sound files you like. A few of the ones I found at freesound.com are these:

- Boiling pot water by Geodylabs (http://bit.ly/BoilingPot1)
- Boiling water by dobroide (http://bit.ly/Boiling2)
- Boiling water by abrez (http://bit.ly/Boiling3)

I downloaded these in the .mp3 file format; this should be fairly cross platform. Copy these into a new folder called sounds in the directory of static_assets too. I only used one of them in the actual world, but you can experiment with the others. Sometimes you don't know if it works until you hear it in the world.

Sound is a node that has to be attached to a View, Image, or Text—React VR's only components. You probably want to attach it to a box, model, or whatever; just wrap the object with a <View>, and put the sound component inside it, as shown:

```
<View>
<Model
    source={{
     obj: asset('teapot2.obj'),
     mtl: asset('teapot2_Mats.mtl'),
     }}
     lit
```

```
        style={{
            transform: [{ translate: [ -5.1, -1, -5.1 ] }]
        }}
    >
    </Model>
    <Sound
        loop
        source={{wav: asset('sounds/211491__abrez__boiling-water.mp3') }}
        />
    </View>
```

One thing that is a bit funny is that the sounds don't come from where our teapot is (the upper left as you first view the world). Why is that? Look at the preceding code; we've simply wrapped the View tag around the Model; so it is transformed differently than the sound.

Some sounds work better than others; you'll have to experiment or record your own. Fixing the transformation is left as an exercise for the reader. (Actually, it's easy, but ensure that you don't paste the transform as a child XML element.) The correct code is this:

```
<View
    style={{
        transform: [{ translate: [-5.1, -1, -5.1] }]
    }}
    >
    <Model
        source={{
            obj: asset('teapot2.obj'),
            mtl: asset('teapot2_Mats.mtl'),
        }}
        lit
    >
    </Model>
    <Sound
        loop
        source={{ wav: asset('sounds/211491__abrez__boiling-water.mp3') }}
    />
</View>
```

Summary

We learned how to build animations both by procedurally changing an object's position and by using the more advanced methods of using timers and the Animated API. We dramatically saw what happens if we use the wrong <View> to animate, and developed a way to make objects animate forever. The Energizer bunny will be proud. We also added sound, which is a very important thing for virtual worlds.

There is a lot you can do with timers; I highly recommend that you study the online documentation and experiment!

So far, we have stayed within React VR. Sometimes, there are things we need to do that React doesn't allow us to do. In the next chapter, we'll go Native (native React, that is)!

Can someone turn off that boiling pot?

9
Do It Yourself – Native Modules and Three.js

React VR makes it easy to do VR without having to know three.js. The three.js is the wrapper class that helps implement WebGL, which itself is a form of the native OpenGL rendering library.

React VR is fairly inclusive, but like all APIs, it can't do everything. Fortunately, React VR anticipated this; if React VR doesn't support a feature and you need it, you can build that feature yourself.

In this chapter, you will cover the following topics:

- Using three.js from inside React VR code
- The basic three.js procedural code
- Setting up three.js to interact with our React VR components
- Using three.js to do things visually that are lower level with three.js

Native modules and views

Maybe you do know three.js and need to use it. **React Native modules** are how your code can directly include raw three.js programming. This is very useful if you need to programmatically create native three.js objects, modify material attributes, or use other three.js code that isn't directly exposed by React VR.

You may have some JavaScript code that does business logic, and don't want to, or can't rewrite that as React VR components. You might need to access three.js or WebVR components from React VR. You might need to build a high-performance database query with multiple threads so that the main rendering loop doesn't slow down. All of these things are possible with React Native.

This is a fairly advanced topic and will not normally be required to write engaging, effective WebVR demos; still, it's fantastic knowing that React VR and React are so extensible.

Making a three.js cube demo

First, let's take a look at a simple box demo. Let's start with a freshly generated site. Go to your node.js command-line interface and kill any *npm start* windows you have running and recreate a new, fresh site by issuing the command:

```
f:\ReactVR>React-vr init GoingNative
```

The first task is to go to the `vr` folder and edit `client.js`. Up to this point, we haven't had to edit this file; it contains boilerplate React VR code. Today, we're going to edit it, as we aren't doing just boilerplate. The bold lines in the following code are the lines we will add to `client.js`:

```
// Auto-generated content.
// This file contains the boilerplate to set up your React app.
// If you want to modify your application, start in "index.vr.js"

// Auto-generated content.
import {VRInstance} from 'react-vr-web';
import {Module} from 'react-vr-web';
import * as THREE from 'three';

function init(bundle, parent, options) {
const scene = new THREE.Scene();
const cubeModule = new CubeModule();

const vr = new VRInstance(bundle, 'GoingNative', parent, {
 // Add custom options here
 cursorVisibility: 'visible',
 nativeModules: [ cubeModule ],
 scene: scene,
 ...options,
 });

const cube = new THREE.Mesh(
new THREE.BoxGeometry(1, 1, 1),
```

```
   new THREE.MeshBasicMaterial()
   );
   cube.position.z = -4;
   scene.add(cube);
   cubeModule.init(cube);

   vr.render = function(timestamp) {
   // Any custom behavior you want to perform on each frame goes here
   //animate the cube
   const seconds = timestamp / 1000;
   cube.position.x = 0 + (1 * (Math.cos(seconds)));
   cube.position.y = 0.2 + (1 * Math.abs(Math.sin(seconds)));
   };
   // Begin the animation loop
   vr.start();
   return vr;
   };

window.ReactVR = {init};
```

We also need to create the object CubeModule. You could put this in a separate file, and should if it gets complicated. For now, we can add it to the bottom of client.js:

```
export default class CubeModule extends Module {
   constructor() {
     super('CubeModule');
   }
   init(cube) {
     this.cube = cube;
   }
   changeCubeColor(color) {
     this.cube.material.color = new THREE.Color(color);
   }
}
```

No other changes are needed. You will now see a bouncing, plain white cube. We haven't changed index.vr.js, so it still displays the **hello** text. This shows that both React VR and Native code, in this case three.js, are running at the same time.

OK, so we put in a bouncing cube. The nice thing about this code is that it shows some high levels of integration; yet, this is done in a very clean way. For example, the line—const scene = new THREE.Scene()—gives you a three.js-accessible scene, so we can do whatever we want with three.js, yet, all of the React VR keywords just work because it will use the existing scene. You don't have to import/export scenes from one side to another and maintain handles/pointers. It's all clean, declarative, as React VR is supposed to be. We have the regular scene and objects created outside of our normal React VR syntax.

In our previous animations, we changed index.vr.js. In this case, with three.js objects, we make those changes directly in this part of client.js; right where the code generator suggests it:

```
vr.render = function(timestamp) {
// Any custom behavior you want to perform on each frame
goes here
```

Making native code interact with React VR

You can really see the power of React VR if we then go ahead and make this object interact with the rest of the world. To do that, we will need to change the index.vr.js. We will also use a `VrButton` for the first time.

> Note the spelling in `VrButton`. I was beating my head against the keyboard for a while on that one. I just naturally type "VR" instead of "Vr," but it does follow the React VR case standard.

> The clue is that in the console you will see `VRButton is not defined`, which normally means that you forgot it in the `import` statement. In this particular case, you'll see an oddity of React; you can type `import { YoMomma } from 'react-vr';` and you won't get an error; try it. React VR is apparently too scared to talk back to YoMomma.

When we click on buttons, an important part of immersion is for them to make a click. Anyone that has their phone on silent, without vibration knows what I mean; you press on the cell phone and hear nothing and think it's broken. So, let's head to `FreeSound.org` and download some clicks.

I found *Switch Flip #1* by *IanStarGem,* and it's Creative Commons licensed. So, let's put that in the `static_assets` folder:

1. First, we will need to include the declaration of our `NativeModule`; usually, you do this at the top after the `import` directives, as follows:

```
// Native Module defined in vr/client.js
const cubeModule = NativeModules.CubeModule;
```

   Note that you could call your object `CubeModule` but you can get confused with the implementation versus definition. It does make it easier to type. JavaScript can be pretty forgiving. That may or may not be a good thing.

2. In any event, in `index.vr.js`, we need to setup our new inital state, or we get a black screen and an error:

```
class GoingNative extends React.Component {
  constructor(props) {
  super(props);
  this.state = { btnColor: 'white', cubeColor: 'yellow' };
  cubeModule.changeCubeColor(this.state.cubeColor);
  }
```

3. In the same file, right below the `render()` statement, change the `<View>` definition to the following (note that we are still 'inside' the view and haven't closed it yet):

```
<View
  style={{
    transform:[{translate: [0, 0, -3]}],
    layoutOrigin: [0.5, 0, 0],
    alignItems: 'center',
  }}>
```

We are cheating slightly here, that is, moving the view backward so that the objects are in front of us.

As React VR is not a CAD system, you can't edit visually, so you've got to think about the positioning of items when you do the code.

Layout graph paper might also help for something complicated.

4. After the `<Pano>` statement, and before the `</View>` closing tag, insert the following (changing the template-generated Text statement):

```
<VrButton
  style={{
    backgroundColor: this.state.btnColor,
    borderRadius: 0.05,
    margin: 0.05,
  }}
  onEnter={() => { this.setState({ btnColor: this.state.cubeColor
}) }}
  onExit={() => { this.setState({ btnColor: 'white' }) }}
  onClick={() => {
    let hexColor = Math.floor(Math.random() *
0xffffff).toString(16);
    // Ensure we always have 6 digits by padding with leading
zeros.
    hexColor = '#' + (('000000' + hexColor).slice(-6));
    this.setState({ cubeColor: hexColor, btnColor: hexColor });
    // Asynchronous call to custom native module; sends the new
color.
    cubeModule.changeCubeColor(hexColor);
  }}
  onClickSound={asset('freesound__278205__ianstargem__switch-
flip-1.wav')}
  >
  <Text style={{
```

```
        fontSize: 0.15,
        paddingTop: 0.025,
        paddingBottom: 0.025,
        paddingLeft: 0.05,
        paddingRight: 0.05,
        textAlign: 'center',
        textAlignVertical: 'center',
      }}>
        button
    </Text>
</VrButton>
```

When you refresh your browser, the cube will still bounce around, but you can click on the button and see the cube change color. When you move the mouse or controller's cursor over the button (visible as a `<Text>` component), you will see the button change to the cube's current color.

One neat thing you could do is pregenerate the new color of the cube in a static variable (so it doesn't go away like let will) and then make the mouse over color be that color.

A default color of white on white should be fixed too.
Go ahead and try that; it's a fun exercise.

When we play the sound, we get the following error in the console of the browser:

```
VrSoundEffects: must load sound before playing
../static_assets/freesound__278205__ianstargem__switch-flip-1.wav
```

You may also see the following error:

```
Failed to fetch audio:
../static_assets/freesound__278205__ianstargem__switch-flip-1.wav
The buffer passed to decodeAudioData contains invalid content which
cannot be decoded successfully.
```

5. The fix for this problem is to make sure that you have the right audio format for your browser. The right formats are:
   1. Audio files need to be mono; this is so they can be transformed into 3D space.
   2. Audio files need to be 48 KHz or lower. This seemed to change between Firefox 55 and 59, but it's safest to be as generic as possible.

6. If your files are the wrong format, or you don't hear the sound, there are two possible fixes:

   1. You can fix these with Audacity or other sound editing tools.
   2. You can let me fix it! I've already downloaded and converted the file for you in the book files. However, if you don't try to do the fix, you won't learn. You could just download only 48 KHz mono files and avoid the conversion, but in practice these are fairly rare. Converting the sounds is easy and free with Audacity, you just have to learn a little bit of the program to do this. Inside the VR button all we need to do is load the modifed, mono sound file:

```
onClickSound={asset('freesound__278205__ianstargem__switch-
flip-48kmono.wav')}
```

I mentioned this in an earlier section, but it bears repeating that if you get unexplained errors and you exclaim "I know the file is there and it plays!", try checking the format of the sound file.

Summing up the code so far

We added a lot of code; let's summarize where we are. React VR can sometimes be confusing, as it is a mixture of JavaScript and XML "ish" code (JSX), so here is the complete and total index.vr.js:

```
import React from 'react';
import {
  AppRegistry,
  Animated,
  asset,
  Easing,
  NativeModules,
  Pano,
  Sound,
  Text,
  View,
  VrButton
} from 'react-vr';

const cubeModule = NativeModules.CubeModule;

class GoingNative extends React.Component {
  constructor(props) {
```

```
    super(props);
    this.state = { btnColor: 'white', cubeColor: 'yellow' };
    cubeModule.changeCubeColor(this.state.cubeColor);
  }
  render() {
    return (
      <View
        style={{
          transform: [{ translate: [0, 0, -3] }],
          layoutOrigin: [0.5, 0, 0],
          alignItems: 'center',
        }}>
        <Pano source={asset('chess-world.jpg')} />
        <VrButton
          style={{
            backgroundColor: this.state.btnColor,
            borderRadius: 0.05,
            margin: 0.05,
          }}
          onEnter={() => { this.setState({ btnColor: this.state.cubeColor
}) }}
          onExit={() => { this.setState({ btnColor: 'white' }) }}
          onClick={() => {
            let hexColor = Math.floor(Math.random() *
0xffffff).toString(16);
            // Ensure we always have 6 digits by padding with leading
zeros.
            hexColor = '#' + (('000000' + hexColor).slice(-6));
            this.setState({ cubeColor: hexColor, btnColor: hexColor });
            // Asynchronous call to custom native module; sends the new
color.
            cubeModule.changeCubeColor(hexColor);
          }}
          onClickSound={asset('freesound__278205__ianstargem__switch-
flip-48kmono.wav')}
        >
          <Text style={{
            fontSize: 0.15,
            paddingTop: 0.025,
            paddingBottom: 0.025,
            paddingLeft: 0.05,
            paddingRight: 0.05,
            textAlign: 'center',
            textAlignVertical: 'center',
          }}>
            button
        </Text>
        </VrButton>
```

```
        </View>
      );
    }
};

AppRegistry.registerComponent('GoingNative', () => GoingNative);
```

In the file, `client.js`, in the `vr` folder (the folder name is lowercase), will be the following:

```
import {VRInstance} from 'react-vr-web';
import {Module} from 'react-vr-web';
import * as THREE from 'three';

function init(bundle, parent, options) {
const scene = new THREE.Scene();
const cubeModule = new CubeModule();
const vr = new VRInstance(bundle, 'GoingNative', parent, {
    cursorVisibility: 'visible',
    nativeModules: [ cubeModule ],
    scene: scene,
    ...options,
  });

  const cube = new THREE.Mesh(
    new THREE.BoxGeometry(1, 1, 1),
    new THREE.MeshBasicMaterial()
  );
  cube.position.z = -4;
  scene.add(cube);

  cubeModule.init(cube);

  vr.render = function(timestamp) {
    const seconds = timestamp / 1000;
    cube.position.x = 0 + (1 * (Math.cos(seconds)));
    cube.position.y = 0.2 + (1 * Math.abs(Math.sin(seconds)));
  };
  vr.start();
  return vr;
};

window.ReactVR = {init};

export default class CubeModule extends Module {
  constructor() {
    super('CubeModule');
  }
  init(cube) {
```

```
    this.cube = cube;
  }
  changeCubeColor(color) {
    this.cube.material.color = new THREE.Color(color);
  }
}
```

Something more visual

We've done some neat interactivity, which is fantastic, although another big reason to use three.js directly is to do something rendering wise that React VR cannot do. Well, actually, React VR can do some amazing things through Native methods, so let's do exactly that.

First, let's change our cube from bouncing around to spinning as well. It'll look more impressive when we add some of the visual effects.

Let's also add a few spheres around. We'll want some things to reflect. I chose reflection as an impressive thing that you cannot really do in real time with WebVR currently, although we can do something really close to it through environment mapping. For a fairly long discussion of what environment mapping is, you can go to: http://bit.ly/ReflectMap.

Add the following code to your existing index.vr.js, below the </VrButton>:

```
<Sphere
  radius={0.5}
  widthSegments={20}
  heightSegments={12}
  style={{
    color: 'blue',
    transform: [{ translate: [-1, 0, -3] }],
  }}
  lit />
<Sphere
  radius={1.5}
  widthSegments={20}
  heightSegments={12}
  style={{
    color: 'crimson',
    transform: [{ translate: [1, -2, -3] }],
  }}
  lit />
```

We'll also add an ambient and directional light to the top of `index.vr.js` inside the top level `<View>`:

```
<AmbientLight  intensity={.3} />
<DirectionalLight
  intensity={.7}
  style={{ transform: [{
    rotateZ: 45
  }]
  }}
/>
```

Go ahead and load that, and make sure that you see a nice blue sphere and big red ball. Note that I'm coding slightly more dense than normal, so this book doesn't kill more trees or photons. Most of our changes are going to be in `client.js`. First, initialize all of the variables we need under `init`:

```
var materialTorus;
var materialCube;
var torusCamera;
var cubeCamera;
var renderFrame;
var torus;
var texture;
var cube;
```

Then, we will set up a custom background to the scene. Interestingly, this doesn't show up when we have a `<Pano>` statement, but that's a good thing as we're coding in `three.js` right now; it doesn't understand VR, so the background isn't quite right. This will show up on the images a little, but fixing that is best left as an exercise by the reader. To setup the custom background for `three.js`, continue adding to the code as follows:

```
var textureLoader = new THREE.TextureLoader();
textureLoader.load('../static_assets/chess-world.jpg', function (texture)
{
  texture.mapping = THREE.UVMapping;
  scene.background = texture;
});
```

Then, we'll create a torus and the cube we already created earlier (remember that this is all still in the init statement):

```
torusCamera = new THREE.CubeCamera(.1, 100, 256);
torusCamera.renderTarget.texture.minFilter =
THREE.LinearMipMapLinearFilter;
  scene.add(torusCamera);

cubeCamera = new THREE.CubeCamera(.1, 100, 256);
cubeCamera.renderTarget.texture.minFilter =
THREE.LinearMipMapLinearFilter;
  scene.add(cubeCamera);
```

What we've done here is created some extra cameras. We will move these cameras to where the torus and our bouncing cube will be, then render those cameras to an off-screen buffer (that won't be visible). Now that we have created those cameras, we can create our cube and torus three.js objects; note that this is a slight change to our earlier cube:

```
  materialTorus = new THREE.MeshBasicMaterial({ envMap:
torusCamera.renderTarget.texture });
  materialCube = new THREE.MeshBasicMaterial({ envMap:
cubeCamera.renderTarget.texture });

torus = new THREE.Mesh(new THREE.TorusKnotBufferGeometry(2, .6, 100, 25),
materialTorus);
  torus.position.z = -10; torus.position.x = 1;
  scene.add(torus);

cube = new THREE.Mesh( new THREE.BoxGeometry(1, 1, 1), materialCube);
  cube.position.z = -4;
  scene.add(cube);

renderFrame = 0;
cubeModule.init(cube);
```

Note that the `cubeModule.init(cube);` statement should have already been there. Now, we just have to actually wrap the faux tinfoil around our objects; we will do this in the `vr.render` function. Here is the entire function:

```
vr.render = function (timestamp) {
    // Any custom behavior you want to perform on each frame goes here
    const seconds = timestamp / 2000;
    cube.position.x = 0 + (1 * (Math.cos(seconds)));
    cube.position.y = 0.2 + (1 * Math.abs(Math.sin(seconds)));
    cube.position.y = 0.2 + (1 * Math.sin(seconds));
```

```
    var time = Date.now();
    torus.rotation.x += 0.01;
    torus.rotation.y += 0.02;

    //we need to turn off the reflected objects,
    //or the camera will be inside.
    torus.visible = false;
    torusCamera.position.copy(torus.position);
    torusCamera.update(vr.player.renderer, scene)
    materialTorus.envMap = torusCamera.renderTarget.texture;
    torus.visible = true;

    cube.visible = false;
    cubeCamera.position.copy(cube.position);
    cubeCamera.update(vr.player.renderer, scene);
    materialCube.envMap = cubeCamera.renderTarget.texture;
    cube.visible = true;

    renderFrame++;

  };
  // Begin the animation loop
  vr.start();
  return vr;
};
```

I changed the box slightly by removing the function `Math.abs(..)` around the sine wave so that it'll rotate in a complete circle; this is so that we can see what is good about reflection maps, and what is bad.

Hopefully, we got everything pasted in. You can watch the display with a grin on your face. Neat chrome knot objects! After you stare at it, you'll note that a few things aren't quite right. You can see the difference between the faked reflections and real reflections in the square box. It'll look a little "off," but the chrome knot looks good.

Check out the red highlight versus the green in the following image:

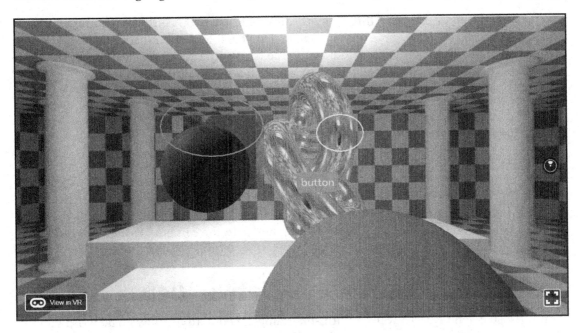

Creating good VR is all about reasonable compromises. In the case of reflections, they can look great, as the preceding image shows, but they can also look just a little disturbing. The box or a flat mirror would be a good example of something not to do. Curved objects look a lot more natural as you can see.

Games and real-time programming are as much about careful design as a faithful recreation of the real world. Remember that we do not create something real; all we have to do is create something which will seem real.

There is a true reflector in three.js called `THREE.Reflector` if you want to build a flat mirror. It is well documented in the three.js examples.

With these techniques, and the React Native bridge, you can do some amazing things with React VR, without having to get deep into regular three.js programming.

Next steps

Now that you can see the basic three.js syntax for materials, you could look at the various three.js samples, and copy some of that code in. Don't just look at the samples on the screen. You will want to also try them in VR. Some game tricks, such as lens reflections or screen space reflections, do not look really good in VR. As always, test, test, and test.

I also changed the color of the button slightly, and we don't have a cursor when we shift into VR mode, so the button press doesn't always work. In the next chapter, I'll show you how to fix this, or you can investigate yourself.

I've also loaded a metal-like reflection texture in the source files, called `static_assets/metal_reflect.jpg`. You don't have to do the camera rendering to get something that looks shiny, especially if it's a dull reflection, and may not want the extra overhead of halving your frame rate (all of those camera renderings do take time). If this is the case, you can do a simple environment map and skip the camera loading and rendering.

Extending React VR — Native Views

You can also extend React VR itself with something called **Native Views**. The word view might make you think of a camera rendering, although the meaning, in this case, is a little different. Think of these more as new React VR objects that are native three.js. They are very useful. You could use the three.js code we just went through to mix in raw three.js programming, but you have limited ability to use declarative programming that way. Is there a more React VR way to do this? You can do this through Native Views.

Extending the language

When you implement a Native View, you can control how properties and code interact with the rest of the runtime code. These injections will usually be visual, although you can inject sound as well.

You can also implement new Native objects. The programming is similar to what we have done so far; you implement base properties, expose the new keyword to the runtime, and then code them as if they were part of the React VR language. There are additional keywords and functions that let you describe your new React VR views in terms of props and types.

To create a native view, there is documentation at: `http://bit.ly/RCTNativeView`.

You are getting to the point now that you should be able to do some amazing things with React VR, and I fully trust that you can pick apart my examples, extend them, and have a fun time.

Summary

In this chapter, we discussed how to use the full power of three.js with React VR. While learning this, we demonstrated where to place native code and the React VR Native bridge. We built `three.js` meshes directly via JavaScript and added sound that made the world seem more alive. We also used React Native Views and the Native bridge to do customized rendering, including a reflection map—we added chrome to VR (as opposed to viewing VR with Chrome). We also showed how to get access to the React VR camera via the `vr.player.renderer` to do more three.js processing.

With a full-blown three.js included, we really can do anything we want with React VR. We should, however, use React VR where it is needed, and three.js where we need a little more detail, otherwise React VR will be icing on a bolt. It would be liable to cause rust and easily fall off.

10
Bringing in the Real Live World

As you learned in the last Chapter 9, *Do it Yourself – Native Modules and Three.js*, we can include native code and JavaScript code into our world. Aside from breathing life into our world by making it more interesting visually, we can also bring the outside world in.

In this chapter, you will learn how to use React and JavaScript to bring the web into the VR world. You will learn how to use your existing high-performance code in VR.

First, we will need a VR world to start in. This time, we're going to Mars!

In this chapter, you will learn the following topics:

- Doing JSON/Web API calls
- The Fetch statement
- **Cross-Origin Resource Sharing (CORS)**
- The **Networking** tab for diagnostics
- The Cylindrical Pano statement
- Justified text, similar to a flexbox (part of React Native)
- Conditional rendering
- Style sheets

Going to Mars (the initial world creation)

You would think there is no weather in space, but actually there is, and we have weather stations there. We will go to Mars to get our weather. This will be a real-time program that will obtain weather data from the Mars Science Laboratory, or its rover called **Curiosity**.

Curiosity is an SUV-sized robotic rover that was sent to Mars on November 26, 2011 and landed on August 6, 2012. If you drove your SUV there, even if you could buy gas, you would take about 670 years to get there. The Mars rover was designed for a two year mission, but its mission was extended, which is fortunate for us.

Driving that SUV to Mars to get the weather report would have been a hassle. I don't even know where the gas stations are.

Creating the initial world

First, as we've done before, go to your directory where you're storing your worlds and create one, as follows:

```
react-vr init MarsInfo
```

Then, download the assets from `https://github.com/jgwinner/ReactVRBook/tree/master/Chapter10/MarsInfo`.

Although I uploaded all of the files to make this work, not just the static assets, you really should try to code this yourself. You don't really learn anything from downloading files and running them.

Making mistakes is what builds character. I uploaded the files and will maintain them just in case there is *too much* character.

Now that we have an initial world, we'll start setting up the web services to obtain data.

Jason and JSON

When you hear people talk about JSON, hopefully, you aren't thinking of this guy:

I found the image on the web, marked creative commons; it's a Jason Voorhees costume (cosplay) from the Montreal Comic-Con. The photo is from Pikawil from Laval, Canada.

On a serious note, JSON is the most common way to bring in the outside world through web services; however, as we've seen ways to include native code and JavaScript, you could integrate your system in a variety of ways.

The other huge advantage of React VR is that it is based on React, so things that you can commonly do with React, you can do in React VR, with some important differences.

Why JSON has nothing to do with React

At first, you might be thinking, *"How do I do AJAX requests in React VR?"*

You don't, not really. React VR and React Native do not have any allegiance to any particular way of fetching data. In fact, as far as React is concerned, it doesn't even know there's a *server* in the picture at all.

React simply renders components using data from only two places: props and state.

That is the academic answer. The real answer is a bit more broad. You can get data any way you feel like it. After having said that, usually most React programmers will use one of these APIs and/or frameworks:

- **Fetch**: Nearly a standard, it is built-in to React, as it is usually already included; refer to `http://bit.ly/FetchAPI` for usage notes and examples
- **Axios**: Axios revolves around promises (asynchronous completion APIs), although it can be used in a simpler way as well for singlethreaded apps; refer to `http://bit.ly/AxiosReadme` for more details
- **Superagent**: If you don't like promises, but like callbacks; refer to `http://bit.ly/SuperagentAPI` for more info

In these examples, we will show fetch, as there is no need to install different modules and set up callbacks. After having said this, you may want to build a slightly more responsive app that uses some type of callback of asynchronous completion so that your app can do something while it waits for data externally. Fetch does do asynchronous completion through promises, so we'll be doing conditional rendering to take advantage of this and maintain a responsive VR app.

You may already have a lot of this code written. React VR, as discussed earlier, is a rendering system for your VR objects, so you can use a variety of external JavaScript systems.

Finding the API -- All the way from Mars

Now, we'll get the weather data all the way from Mars. No, I'm not really joking. Refer to `http://bit.ly/MarsWeatherAPI`, which describes the API and gives a little science background, if you are interested. This API is set up to consume XML data from, and return it in, a JSON or JSONP format. The following is the resulting data, which you can also get by referring to: `http://marsweather.ingenology.com/v1/latest/`.

```
{
  "report": {
    "terrestrial_date": "2019-04-21",
    "sol": 2250,
    "ls": 66.0,
    "min_temp": -80.0,
    "min_temp_fahrenheit": -112.0,
    "max_temp": -27.0,
    "max_temp_fahrenheit": -16.6,
    "pressure": 878.0,
    "pressure_string": "Higher",
```

```
    "abs_humidity": null,
    "wind_speed": null,
    "wind_direction": "--",
    "atmo_opacity": "Sunny",
    "season": "Month 4",
    "sunrise": "2019-04-21T11:02:00Z",
    "sunset": "2019-04-21T22:47:00Z"
  }
}
```

We can fairly easily turn this into our JSON object. First, let's test the connectivity and make a sanity check to the actual JSON text returned. We tested the preceding JSON data in a browser, but we need to test the code to make sure that it works. To do this, follow these steps:

1. In `index.vr.js` find the MarsInfo `Component {` declaration to add the following:

```
export default class MarsInfo extends Component {
    componentDidMount() {
        fetch(`http://marsweather.ingenology.com/v1/latest/`,
            {
                method: 'GET'
            })
            .then(console.log(result))
    }

    render() {
```

2. Paste this in and run it.

3. Open the console in the browser (*Ctrl+Shift+K* in Firefox Nightly). Although the code we just showed is really reasonable, and runs fine in the browser, when we run this, we will get an error:

```
⚠ ▶ ▶ TypeError: NetworkError when attempting to fetch resource.                          Networking.js:103:8
⚠ Cross-Origin Request Blocked: The Same Origin Policy disallows reading the remote resource at
  http://marsweather.ingenology.com/v1/latest/. (Reason: CORS header 'Access-Control-Allow-Origin' missing).
⚠ THREE.WebGLProgram: gl.getProgramInfoLog()                                              three.js:11872:3
```

What is the problem? It's CORS. This is a mechanism to make Cross-Origin or web content that doesn't come from the same server safe and secure. Essentially, it is a way for web servers to say, "I'm OK to be embedded in another web page." Your bank, for example, would not want to have your banking details embedded inside some other site's web page; your checking account could be compromised easily that way, and you'd think you were logging into your real bank—and you would be.

Note that I could have used an API that did not give these errors, but you may well run into the same problem with your own content, so we will discuss how to spot a CORS problem and how to fix it.

4. To find out why we got this error, we need to look at the protocol headers; open the **Network** tab by clicking on **Tools ->Web Developer ->Network**:

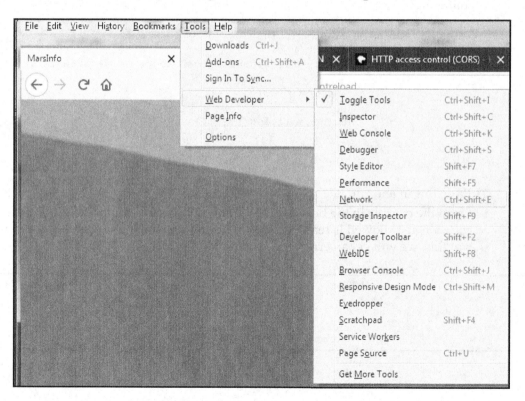

This window is very valuable for figuring out native JSON request issues and website integrations.

5. Once you bring up the console, you'll see the different HTTP actions; click on the one that didn't complete:

We will then take a look at the data that is returned.

6. Look at the right-hand side of the following screenshot; here, you can click on a response and headers to check the data. We can see that the website does return the data; however, our browser (Firefox) has blocked it from showing by generating the CORS error:

```
Render() main thread, photo collection: ▼ {…}
                                        ▼ photos: [...]
                                          ▼ [0...99]
                                            ▼ 0: {…}
                                              ▶ camera: Object { id: 20, name: "FHAZ", rover_id: 5, … }
                                                earth_date: "2015-12-18"
                                                id: 529979
                                                img_src: "http://mars.jpl.nasa.gov/msl-raw-images/proj/msl/redops
                                              ▼ rover: {…}
                                                ▶ cameras: Array [ {…}, {…}, {…}, … ]
                                                  id: 5
                                                  landing_date: "2012-08-06"
                                                  launch_date: "2011-11-26"
                                                  max_date: "2017-10-03"
                                                  max_sol: 1834
                                                  name: "Curiosity"
                                                  status: "active"
                                                  total_photos: 321721
                                                ▶ __proto__: Object { … }
                                                sol: 1197
```

The code was correct, but the website does not include the important CORS headers, so per CORS security rules, the website blocks it. You can read more about CORS at: `http://bit.ly/HTTPCORS`.

If you get this error, there may be a solution by adding headers to the request. To add headers, you need to modify the `fetch` request; the `fetch` request also allows a mode of `'cors'`. However, for whatever reason, for this particular website, the `'cors'` option didn't seem to work for me; for other websites, it might work better. The syntax for this is as follows:

```
fetch(`http://marsweather.ingenology.com/v1/latest/`,
    {
        method: 'GET',
        mode: 'cors',
    })
```

To have more control over exactly what we are requesting, create a header object and pass it into the `fetch` command. This can also be used for what is called a **preflight check**, which is simply two requests: one to find out whether CORS is supported, and the second request will include values from the first request.

7. To construct a request or preflight request, set the headers as follows:

```
var myHeaders = new Headers();
myHeaders.append('Access-Control-Request-Method', 'GET');
myHeaders.append('Access-Control-Request-Headers', 'Origin,
Content-Type, Accept');

fetch(`http://marsweather.ingenology.com/v1/latest/`,
    {
        headers: myHeaders,
        method: 'GET',
        mode: 'cors',
    })
```

The header value `'Access-Control-Request-Headers'` can be set to custom header options that the server will return (if it supports CORS) to validate to the client code that this is a valid CORS request. As of 2016, the spec was modified to include wild cards, but not all servers will be updated. You may need to experiment and use the **Network** tab to see what's going on if you get a CORS error.

In this case, we will need to use options for a "preflight" check—but even after making a modification to the React VR networking code, this didn't work with `marsweather.ingenology.com` so, it's quite likely that their server has not been upgraded to modern web security standards.

This can happen! In our case, there really is no general fix. I did find a Firefox plugin that will allow you to bypass CORS restrictions (remember, the problem isn't from the server, it's the browser that shuts down your code when seeing the payload the server *already* sent), but this would require people to download plugins and fiddle with them.

We need to find a better API. NASA has a fantastic catalog of web APIs, and we will use their Mars rover camera API. You can fetch any of the hundreds of thousands of photos all for free. Once we use a different web API, we will get the proper CORS headers we've been looking for, and it all works just fine. Once we ask a server that has modern security standards, we will note that it automatically includes the **access-control-allow-origin** that Firefox needs (here wildcarded), as seen in the following image, taken from the **Network** tab:

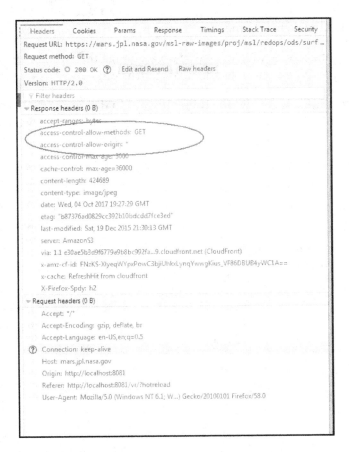

So, instead of seeing the weather on Mars, we'll look at actual pictures.

A better API from NASA

To take a look at some great web APIs, you can go to: `http://bit.ly/NasaWebAPI` and see the list of APIs that you can use, or better yet, use some web APIs you've already written. React VR makes it very easy to integrate these through the power of React and React Native. We will use the Mars photo API. To enable it, you will probably need a Developer key. When you make the requests, you can add your API key to the URL or use `DEMO_KEY`. This becomes part of the API call, for example, `https://api.nasa.gov/mars-photos/api/v1/rovers/curiosity/photos?sol=1000&api_key=DEMO_KEY`. Note that there is no period on the end of the URL.

If you start getting errors while developing your code, you might be using the `DEMO_KEY` a little too much; it is very quick and easy to get your own Developer API; instructions for that can be found at the website I mentioned at: `http://bit.ly/NasaWebAPI`.

To fetch the data from NASA, all we have to do is change the `fetch` command slightly, as follows; we won't need the custom headers, as it turns out:

1. Change `index.vr.js` to the following, up to the `render()` statement:

```
export default class MarsInfo extends Component {
    constructor() {
        super();
        this.state = {
            currentPhoto: 2,
            photoCollection: { photos: []}
        };
    };
    componentDidMount() {
fetch('https://api.nasa.gov/mars-photos/api/v1/rovers/curiosity
/photos?sol=1197&api_key=DEMO_KEY',
            { method: 'GET' })
            .then(response => response.json())
            .then(console.log("Got a response"))
            .then(json => this.setState({ photoCollection:json
})))

    };
```

This is all we have to do to obtain the data from Mars, via NASA and put it in a collection. Amazing! The following are a few notes on what we did:

- The `photoCollection` object is initialized to be an empty array (collection). This is so that we can use similar code before and after we get data.
- You should still check for failures, however.
- The `currentPhoto` value we initialize to 2 as sort of a "cheat." The reason this is cheating is that when I was writing this book, if you let `currentPhoto` default to the first image, your first view of Mars was pretty boring. The first couple of images were test images and fairly plain, so I'll have you change `currentPhoto` to 2, so we can see something interesting. You might do the same thing if you have an API that returns specific data you want to show someone.
- This code just obtains data; it doesn't render it. For that, we will develop a separate object to keep our code modular.

2. For debugging purposes, we'll also add a line in the `render()` thread to see exactly what data we have. Insert the following `console.log` statement:

```
render() {
    console.log("Render() main thread, photo collection:",
this.state.photoCollection);
    return (
```

This can be very handy for working out the rendering code and understanding the current state and how it changes. Run this code, and we can see the object that is returned in the console. First, we get a line from the `render()` thread that shows us an empty `photo collection`:

```
Running application "MarsInfo" with appParams: {"initialProps":{},"rootTag":1}. __DEV_
Render() main thread, photo collection: ▼ {…}
                                          ▼ photos: []
                                            length: 0
                                          ▶ __proto__: Array []
                                          ▶ __proto__: Object { … }
```

Note that the `photo collection` is empty; this makes sense as we initialized it that way. After a few seconds delay—during which you *can view the virtual world*—you will see another `render()` update and changed data:

```
Render() main thread, photo collection: ▼ {…}
                                         ▼ photos: […]
                                          ▼ [0..99]
                                           ▼ 0: {…}
                                            ▶ camera: Object { id: 20, name: "FHAZ", rover_id: 5, … }
                                              earth_date: "2015-12-18"
                                              id: 529979
                                              img_src: "http://mars.jpl.nasa.gov/msl-raw-images/proj/msl/redops
                                            ▼ rover: {…}
                                             ▶ cameras: Array [ {…}, {…}, {…}, … ]
                                               id: 5
                                               landing_date: "2012-08-06"
                                               launch_date: "2011-11-26"
                                               max_date: "2017-10-03"
                                               max_sol: 1834
                                               name: "Curiosity"
                                               status: "active"
                                               total_photos: 321721
                                             ▶ __proto__: Object { … }
                                               sol: 1197
                                             ▶ proto  : Object { … }
```

In this particular case (day 1,1197), there were a *lot* of images. JSON handles this very well, slicing (ouch, bad pun) and dicing the data, all while we look around in our VR world.

Another thing to note is that the `render()` loop is called just twice. If you are used to a game development paradigm, this may seem weird since, as we discussed, to build a sense of immersion, we will need more than 60 frames per second. How can we do that if we rendered just twice?

React VR doesn't do the actual image generation, three.js does. When React VR "renders," it just takes the React VR syntax and applies any props or state changes and calls `render()` for those objects that have changed once.

To display the data we've retrieved, we'll build a new object.

3. Create a new file, called `CameraData`, and make it a separate component. We'll also change the `render()` method in `index.vr.js`.

Everyone needs a style(sheet)

Styles aren't just for your hair; in this case, it will help to use a style sheet to make our code simpler, cleaner, and easier to maintain. Style reuse is very easy. Styles aren't a separate language; they are JavaScript like everything else in React. All of the core objects in React VR accept a prop named `styles`. We will define this style in our file and reuse it.

Create the following style definitions so that we can use them for the `CameraData.js` component (note that you can put this anywhere in the file):

```
const styles = StyleSheet.create({
    manifestCard: {
        flex: 1,
        flexDirection: 'column',
        width: 2,
        alignItems: 'center',
        justifyContent: 'center',
        backgroundColor: 'green',
        opacity: 0.8,
        borderRadius: 0.1,
        borderColor: '#000',
        borderWidth: 0.02,
        padding: 0.1,
        layoutOrigin: [-1, 0.3],
        transform: [
            {
                rotateY: -30,
                translate: [1, 0, -2]
            }
        ]
    },

    manifestText: {
        textAlign: 'center',
        fontSize: 0.1
    },
    frontCard: {
        flex: 1,
        flexDirection: 'column',
        width: 2,
        alignItems: 'center',
        justifyContent: 'center',
        backgroundColor: 'green',
        borderRadius: 0.1,
        borderColor: '#000',
        borderWidth: 0.02,
        padding: 0.05,
```

```
            transform: [{ translate: [-1, 1, -3] }],
    },
    panoImage: {
        width: 500,
        height: 500,
        layoutOrigin: [-.5, 0],
    },
    baseView: {
        layoutOrigin: [0, 0],
    },
});
```

 If you omit the `width` style, objects will transform and move completely differently. I'm not sure yet if this is a bug or is a different type of layout style, but note that if your `transform` statements are not moving a text or view object, it might be because you don't have a `width:` prop for your text style.

Building the image and status UI

Next, we will need to render the camera data in two different ways. The first, when we have no `CameraData`, yet, in other words, right when the app starts up, or if we don't have an internet connectivity; and the second, when we obtain the data and need to display it. We also want to keep these routines fairly modular so that when a state change is initiated we can easily redraw the objects that need it.

Note that a lot of this is done automagically by React VR. If an object's props or state do not change, it is not told to render itself. In this case, our main thread already has the JSON handling to modify the change, so nothing in the main loop has to be created to re-render the camera data.

1. Add the following code:

```
export default class CameraData extends Component {
    render() {
        if (!this.props) {
            return this.renderLoadingView();
        }
        var photos = this.props.photoCollection.photos;
        if (!photos) {
            return this.renderLoadingView();
        }
        var photo = photos[this.props.currentPhoto];
        if (!photo) {
```

```
            return this.renderLoadingView();
    }
    return this.renderPhoto(photo);
};
```

Note that we aren't finished with the component, so don't type the final `}`; yet. Let's discuss what we added. The previous main `render()` loop essentially checks what values are valid and calls one of two routines to actually do the rendering, either `renderPhoto(photo)` or `renderLoadingView()`. We can assume that if we don't have a photo, we are in the process of loading it. The nice thing about the preceding code is that we are checking our props and making sure that they are valid before using them.

> Many computer courses and self-help books strip out error handling to *"concentrate on the important things"*.
> Error handling is the *most* important thing in your app.
>
> In this case, it's particularly important as while we are retrieving data, we don't have the photographs loaded yet, so we have nothing to display. We'll get an error if we don't handle this. What I have stripped out are `console.log` statements; if you download the source code for the book, you will find more extensive comments and trace statements.

Now, let's move on to the actual rendering. This looks deceptively simple, mostly as all of the hardwork to serialize, fetch, and selectively render has already been done. This is what programming should strive to be—clean, robust, easy to understand, and maintain.

> Some of these code samples are getting long, so I'm putting closing braces and tags at the end of the object they are closing. I would recommend that you buy a large desktop screen and code in a more expansive way; when you spend an hour tracking down a missing or out of place `/>`, you will appreciate a large format display device. It just helps productivity.

2. Add the following code:

```
renderLoadingView() {
    console.log('CameraData props during renderLoadingView',
this.props);
    return (
        <View style={styles.frontCard} >
            <Text style={styles.manifestText}>Loading</Text>
            <Text style={styles.manifestText}>image data</Text>
            <Text style={styles.manifestText}>from NASA</Text>
```

```
                        <Text style={styles.manifestText}>...</Text>
                </View>
            );
        };
        renderPhoto(photo) {
        return (
            <View style={styles.baseView}>
                <CylindricalPanel
                    layer={{
                        width: 1000,
                        height: 1000,
                        density: 4680,
                        radius: 20 }}>
                    <Image
                        source={{ uri: photo.img_src }}
                        style={styles.panoImage}>
                    </Image>
                </CylindricalPanel>
                <Model
                    source={{
                        obj: asset('ArrowDown.obj'),
                        mtl: asset('ArrowDown.mtl'), }}
                    lit
                    style={{
                        transform: [{ translate: [-2.5, -1, -5.1] }] }} />
                <Model
                    source={{
                        obj: asset('ArrowUp.obj'),
                        mtl: asset('ArrowUp.mtl'), }}
                    lit
                    style={{
                        transform: [{ translate: [1.3, -1, -5.1] }] }} />
                <View style={styles.manifestCard}>
                    <Text style={styles.manifestText}>
                        {photo.camera.full_name}</Text>
                    <Text style={styles.manifestText}>
                        {photo.rover.name} Rover #{photo.rover.id}</Text>
                    <Text style={styles.manifestText}>
                        Landed on: {photo.rover.landing_date}</Text>
                    <Text style={styles.manifestText}>
                        Launched on: {photo.rover.launch_date}</Text>
                    <Text style={styles.manifestText}>
                        Total Photos: {photo.rover.total_photos}</Text>
                    <Text style={styles.manifestText}>
                        Most recent: {photo.rover.max_date} Latest earth
date</Text>
                    <Text style={styles.manifestText}>
                        Viewing: {photo.rover.max_sol} Mars Sol</Text>
```

```
        <Text style={styles.manifestText}>
            Taken: {photo.earth_date} Earth (GMT)</Text>
    </View>
  </View>
);
}
}
```

If you've typed in all of the code so far, when the world loads, you will see a green dialog box that informs you that it's receiving data. After a few seconds, that will be replaced by photo 2 and detailed meta-info about the data that came to you from Mars, as follows:

If you want to open two virtual words at the same time, for example, to check on some imports without incurring the round trip web hits that we're in the middle of programming, you can do it by going to your second world that's set up, instead of npm start, using the react-native start --port 9091 command.

I mentioned this briefly earlier, but it's important to note how multithreaded React really is; the elements change their rendering when their props or state change, without being told to. It's multithreaded without a change of code. This allows you to move the camera around and look while the world fills in its data.

This makes the virtual world seem more "real"; it responds to input just as if it was reality. It is—we created a Virtual Reality.

How (not to) to make people sick

You may have noted that we put the user interface for this—the icons and the screens—a little far out; so far, we've put everything at least five meters out. Why is that?

It's because of accommodation-vergence conflict.

When your eyes 'point' at something, like we discussed in `Chapter 1`, *What is Virtual Reality, Really?*, and if that something is really close to your face, your eyes will attempt to focus on it. However, your HMD is a fixed focus device, and always shows things in focus, no matter how close or far away they are. In the real world, something that is, say, closer than 3 to 4 feet will require your eyes to focus more than something say 10 feet away.

So, your eyes will converge on an image that you should have to focus more on, but what you are looking at is already in focus (as everything is), so there is a difference between what you expect to see in the real world and what you see in the HMD.

This doesn't cause any actual vision issues—everything is sharp and in focus.

What you can get would be eye strain and a vague feeling of discomfort, which is worse the longer you use the HMD.

The way to avoid this is to try to always put UI elements at least as far away as we have in this example. Don't put floating screens where a pair of glasses would be, for example. If you do, people will look at them, and their eyes will expect to have to focus on something say six inches away, but from a focus standpoint, the item is more than arms-length away. This will strain your users.

This is why most VR has you looking at large screens that are far away to make a selection. About the closest you would want to make a UI element might be on a wrist, and even that is a little risky.

I do feel that the more people use VR, the more their eyes and focusing will retrain, however, I do not know of any medical studies that show this effect. I only mention it because I have a nearsighted eye and a farsighted eye; when I put glasses on, my focusing changes. What is funny is that if I put on glasses *without any glass*, my focusing still changes. I feel the human brain is infinitely adaptable and that we can overcome the accommodation-vergance conflict.

Your user's mileage may vary, however, so don't make them tired by putting things at a close distance (less than a meter) to their face.

Summary

In this chapter, you learned quite a few things. We've taken our worlds and made them truly interactive by building web service calls that consume JSON APIs. We've seen a few ways to obtain data and used the more or less built-in `fetch` statement. These API calls are now asynchronous, so we can look around our world and admire Mars while the camera data we're asking for is loading.

We've seen how to build secure worlds by handling cross-site scripting issues. We've created justified text and built conditional rendering. We've also discussed error handling.

Doing all of this takes some time, and we've had a few times where during development we spent hours trying to line up objects. I got shut down a few times because I was exceeding the `DEMO_KEY` number of retrievals during one hour. That's why I recommend that you get your own API key, then you can request a lot more images.

This chapter has been fairly long, and the world, while retrieving real-world data, is not totally interactive yet. In the next chapter, you will learn how to make your worlds interact to our input. This is why I built in the + and - arrows in the preceding view. Check out the next chapter to find how to hook them up to a page through our Mars data. I'll show a different world, but show ways to make the buttons interactive. It'll be your exercise to come up with and make simple prop changes to make the plus and minus buttons real.

11
Take a Walk on the Wild Side

We've built some real, yet small, worlds so far in the chapters up to here.

There has been something missing, however. At the start, I've talked about VR as being something that you can interact with — a reality, even if it doesn't look real. So far, most of what we've been doing is looking and seeing things, but we can't move around.

In this chapter, we will do exactly that.

You will learn the following topics:

- Using NPM to add components
- The Gaze button
- Using a Gaze button to trigger an event
- Adding in JavaScript files
- Converting the JavaScript files to build geometry on the fly
- Moving the point of view in the world we've created
- Moving makes things seem more real
- A little more about VR controllers

Going loco–VR locomotion

I used to get carsick as a kid. VR can do this to you too — the reasons for this were discussed earlier while introducing VR, but this is a very important topic, so it bears repeating.

If you move a point of view, independently of what the user is doing (user agency), the brain knows that it didn't move. Yet, the brain also sees the world moving through your (VR) eyes. The brain then relies on a very ancient, important survival characteristic—you will think you've been poisoned.

When you've been poisoned, your body is very good at emesis. In less clinical terms, you throw up. Your body figures that something is trying to kill you, so it just gets rid of whatever is in your stomach as a panic reaction.

So, how do you move around in VR? How to enable VR locomotion without making people loco?

Types of VR locomotion

A discussion of VR locomotion wouldn't be complete without discussing VR controllers at least a little bit. What you've got in your hands, under your feet, holding you up, or letting you roll around in obviously makes a huge difference.

We are discussing WebVR, which, while very easy for people to get into, probably means that your users may not have all of the various types of VR gear handy. If you do have gear handy, you may still find that for your app, simpler types of locomotion are better, and they are certainly faster to code.

When discussing equipment, people discuss **Degrees of Freedom (DOF)**. This really is less about strictly considering degrees of freedom but mostly about what is tracked.

If you have a handheld device, you may have only **3DOF**; this means that the electronics can track whether you spin it around its center or not. A **6DOF** controller is tracked that way, but it can also detect whether it is moving around, in other words, translating. Usually, each of these has 3 degrees.

A 6DOF controller is much more lifelike; you can reach out and touch things. However, they require some form of tracking, which, for the current state of the industry, usually means external trackers such as the Vive lighthouses or the Oculus cameras.

There is a third type of tracking called *inside out* tracking, which simply means that the headset itself sees the controllers and figures out where they are. They do use cameras, just not external cameras scattered about the room.

It's difficult to categorize types of locomotion as things that work without controllers; it may also work great with controllers (teleportation).

I won't really include moving your head around (or mousing around), although that is movement; without that, a VR system isn't really VR (in my definition). However, there have been VR headsets that did not include this feature—or don't do it well. This is the real breakthrough for high-end cell phones (for Samsung Gear VR and Google Daydream) and for the PC headsets, Vive and Rift.

Consider the following types of VR Locomotion:

- **Gaze detection**: You look at something, and it activates an effect, a blink, or makes you move
- **Vehicles/Cockpit locomotion**: Your view shows walls or details of a cockpit
  - Can move with gaze detection
  - With controllers (joysticks, and so on)
  - Timed/artificial (push a button or move the player after a time)
  - Only a slight chance of getting ill

- **Room scale**:
  - Walk around (up to bounds)
  - Very low chance of getting ill
  - Requires hardware

- **Teleportation or blinks**:
  - Usually with Gaze or with 3DOF or 6DOF controllers
  - Teleportation can also be done in small steps—removing motion (vection); this makes it feel like you are moving, but won't make you sick

- **Treadmills**:
  - A device you stand on and move your feet, and it detects how you move
  - There are hang glider simulators as well as flight simulators, where you lay down or sit down and fly by shifting your body weight
  - All of these are large and expensive, usually limited to VR arcades

- **Tracked 6DOF controller movement paradigms**:
  - Vive/Rift usually use teleportation, and the 6DOF controllers make it easy
  - There are many other ways to move with 6DOF controllers; one good list can be found at http://bit.ly/VRLoco

- **Artificial locomotion/rails**:
  - Once you've used your UI to indicate what to do, the VR system moves you along a path.
  - Gaze/head controlled turning is in this category.
  - Very easy to make people sick.
  - It can be irritating — if your head turns, just change the way you move; even if you don't get sick, you'll feel as if you are being carried away. Still, it can work with careful implementation.

The preceding ways to move around are, of course, constrained by how much hardware you have. Another constraint is how large you want your audience to be. If you design your VR app to be **room scale** (natural walking around), you've excluded every mobile phone user. Yet, by the same token, if you've decided on a gaze teleportation system, people that do have room scale VR will feel frustrated that they cannot just walk around.

WebVR is currently more aimed at mobile VR, with room scale being a large programming challenge. It is possible, but is not built in 'out of the box' with React-VR, and for that matter WebVR. Looking from the point of view of hardware is available:

- **No equipment** (Google Cardboard):
  - Natural locomotion (pan/tilt)–small amounts only
  - Gaze detection
  - Artificial movement ('rails' movement, like you are on a rail) either by timer or gaze detection
- **VR Headset with controller** (Gear VR, Daydream, others):
  - Now we have better ways, but can still do all the previous ways:
    - Natural locomotion (pan/tilt) - small amounts only
    - Gaze detection
    - Artificial movement ('rails' movement, like you are on a rail) either by timer or gaze detection
  - Cockpit locomotion
  - Teleport via controller
  - Joystick/controller

- **PC VR–Vive/Rift**:
    - Now we have better ways, but can still do all the previous ways:
        - Natural locomotion (pan/tilt)–small amounts only
        - Gaze detection
        - Artificial movement ('rails' movement, like you are on a rail) either by timer or gaze detection
        - Cockpit locomotion
        - Teleport via controller
        - Joystick/controller (on the tracked 6DOF controllers)
    - Tracked 6DOF controller movement paradigms
    - Room scale walking
- **High-end equipment**:
    - Omni virtual treadmill or other treadmill

Avoiding the ghost effect

There is another reason why we want people to be able to move around without some type of user agency; without movement, it really isn't Virtual Reality. In reality, we all move around; cats move their heads sideways when stalking. If you're intrigued or curious, you tilt your head. With 360 video, one of the challenges is that you can only look around; you can't move. Tilting your head really does nothing.

What happens with 360 video, as detailed as it can be, is that you feel like a disembodied ghost. You can't look down and see yourself (you might see the camera rig though), you can't move around, you can't reach out and touch something, and you can't move your point of view. If you tilt your head, or move side-to-side, there is no parallax effect.

I really like 360 video, but I also feel that it isn't really VR, as ultimately you feel disembodied, essentially a chained ghost. Sure, the video might move, but you can't change how it moves; you're just along for the ride.

One of the subtle things I was very impressed with WebVR is that if you tilt your head, the VR view does shift slightly, as if you are moving your head to the side. It's a subtle effect; it isn't room scale VR, where you can just walk around, but it is a type of VR. You don't feel like a disembodied ghost.

Allowing people to explore their environment is important; without that, you really do feel like a ghost. For our example, we will use a teleport movement metaphor and allow people to explore a maze.

Without the ability to interact with the world and move around, you feel like a disembodied ghost. Although it's taken us nearly the entire book to get to this point, the ability to interact with your environment and world is one of the most important things in VR.

You will be able to do that in this chapter with any WebVR client. If we knew everyone had an HTC Vive or a room scale Oculus Rift, we could show you code to walk around the maze, although this brings up some interesting UI issues — what if someone walks through a hedge? Until we get full haptic head to toe suits, you can walk through a virtual wall. There are ways of using the user interface to counteract this, such as fading the screen to black briefly and then teleporting the user back to the start, just allowing them to cheat (not good), or other interesting ways around this.

For now, we will simply allow the user to move to the next cell/open spot in the maze, and to that location only. We will use gaze selection, meaning that when you stare at a UI element, we'd know you've *clicked* on it. This will work with all VR devices on the market, and this really is the best place to start at. More sophisticated UI elements would need to check to see what kind of VR controllers and tracking the user has and enable the proper movement as appropriate. This is a little beyond the scope of this book.

Before we discuss how to move in our world, we will need something interesting to move around in. For example, perhaps we were strolling through the forest and found our way blocked by a maze or it is early morning and we wanted to get to a small lake and see the early morning fog.

Let's build that maze.

Building a maze

There are a few ways we could build a maze. The most straightforward way would be to fire up our 3D modeler package (say, Blender) and create a labyrinth out of polygons. This would work fine and could be very detailed.

However, it would also be very boring. Why? The first time we get through the maze will be exciting, but after a few tries, you'll know the way through. When we construct VR experiences, you usually want people to visit often and have a fun time every time.

A modeled labyrinth would be boring. Life is too short to do boring things.

So, we want to generate a Maze randomly. This way, you can change the Maze every time so that it'll be fresh and different. The way to do that is through random numbers to ensure that the Maze doesn't shift around us, so we want to actually do it with pseudo-random numbers. To start doing that, we'll need a basic application created. Please go to your VR directory and create an application called 'WalkInAMaze':

```
react-vr init WalkInAMaze
```

Almost random–pseudo random number generators

To have a chance of replaying value or being able to compare scores between people, we really need a pseudo–random number generator. The basic JavaScript Math.random() is not a pseudo–random generator; it really gives you a totally random number every time. We need a pseudo–random number generator that takes a seed value. If you give the same seed to the random number generator, it will generate the same sequence of random numbers. (They aren't completely random, but are very close.) Random number generators are a complex topic; for example, they are used in cryptography, and if your random number generator isn't completely random, someone could break your code.

We aren't so worried about that, we just want repeatability. Although the UI for this may be a bit beyond the scope of this book, creating the Maze in a way that clicking on *Refresh* won't generate a totally different Maze is really a good thing and will avoid frustration on the part of the user. This will also allow two users to compare scores; we could persist a *board number* for the Maze and show this. This may be out of scope for our book; however, having a predictable Maze will help immensely during development. If it wasn't for this, you might get lost while working on your world. (Well, probably not, but it makes testing easier.)

Including library code from other projects

Up to this point, I've shown you how to create components in React VR (or React). JavaScript interestingly has a historical issue with include. With C++, Java, or C#, you can include a file in another file or make a reference to a file in a project. After doing that, everything in those other files, such as functions, classes, and global properties (variables), are then usable from the file that you've issued the include statement in.

With a browser, the concept of "including" JavaScript is a little different. With Node.js, we use `package.json` to indicate what packages we need. To bring those packages into our code, we will use the following syntax in your .js files:

```
var MersenneTwister = require('mersenne-twister');
```

Then, instead of using `Math.random()`, we will create a new random number generator and pass a seed, as follows:

```
var rng = new MersenneTwister(this.props.Seed);
```

From this point on, you just call `rng.random()` instead of `Math.random()`.

For now, we can just use `npm install <package>` and the `require` statement for properly formatted packages. In the next chapter, we'll discuss upgrades and modify `package.json` to make sure that the code ships and updates properly. Much of this can be done for you by executing the `npm` command:

```
npm install mersenne-twister --save
```

Remember, the --save command to update our manifest in the project. While we are at it, we can install another package we'll need later:

```
npm install react-vr-gaze-button --save
```

Now that we have a good random number generator, let's use it to complicate our world.

The Maze render()

How do we build a `Maze`? I wanted to develop some code that dynamically generates the `Maze`; anyone could model it in a package, but a VR world should be living. Having code that can dynamically build `Maze` in any size (to a point) will allow a repeat playing of your world.

There are a number of JavaScript packages out there for printing mazes. I took one that seemed to be everywhere, in the public domain, on GitHub and modified it for HTML. This app consists of two parts: `Maze.html` and `makeMaze.JS`. Neither is React, but it is JavaScript. It works fairly well, although the numbers don't really represent exactly how wide it is.

First, I made sure that only one **x** was displaying, both vertically and horizontally. This will not print well (lines are usually *taller* than *wide*), but we are building a virtually real `Maze`, not a paper `Maze`.

The `Maze` that we generate with the files at `Maze.html` (`localhost:8081/vr/maze.html`) and the JavaScript file—`makeMaze.js`—will now look like this:

```
x1xxxxxxx
x   x   x
xxx x x x
x x   x x
x xxxxx x
x x   x x
x x x x x
x   x   2
xxxxxxxxx
```

It is a little hard to read, but you can count the squares vs. **xs**. Don't worry, it's going to look a lot fancier. Now that we have the HTML version of a `Maze` working, we'll start building the hedges.

This is a slightly larger piece of code than I expected, so I broke it into pieces and loaded the `Maze` object onto GitHub rather than pasting the entire code here, as it's long. You can find a link for the source at: `http://bit.ly/VR_Chap11`

Adding the floors and type checking

One of the things that look odd with a 360 Pano background, as we've talked about before, is that you can seem to "float" against the ground. One fix, other than fixing the original image, is to simply add a floor. This is what we did with the Space Gallery, and it looks pretty good as we were assuming we were floating in space anyway.

For this version, let's `import` a ground square. We could use a large square that would encompass the entire `Maze`; we'd then have to resize it if the size of the `Maze` changes. I decided to use a smaller cube and alter it so that it's "underneath" every cell of the `Maze`. This would allow us some leeway in the future to rotate the squares for worn paths, water traps, or whatever.

To make the floor, we will use a simple cube object that I altered slightly and is UV mapped. I used Blender for this. We also `import` a `Hedge` model, and a `Gem`, which will represent where we can teleport to. Inside 'Maze.js' we added the following code:

```
import Hedge from './Hedge.js';
import Floor from './Hedge.js';
import Gem from './Gem.js';
```

Then, inside the `Maze.js` we could instantiate our floor with the code:

```
<Floor X={-2} Y={-4}/>
```

Notice that we don't use 'vr/components/Hedge.js' when we do the import; we're inside Maze.js. However, in index.vr.js to include the Maze, we do need:

```
import Maze from './vr/components/Maze.js';
```

It's slightly more complicated though. In our code, the Maze builds the data structures when props have changed; when moving, if the maze needs rendering again, it simply loops through the data structure and builds a collection (mazeHedges) with all of the floors, teleport targets, and hedges in it. Given this, to create the floors, the line in `Maze.js` is actually:

```
mazeHedges.push(<Floor {...cellLoc} />);
```

Here is where I ran into two big problems, and I'll show you what happened so that you can avoid these issues. Initially, I was bashing my head against the wall trying to figure out why my floors looked like hedges. This one is pretty easy—we imported `Floor` from the `Hedge.js` file. The floors will look like hedges (did you notice this in my preceding code? If so, I did this on purpose as a learning experience. Honest).

This is an easy fix. Make sure that you code `import Floor from './floor.js';` note that `Floor` not type-checked. (It is, after all, JavaScript.) I thought this was odd, as the `hedge.js` file exports a `Hedge` object, not a `Floor` object, but be aware you can rename the objects as you `import` them.

The second problem I had was more of a simple goof that is easy to occur if you aren't really thinking in React. You may run into this. JavaScript is a lovely language, but sometimes I miss a strongly typed language. Here is what I did:

```
<Maze SizeX='4' SizeZ='4' CellSpacing='2.1' Seed='7' />
```

Inside the `maze.js` file, I had code like this:

```
for (var j = 0; j < this.props.SizeX + 2; j++) {
```

After some debugging, I found out that the value of `j` was going from 0 to 42. Why did it get 42 instead of 6? The reason was simple. We need to fully understand JavaScript to program complex apps. The mistake was in initializing SizeX to be `'4'`; this makes it a string variable. When calculating `j` from 0 (an integer), React/JavaScript takes 2, adds it to a string of `'4'`, and gets the 42 string, then converts it to an integer and assigns this to `j`.

When this is done, very weird things happened.

When we were building the Space Gallery, we could easily use the `'5.1'` values for the input to the box:

```
<Pedestal MyX='0.0' MyZ='-5.1'/>
```

Then, later use the transform statement below inside the class:

```
transform: [ { translate: [ this.props.MyX, -1.7, this.props.MyZ] } ]
```

React/JavaScript will put in the string values into `This.Props.MyX`, then realize it needs an integer, and then quietly do the conversion. However, when you get more complicated objects, such as our `Maze` generation, you won't get away with this.

Remember that your code isn't "really" JavaScript. It's processed. At the heart, this processing is fairly simple, but the implications can be a killer.

 Pay attention to what you code. With a loosely typed language such as JavaScript, with React on top, any mistakes you make will be quietly converted to something you didn't intend.

You are the programmer. Program correctly.

So, back to the `Maze`. The `Hedge` and `Floor` are straightforward copies of the initial `Gem` code. Let's take a look at our starting `Gem`, although note it gets a lot more complicated later (and in your source files):

```
import React, { Component } from 'react';
import {
    asset,
    Box,
    Model,
    Text,
    View
} from 'react-vr';

export default class Gem extends Component {
    constructor() {
        super();
        this.state = {
            Height: -3 };
    }
    render() {
        return (
            <Model
                source={{
                    gltf2: asset('TeleportGem.gltf'),
                }}
                style={{
                    transform: [{ translate: [this.props.X,
this.state.Height, this.props.Z] }]
                }}
```

```
            />
        );
    }
}
```

The `Hedge` and `Floor` are essentially the same thing. (We could have made a prop be the file loaded, but we want a different behavior for the `Gem`, so we will edit this file extensively.)

To run this sample, first, we should have created a directory as you have before, called `WalkInAMaze`. Once you do this, download the files from the Git source for this part of the chapter (`http://bit.ly/VR_Chap11`). Once you've created the app, copied the files, and fired it up, (go to the `WalkInAMaze` directory and type `npm start`), and you should see something like this once you look around - except, there is a bug. This is what the maze should look like (if you use the file `'MazeHedges2DoubleSided.gltf'` in `Hedge.js`, in the `<Model>` statement):

Now, how did we get those neat-looking hedges in the game? (OK, they are pretty low poly, but it is still pushing it.) One of the nice things about the pace of improvement on web standards is their new features. Instead of just .obj file format, React VR now has the capability to load glTF files.

Using the glTF file format for models

glTF files are a new file format that works pretty naturally with WebGL. There are exporters for many different CAD packages. The reason I like glTF files is that getting a proper export is fairly straightforward. Lightwave OBJ files are an industry standard, but in the case of React, not all of the options are imported. One major one is transparency. The OBJ file format allows that, but at of the time of writing this book, it wasn't an option. Many other graphics shaders that modern hardware can handle can't be described with the OBJ file format.

This is why glTF files are the next best alternative for WebVR. It is a modern and evolving format, and work is being done to enhance the capabilities and make a fairly good match between what WebGL can display and what glTF can export.

This is, however, a chapter on interacting with the world, so I'll give a brief mention on how to export glTF files and provide the objects, especially the `Hedge`, as glTF models.

The nice thing with glTF from the modeling side is that if you use their material specifications, for example, for Blender, then you don't have to worry that the export won't be quite right. Today's **physically Based Rendering (PBR)** tends to use the metallic/roughness model, and these import better than trying to figure out how to convert PBR materials into the OBJ file's specular lighting model. Here is the metallic-looking `Gem` that I'm using as the gaze point:

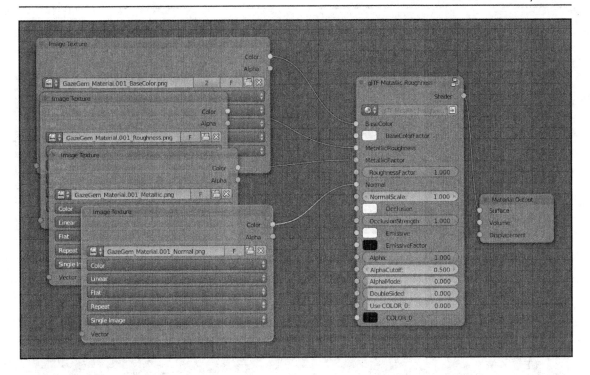

Using the glTF Metallic Roughness model, we can assign the texture maps that programs, such as Substance Designer, calculate and import easily. The resulting figures look metallic where they are supposed to be metallic and dull where the paint still holds on.

I didn't use Ambient Occlusion here, as this is a very convex model; something with more surface depressions would look fantastic with Ambient Occlusion. It would also look great with architectural models, for example, furniture.

To convert your models, there is user documentation at `http://bit.ly/glTFExporting`. You will need to download and install the Blender glTF exporter. Or, you can just download the files I have already converted. If you do the export, in brief, you do the the following steps:

1. Download the files from `http://bit.ly/gLTFFiles`. You will need the `gltf2_Principled.blend` file, assuming that you are on a newer version of Blender.
2. In Blender, open your file, then link to the new materials. Go to **File->Link**, then choose the `gltf2_Principled.blend` file. Once you do that, drill into "NodeTree" and choose either glTF Metallic Roughness (for metal), or glTF specular glossiness for other materials.

3. Choose the object you are going to export; make sure that you choose the Cycles renderer.

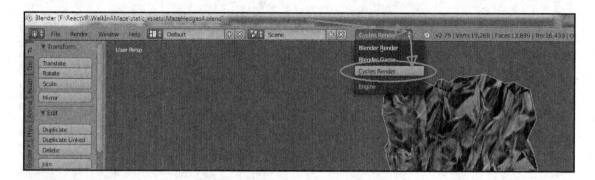

4. Open the Node Editor in a window (like you did for images in earlier chapters). Scroll down to the bottom of the Node Editor window, and make sure that the box **Use Nodes** is checked.

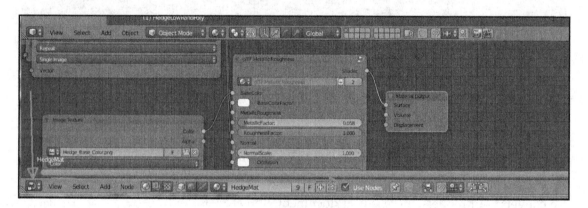

5. Add the node via the nodal menu, **Add->Group->**glTF Specular Glossiness or Metallic Roughness.

6. Once the node is added, go to **Add->Texture->Image texture**. Add as many image textures as you have image maps, then wire them up. You should end up with something similar to this diagram.

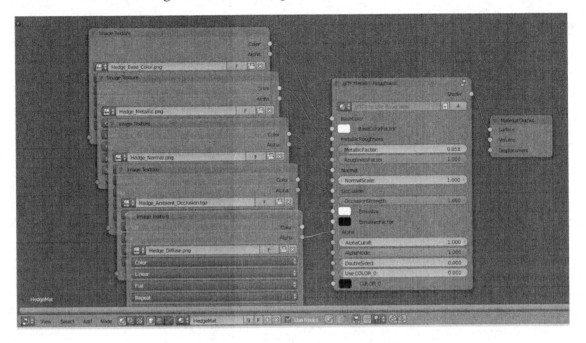

7. To export the models, I recommend that you disable camera export and combine the buffers, unless you think you will be exporting several models that share geometry or materials. The **Export** options I used are as follows:

Now, to include the exported glTF object, use the `<Model>` component as you would with an OBJ file, except you have no MTL file. The materials are all described inside the .glTF file. To include the exported glTF object, you just put the filename as a gltf2 prop in the `<Model`:

```
<Model
  source={{ gltf2: asset('TeleportGem2.gltf'),}}
...
```

To find out more about these options and processes, you can go to the glTF export web site at: `http://bit.ly/WebGLTF`. This site also includes tutorials on major CAD packages and the all important glTF shaders (for example, the Blender model I showed earlier).

I have loaded several .OBJ files and .glTF files at `http://bit.ly/VR_Chap11` so you can experiment with different combinations of low poly and transparency. When glTF support was added in React VR version 2.0.0, I was very excited as transparency maps are very important for a lot of VR models, especially vegetation; just like our hedges. However, it turns out there is a bug in WebGL or three.js that does not render the transparency properly. As a result, I have gone with a low polygon version in the files on the GitHub site; the pictures, above, were with the file `MazeHedges2DoubleSided.gltf` in the `Hedges.js` file (in vr/components).

 If you get 404 errors, check the paths in the glTF file. It depends on which exporter you use—if you are working with Blender, the gltf2 exporter from the Khronos group calculates the path correctly, but the one from Kupoman has options, and you could export the wrong paths.

Animation — VR Buttons

OK! We want to animate something. To do that, we will use the VRButton. It activates when one of the following things occur:

- Button A on an XBox Gamepad
- Space button on a keyboard
- Left click with a Mouse
- Touch on a screen

Unfortunately, our "lowest common denominator" is a Google Cardboard, which may, or may not, have a button. You don't want to have to stick your finger inside and try to touch the screen. (After having said that, the newer VR headsets have a little lever arm that pokes the screen, even in the actual cardboard versions). What we will use is a *Gaze button*. When a mouse pointer or center of the screen (marked by a small dot) go over your object, events will be called, and our code will handle this.

The Gaze button is also packaged into a nice `<GazeButton>` object in the npm ecosystem. Please refer to the web page at: `http://bit.ly/GazeButton`. To use it, we'll need to understand what it does, and how we can let the View know that a `Gem` has been "touched" (or looked at for two seconds). We installed it earlier in the chapter; if you haven't up to now, we install it by using Node.js command prompt and entering:

```
npm install react-vr-gaze-button
```

We could use VR Button, but then we'd have to handle entering the object, leaving it, counting down, and so on. The `GazeButton` does all of this for us. Note that the way it expects children is a bit different to what we have been used to up to now.

Your `Gem.js` code (note the capital) should now be as follows:

```
import GazeButton from 'react-vr-gaze-button'
export default class Gem extends Component {

  constructor() {
    super();
    this.state = {
      Height: -3,
      buttonIsClicked: false
    };
  }
  onGemClicked() {
    this.setState({ buttonIsClicked: true });
    console.log("Clicked on gem " + this.props.X + " x " + this.props.Z);
  }
  render() {
    const { buttonIsClicked } = this.state
    return (
      <GazeButton onClick={() => this.onGemClicked()}
        duration={2000}>
        {time => (

          <Model
            source={{
              gltf2: asset('TeleportGem.gltf'),
            }}
```

```
              style={{
                transform: [{ translate: [0, -1, 0] }]
              }}
              style={{
                transform: [{ translate:
                    [this.props.X, this.state.Height, this.props.Z] }]
              }}
            />
          )}
        </GazeButton>
      );
    }
  }
```

Now, when we try this on the desktop, it seems to work, but on a mobile phone (I tried it with Samsung GearVR), there is no cursor and nothing to click on. We need to implement a raycaster (even without controls).

There are so many different kinds of VR control systems, as we discussed briefly at the start of the chapter, where the default is "no" VR input device, including a center of the screen cursor.

The implementation of a proper control system is in our hands.

When you are using a desktop browser to do your initial development, you get a mouse cursor (including a *hand* cursor when over a tracked component), which can imply a gaze cursor is built in; they aren't. Just be aware there is a valid reason for this.

Raycasters

A **raycaster** shoots a ray out into the world and calculates what it touches. You usually see these as glowing lines from VR controllers. Without a controller, the raycaster will cast a ray from the center of the screen; this is exactly what we need to implement our Gaze button.

In this case, as we did with the button, there is already a `simple-raycaster` out there. If you haven't yet, you need to install it from npm via the following command:

```
npm install --save simple-raycaster
```

You might want to skip the `--save` while experimenting with packages; if you do, remember to update your `package.json` file manually or via the appropriate tools.

Implementation of the `simple-raycaster` is pretty easy. In `client.js`, below the existing `import` line (VRInstance), add the following `import` statement:

```
import * as SimpleRaycaster from "simple-raycaster";
```

Where it says `// Add custom options here`, insert the following lines:

```
raycasters: [
    SimpleRaycaster // Add SimpleRaycaster to the options
],
cursorVisibility: "auto", // Add cursorVisibility
```

On your PC, things get a little strange at this point—the center of the screen will activate (and drop) the gems, even if you don't click. That's the entire point.

If we had more pages, we would make the gems spin when your gaze enters them. For now, we will give this exercise up to the reader.

You'll want to start an animation during the `onClick` handler.

So far, we've shown how to get events when a gem is gazed at. That's good, we can use the event to trigger a movement, but how do we move?

One thing that is a little odd, is that React VR has no way to move the camera as many graphics systems do. To move the current point of view, you translate the `<View>` at the start of the `index.vr.js` to the opposite direction; this moves everything in the world the other way, which makes it look like you are moving forward. To move a point of view, we need to pass on the click event from the `Gem` to its parent's parent (the top level View).

Props, state, and events

React, and thus React VR, at its core, handles props, events, and state in a predictable, deterministic manner and this is what makes React apps consistent, clean, and easy to maintain.

Props are created when an object is declared and should not change over the life of the object. If an object needs to change, for example, our teleport gems, then you should assign these values to state. This enforces a top-down, unidirectional data flow. If a component needs the same state in different areas, then that state should be lifted up to the highest parent.

This causes interesting issues if you want a subcomponent to let a parent component know about an event or change its state based on an event at a lower level.

There are several ways of handling this; it can be a complicated subject in the React world. React VR doesn't differ from React Native or React in how state, props, and events are handled. A good place to start is the React Documentation, on *State and Lifecycle*.

Essentially, in a React app, there should be a single source of truth for something that changes. If a parent doesn't care, for example, if a Gem is higher or lower (stepped on or not), then you do not need to have that parent keep track of its children's height. Keeping state at a level as low as possible is the right decision. The height can be calculated from "have we stepped on the Gem", and so shouldn't be a prop that is passed down. (You might consider a *starting height*, though, as a prop; good programming says not to hardcode values, even though in a lot of the book files, we have for brevity.)

With our maze world, we have a quandary. We move the point of view by changing the <View> node at the top of our world tree. Yet, as we click on each <Gem>, we want the view to change.

We could handle this with context; a number of libraries, such as Redux or MobX, use context under the covers. There are event libraries that use context and other abilities. Context, however, is a bit of an advanced concept and a bit of overkill for what we are doing.

In this particular case, we will simply pass a `callback` function down the child tree. The reasons we will do this are as follows:

- At this point, our app is fairly small from a hierarchy view, only three levels.
- The `Maze` itself may need to know when the user has gotten to the end (for example, to display fireworks or update a high score). The `Gem` doesn't know this. If the `Gem` sent the notification directly to the View, the `Maze` would never know.
- We could bring in additional libraries, but this is a straightforward project, and too many external dependencies in an open source world can break things. This isn't a big problem usually, though—if something breaks, it's open source; go fix it.

 If, while looking for external packages, you do break things, you need to uninstall the offending package, then restart your Node.js server by running the following command:

```
npm start -- --reset-cache
```

`npm cache clean --force` does *not* do this cache reset. The error message you get should point this out if you forget.

Making updates flow up river

Although updates ripple down, we need to pass the information up. How do we do that? Easy, with a functional `callback`.

In `index.vr.js`, create a couple of routines and do an all important binding of these routines to this—the `WalkInAMaze` component. I'm just showing the changed lines at this point:

```
constructor(props) {
  super(props);
  this.state = {
    // ... existing member state initialization
  }
  this.handleClickGem = this.handleClickGem.bind(this);
};

onClickFloor(X, Z) {
  this.setState({ newX: X, newZ: Z });
}
```

```
handleClickGem(X, Z) {
  this.setState({ newX: X, newZ: Z });
};
```

Inside our Gem.js, we already have an onClick method. We just need to add a few new props:

```
onGemClicked() {
    this.setState({ buttonIsClicked: true });
    //send it to the parent
    this.props.onClickGem(this.props.X, this.props.Z);
}
```

Now, what's this this.props.onClickGem? This is a prop, which is a function, that is passed from the parent. Where we create the Gem, we just insert this following prop (the inserted line in bold—not that source code can be bold):

```
. . .
mazeHedges.push(<Gem {...cellLoc}
  onClickGem={this.handleClickGem}
  />);
```

OK, where do we get this.handleClickGem? In this (simple) case, the Maze won't be doing anything with the event, just passing it through. In Maze.js, we will add a handler:

```
constructor(props) {
  super(props);
  // existing code here doesn't change
  // at the bottom:
  this.handleClickGem = this.handleClickGem.bind(this);
}

handleClickGem(X, Z) {
  this.props.onClickGem(X, Z);
}
```

Now, we note another prop here. This is, of course, passed to us by the maze's parent; so, in index.vr.js, add the (bold) line:

```
<Maze sizeX={this.state.sizeX} sizeZ={this.state.sizeZ}
  cellSpacing={this.state.cellSpacing} seed={this.state.seed}
  onClickGem={this.handleClickGem} />
```

That's pretty much it. What happens when the Gem's VR Gaze button detects a click? It calls the prop, which is a function. This causes the maze's `handleClickGem` to be called; it, in turn, calls `handleClickGem()` inside `index.vr.js`. This routine (pun intended) then sets internal state. This state causes the view to be re-rendered:

```
handleClickGem(X, Z) {
      this.setState({ startX: -X, startZ: -Z });
   };
```

That's all it takes. Note that you don't just set the state with `this.startX = -X`, you need to call `this.setState()` as shown in the preceding code. This routine will then handle the rippling down of the `render()` updates.

These are big files, and we just made a lot of changes. I called out important lines in the above, but I highly recommend you download the source files from `http://bit.ly/VR_Chap11` and take a look at what we have done. In it, I've built a 4x4 maze that should have reasonable frame rate on most PC's and mobile devices. You can experiment with some other versions of the various objects (hedges that look like hedges or low poly hedges).

Where to go from here?

This is a pretty basic game, but there is a lot you could do with it. Some things we've discussed before, that would be easy to include, are the following:

- Our teleporting is a bit abrupt. We should have a sound, or even do two updates (by changing the `HandleClickGem()` routine) to either add a brief animation or a two-step teleport. Note that it is generally not a good idea to smoothly animate the view itself; this makes people sick, as their eyes say they are moving but their body says not.
- The number of gems clicked on could become a score. This gives us an advantage to go slower, step by step and click on all the gems.
- You could time how long it takes to get to the exit, and lower numbers could increase your score. This gives an advantage to go faster and skip the teleport gems. The two goals here are exclusive, which, with balancing, can make it fun.
- You could include buttons at the front of the maze to increase/decrease the size or generate different random numbers (and display them).
- The scores and the random numbers could be loaded into a high score API.
- Event passing libraries, such as `eventing-bus`, make the passing of `props` a lot easier. My goal was to show you the React VR way of doing it.

Summary

In this chapter, we learned the final pieces to build complete apps and games on the web; coupled with what we learned earlier, our journey is nearly complete; this is really just the first step toward bringing reality to the web. The topics we covered included how to move in a VR world, including basic teleport mechanics. We discussed Gaze buttons and using ray casting to implement them. We discussed the important mechanics of `props`, `state`, and events. To implement these flows, we went over the important React philosophy of pushing `state` up and handling events down stream. We also discussed using pseudo random number generators to make sure that our `props` and `state` didn't change chaotically. All together, we now know how to create, move around in, and make worlds react to us.

In the next chapter, we'll discuss where to go from here, how to upgrade React VR, and how to publish your virtual worlds on the internet.

12

Publishing Your App, and Where to Go from Here

It is fun to develop and experience virtual worlds at home. Eventually though, you want the world to see your world. To do that, we need to package and publish our app. In the course of development, upgrades to React may come along; before publishing, you will need to decide whether you need to "code freeze" and ship with a stable version, or upgrade to a new version. This is a design decision.

At some point, you will need to upgrade, and you will need to publish. This chapter will explain how to do both as well as how to organize your code and check your dryer, and your code, for lint. We will cover these topics here:

- Types of upgrades: Rip and Replace or "Facelift" upgrade, or "Upgrade in place"
- How to ensure that proper versions of your components are present
- Development versus non-development versions, components, and libraries
- Distribution licenses
- Linking and embedding VR content
- Publishing to common web hosts and Content Delivery Networks.
- Where VR is going in the next 5 years

Upgrading React VR

One of the neat things, although it can be frustrating, is that web projects are frequently updated. During the writing of this book, React VR was updated. There are a couple of different ways to do an upgrade:

- You can install/create a new app with the same name
  - You will then go to your old app and copy everything over
    - This is a **facelift** upgrade or *Rip and Replace*
- Do an update. Mostly, this is an update to `package.json`, and then delete `node_modules` and rebuild it. This is an **upgrade in place**.

It is up to you which method you use, but the major difference is that an upgrade in place is somewhat easier—no source code to modify and copy—but it may or may not work. A Facelift upgrade also relies on you using the correct `react-vr-cli`. There is a notice that runs whenever you run React VR from the Command Prompt that will tell you whether it's old:

```
Current CLI version is 0.3.0, but the latest available version is 0.3.5
You can upgrade your CLI with:
  npm update -g react-vr-cli
```

The error or warning that comes up about an upgrade when you run React VR from a Command Prompt may fly by quickly. It takes a while to run, so you may go away for a cup of coffee.

Pay attention to red lines, seriously.

To do an upgrade in place, you will typically get an update notification from Git if you have subscribed to the project. If you haven't, you should go to: `http://bit.ly/ReactVR`, create an account (if you don't have one already), and click on the eyeball icon to join the watch list. Then, you will get an email every time there is an upgrade. We will cover the most straightforward way to do an upgrade—upgrade in place, first.

Upgrading in place

How do you know what version of React you have installed? From a Node.js prompt, type this:

> `npm list react-vr`

Also, check the version of `react-vr-web`:

> `npm list react-vr-web`

Check the version of `react-vr-cli` (the command-line interface, really only for creating the *hello world* app).

> `npm list react-vr-cli`

Check the version of `ovrui` (open VR's user interface):

> `npm list ovrui`

You can check these against the versions on the documentation. If you've subscribed to React VR on GitHub (and you should!), then you will get an email telling you that there is an upgrade. Note that the CLI will also tell you if it is out of date, although this only applies when you are creating a new application (folder/website).

The release notes are at: `http://bit.ly/VRReleases`. There, you will find instructions to upgrade. The upgrade instructions usually have you do the following:

1. Delete your `node_modules` directory.
2. Open your `package.json` file.
3. Update `react-vr`, `react-vr-web`, and `ovrui` to "New version number" for example, 2.0.0.
4. Update `react` to "a.b.c".
5. Update `react-native to` "~d.e.f".
6. Update `three` to "^g.h.k".
7. Run `npm` install or yarn.

 Note the ~ and ^ symbols; ~version means *approximately equivalent to version* and ^version means *compatible with version*. This is a help, as you may have other packages that may want other versions of `react-native` and `three`, specifically. To get the values of {a...k}, refer to the release notes.

I have also found that you may need to include these modules in the
`devDependencies` section of `package.json`:

```
"react-devtools": "^2.5.2",
"react-test-renderer": "16.0.0",
```

You may see this error:

```
module.js:529
  throw err;
  ^
Error: Cannot find module './node_modules/react-native/packager/blacklist'
```

If you do, make the following changes in your projects root folder in the

`rncli.config.js` file.

Replace the `var blacklist = require('./node_modules/react-native/packager/blacklist');` line with `var blacklist = require('./node_modules/metro-bundler/src/blacklist');`.

Third-party dependencies

If you have been experimenting and adding modules with `npm install <something>`,
you may find, after an upgrade, that things do not work. The `package.json` file also needs
to know about all the additional packages you installed during experimentation. This is the
project way (npm way) to ensure that Node.js knows we need a particular piece of software.
If you have this issue, you'll need to either repeat the `install` with the—save parameter,
or edit the `dependencies` section in your `package.json` file. For example (bold line mine),
when we were experimenting with random numbers in the last chapter, we could add this
line manually:

```
{
  "name": "WalkInAMaze",
  "version": "0.0.1",
  "private": true,
  "scripts": {
    "start": "node -e \"console.log('open browser at
http://localhost:8081/vr/\\n\\n');\" && node node_modules/react-
native/local-cli/cli.js start",
    "bundle": "node node_modules/react-vr/scripts/bundle.js",
    "open": "node -e \"require('xopen')('http://localhost:8081/vr/')\"",
    "devtools": "react-devtools",
    "test": "jest"
```

```
  },
  "dependencies": {
    "ovrui": "~2.0.0",
    "react": "16.0.0",
    "react-native": "~0.48.0",
    "three": "^0.87.0",
    "react-vr": "~2.0.0",
    "react-vr-web": "~2.0.0",
    "mersenne-twister": "^1.1.0"
  },
  "devDependencies": {
    "babel-jest": "^19.0.0",
    "babel-preset-react-native": "^1.9.1",
    "jest": "^19.0.2",
    "react-devtools": "^2.5.2",
    "react-test-renderer": "16.0.0",
    "xopen": "1.0.0"
  },
  "jest": {
    "preset": "react-vr"
  }
}
```

Again, this is the manual way; a better way is to use `npm install <package> -save`.

The `-s` qualifier saves the new package you've installed in `package.json`. The manual edits can be handy to ensure that you've got the right versions if you get a version mismatch.

> If you mess around with installing and removing enough packages, you will eventually mess up your modules. If you get errors even after removing `node_modules`, issue these commands:
>
> `npm cache clean --force`
>
> `npm start -- --reset-cache`
>
> The cache clean won't do it by itself; you need the `reset-cache`, otherwise, the problem packages will still be saved, even if they don't physically exist!

Really broken upgrades – rip and replace

If, however, after all that work, your upgrade *still* does not work, all is not lost. We can do a *rip and replace* upgrade. Note that this is sort of a "last resort", but it does work fairly well. Follow these steps:

1. Ensure that your `react-vr-cli` package is up to date, globally:

```
[F:\ReactVR]npm install react-vr-cli -g
C:\Users\John\AppData\Roaming\npm\react-vr ->
C:\Users\John\AppData\Roaming\npm\node_modules\react-vr-
cli\index.js
+ react-vr-cli@0.3.6
updated 8 packages in 2.83s
```

This is important, as when there is a new version of React, you may not have the most up-to-date `react-vr-cli`. It will tell you when you use it that there is a newer version out, but that line frequently scrolls by; if you get bored and don't note, you can spend a lot of time trying to install an updated version, to no avail.

> An npm generates a lot of verbiage, but it is important to read what it says, especially red formatted lines.

2. Ensure that all CLI (DOS) windows, editing sessions, Node.js running CLIs, and so on, are closed. (You shouldn't need to reboot, however; just close everything using the old directory).

3. Rename the *old* code to `MyAppName140` (add a version number to the end of the old `react-vr` directory).

4. Create the application, using `react-vr init MyAppName`, in other words, the original app name.

5. The next step is easiest using a diff program (refer to `http://bit.ly/WinDiff`). I use Beyond Compare, but there are other ones too. Choose one and install it, if needed.

6. Compare the two directories, `.\MyAppName` (new) and `.\MyAppName140`, and see what files have changed.

7. Move over any new files from your old app, including assets (you can probably copy over the entire static_assets folder).

8. Merge any files that have changed, except `package.json`. Generally, you will need to merge these files:
   - `index.vr.js`
   - `client.js` (if you changed it)

9. For `package.json`, see what lines have been added, and install those packages in the new app via npm `install <missed package> --save`, or start the app and see what is missing.

10. Remove any files seeded by the *hello world* app, such as `chess-world.jpg` (unless you are using that background, of course).

11. Usually, you don't change the `rn-cli.config.js` file (unless you modified the seeded version).

Most code will move directly over. Ensure that you change the application name if you changed the directory name, but with the preceding directions, you won't have to.

The preceding list of upgrade steps may be slightly easier if there are massive changes to React VR; it will require some picking through source files. The source is pretty straightforward, so this should be easy in practice.

I found that these techniques will work best if the automatic upgrade did not work.

The best time to do an upgrade

As mentioned earlier, the time to do a major upgrade probably is not right before publishing the app, unless there is some new feature you need. You want to adequately test your app to ensure that there aren't any bugs.

I'm including the upgrade steps here, though, but not because you should do it right before publishing.

Getting your code ready to publish

Honestly, you should never put off organizing your clothes until, oh, wait, we're talking about code. You should never put off organizing your code until the night you want to ship it. Even the code you think is throw away may end up in production. Learn good coding habits and style from the beginning.

Good code organization

Good code, from the very start, is very important for many reasons:

- If your code uses sloppy indentation, it's more difficult to read. Many code editors, such as Visual Studio Code, Atom, and Webstorm, will format code for you, but don't rely on these tools.
- Poor naming conventions can hide problems.
- An improper case on variables can hide problems, such as using `this.State` instead of `this.state`.
- Most of the time spent coding, as much as 80%, is in maintenance. If you can't read the code, you can't maintain it. When you're a starting out programmer, you frequently think you'll always be able to read your own code, but when you pick up a piece years later and say *"Who wrote this junk?"* and then realize it was *you*, you will quit doing things like a, b, c, d variable names and the like.
- Most software at some point is maintained, read, copied, or used by someone other than the author.
- Most programmers think code standards are for "the other guy," yet complain when they have to code well. Who then does?
- Most programmers will immediately ask for the code documentation and roll their eyes when they don't find it. I usually ask to see the documentation they wrote for their last project. Every programmer I've hired usually gives me a deer in the headlights look. This is why I usually require good comments in the code.
    - A good comment is not something like this:

        ```
        //count from 99 to 1
        for (i=99; i>0; i--)
            . . .
        ```

    - A good comment is this:

        ```
        //we are counting bottles of beer
        for (i=99; i>0; i--)
            . . .
        ```

Cleaning the lint trap (checking code standards)

When you wash clothes, the lint builds up and will eventually clog your washing machine or dryer, or cause a fire. In the PC world, old code, poorly typed names, and all can also build up.

Refactoring is one way to clean up the code. I *highly* recommend that you use some form of version control, such as Git or bitbucket to check your code; while refactoring, it's quite possible to totally mess up your code and if you don't use version control, you may lose a lot of work.

A great way to do a code review of your work, before you publish, is to use a **linter**. Linters go through your code and point out problems (crud), improper syntax, things that may work differently than you intend, and generally try to pick up your room after you, like your mom does. While you might not like it if your mom does that, these tools are invaluable. Computers are, after all, very picky and why not use the machines against each other?

One of the most common ways to let software check your software for JavaScript is a program called **ESLint**. You can read about it at: http://bit.ly/JSLinter. To install ESLint, you can do it via npm like most packages—npm install eslint --save-dev.

The --save-dev option puts a requirement in your project while you are developing. Once you've published your app, you won't need to pack the ESLint information with your project!

There are a number of other things you need to get ESLint to work properly; read the configuration pages and go through the tutorials. A lot depends on what IDE you use. You can use ESLint with Visual Studio, for example.

Once you've installed ESLint, you need to configure a local configuration file. Do this with

```
eslint --init.
```

The --init command will display a prompt that will ask you how to configure the rules it will follow. It will ask a series of questions, and ask what style to use. AirBNB is fairly common, although you can use others; there's no wrong choice. If you are working for a company, they may already have standards, so check with management. One of the prompts will ask if you need React.

React VR coding style

Coding style can be nearly religious, but in the JavaScript and React world, some standards are very common. AirBNB has one good, fairly well–regarded style guide at: `http://bit.ly/JStyle`.

For React VR, some style options to consider are as follows:

- Use lowercase for the first letter of a variable name. In other words, this.props.currentX, not this.props.CurrentX, and don't use underscores (this is called **camelCase**).
- Use **PascalCase** only when naming constructors or classes.
- As you're using PascalCase for files, make the filename match the class, so

  `import MyClass from './MyClass'.`

- Be careful about 0 vs {0}. In general, learn JavaScript and React.
- Always use `const` or let to declare variables to avoid polluting the global namespace.
- Avoid using ++ and --. This one was hard for me, being a C++ programmer. Hopefully, by the time you've read this, I've fixed it in the source examples. If not, do as I say, not as I do!
- Learn the difference between == and ===, and use them properly, another thing that is new for C++ and C# programmers.

In general, I highly recommend that you pour over these coding styles and use a linter when you write your code:

```
F:\ReactVR\WalkInAMaze>npm install eslint
npm WARN react-native@0.48.4 requires a peer of react@16.0.0-alpha.12 but none was installed.
npm WARN optional SKIPPING OPTIONAL DEPENDENCY: fsevents@1.1.2 (node_modules\fsevents):
npm notsup SKIPPING OPTIONAL DEPENDENCY: Unsupported platform for fsevents@1.1.2: wanted {"os":"darwin","arch":"any
"} (current: {"os":"win32","arch":"x64"})

+ eslint@4.9.0
added 157 packages in 33.425s

F:\ReactVR\WalkInAMaze>eslint --init
? How would you like to configure ESLint? Use a popular style guide
? Which style guide do you want to follow? Airbnb
? Do you use React? Yes
? What format do you want your config file to be in? JavaScript
Checking peerDependencies of eslint-config-airbnb@latest
? The style guide "airbnb" requires eslint@^4.9.0. You are currently using eslint@4.8.0.
  Do you want to upgrade? Yes
Local ESLint installation not found.
Installing eslint-config-airbnb@latest, eslint@^4.9.0, eslint-plugin-import@2.7.0, eslint-plugin-jsx-a11y@^6.0.2, eslin
t-plugin-react@^7.4.0
npm notice save eslint is being moved from dependencies to devDependencies
npm WARN react-native@0.48.4 requires a peer of react@16.0.0-alpha.12 but none was installed.
npm WARN optional SKIPPING OPTIONAL DEPENDENCY: fsevents@1.1.2 (node_modules\fsevents):
npm notsup SKIPPING OPTIONAL DEPENDENCY: Unsupported platform for fsevents@1.1.2: wanted {"os":"darwin","arch":"any
"} (current: {"os":"win32","arch":"x64"})

+ eslint@4.9.0
+ eslint-plugin-react@7.4.0
+ eslint-config-airbnb@16.1.0
+ eslint-plugin-import@2.7.0
+ eslint-plugin-jsx-a11y@6.0.2
added 152 packages and updated 1 package in 41.19s
Successfully created .eslintrc.js file in F:\ReactVR\WalkInAMaze
ESLint was installed locally. We recommend using this local copy instead of your globally-installed copy.

F:\ReactVR\WalkInAMaze>_
```

Third-party dependencies

For your published website/application to really work reliably, we also need to update `package.json`; this is sort of the "project" way to ensure that Node.js knows we need a particular piece of software. We will edit the `"dependencies"` section to add the last line,(bold emphasis mine, bold won't show up in a text editor, obviously!):

```
{
    "name": "WalkInAMaze",
    "version": "0.0.1",
    "private": true,
    "scripts": {
      "start": "node -e \"console.log('open browser at
http://localhost:8081/vr/\\n\\n');\" && node node_modules/react-
native/local-cli/cli.js start",
      "bundle": "node node_modules/react-vr/scripts/bundle.js",
      "open": "node -e \"require('xopen')('http://localhost:8081/vr/')\"",
      "devtools": "react-devtools",
      "test": "jest"
    },
    "dependencies": {
      "ovrui": "~2.0.0",
      "react": "16.0.0",
```

```
      "react-native": "~0.48.0",
      "three": "^0.87.0",
      "react-vr": "~2.0.0",
      "react-vr-web": "~2.0.0",
      "mersenne-twister": "^1.1.0"
   },
   "devDependencies": {
      "babel-jest": "^19.0.0",
      "babel-preset-react-native": "^1.9.1",
      "jest": "^19.0.2",
      "react-devtools": "^2.5.2",
      "react-test-renderer": "16.0.0",
      "xopen": "1.0.0"
   },
   "jest": {
      "preset": "react-vr"
   }
}
```

This is the manual way; a better way is to use `npm install <package> -s`.

The `-s` qualifier saves the new package you've installed in `package.json`. The manual edits can be handy to ensure that you've got the right versions, if you get a version mismatch.

If you mess around with installing and removing enough packages, you will eventually mess up your modules. If you get errors, even after removing `node_modules`, issue these commands:

```
npm start -- --reset-cache
npm cache clean --force
```

The cache clean won't do it by itself; you need the reset–cache, otherwise the problem packages will still be saved, even if they don't physically exist!

Bundling for publishing on the web

Assuming that you have your project dependencies set up correctly to get your project to run from a web server, typically through an ISP or service provider, you need to "bundle" it. React VR has a script that will package up everything into just a few files.

Note, of course, that your desktop machine counts as a "web server", although I wouldn't recommend that you expose your development machine to the web. The better way to have other people experience your new Virtual Reality is to bundle it and put it on a commercial web service.

Packaging React VR for release on a website

The basic process is easy with the React VR provided script:

1. Go to the VR directory where you normally run `npm start`, and run the `npm run bundle` command:

```
F:\ReactVR\WalkInAMaze>npm run bundle

> WalkInAMaze@0.0.1 bundle F:\ReactVR\WalkInAMaze
> node node_modules/react-vr/scripts/bundle.js

Loading dependency graph, done.
Loading dependency graph, done.
bundle: start
bundle: finish
bundle: Writing bundle output to: F:\ReactVR\WalkInAMaze\vr\build\index.bundle.js
bundle: Done writing bundle output
bundle: start
bundle: finish
bundle: Writing bundle output to: F:\ReactVR\WalkInAMaze\vr\build\client.bundle.js
bundle: Done writing bundle output
Production versions were successfully built.They can be found at F:\ReactVR\WalkInAMaze\vr\build

F:\ReactVR\WalkInAMaze>
```

2. You will then go to your website the same way you normally upload files, and create a directory called `vr`.

3. In your project directory, in our case `f:\ReactVR\WalkInAMaze`, find the following files in `.\VR\Build`:

   ```
   client.bundle.js
   index.bundle.js
   ```

4. Copy those to your website.

5. Make a directory called `static_assets`.

6. Copy all of your files (that your app uses) from `AppName\static_assets` to the new `static_assets` folder.

7. Ensure that you have MIME mapping set up for all of your content; in particular, .obj, .mtl, and .gltf files may need new mappings. Check with your web server documentation:

   - For gltf files, use `model/gltf-binary`
   - Any .bin files used by gltf should be `application/octet-stream`
   - For .obj files, I've used `application/octet-stream`

- The official list is at `http://bit.ly/MimeTypes`
- Very generally, `application/octet-stream` will send the files "exactly" as they are on the server, so this is sort of a general purpose "catch all"

8. Copy the `index.html` from the root of your application to the directory on your website where you are publishing the app; in our case, it'll be the `vr` directory, so the file is alongside the two .js files.

9. Modify `index.html` for the following lines (note the change to `./index.vr`):

```html
<html>
  <head>
    <title>WalkInAMaze</title>
    <style>body { margin: 0; }</style>
    <meta name="viewport" content="width=device-width, initial-scale=1, user-scalable=no">
  </head>
  <body>
    <!-- When you're ready to deploy your app, update this line
to point to your compiled client.bundle.js -->
    <script src="./client.bundle?platform=vr"></script>
    <script>
      // Initialize the React VR application
      ReactVR.init(
        // When you're ready to deploy your app, update this
line to point to
        // your compiled index.bundle.js
        './index.vr.bundle?platform=vr&dev=false',
        // Attach it to the body tag
        document.body
      );
    </script>
  </body>
</html>
```

Note for a production release, which means if you're pointing to a prebuilt bundle on a static web server and not the React Native bundler, the dev and platform flags actually won't do anything, so there's no difference between `dev=true`, `dev=false`, or even `dev=foobar`.

Obtaining releases and attribution

If you used any assets from anywhere on the web, ensure that you have the proper release. For example, many Daz3D or Poser models do not include the rights to publish the geometry information; including these on your website as an OBJ or glTF file may be a violation of that agreement. Someone could easily download the model, or nearly all the geometry fairly easily, and then use it for something else.

I am not a lawyer; you should check with wherever you get your models to ensure that you have permission, and if necessary, attribute properly.

Attribution licenses are a little difficult with a VR world, unless you embed the attribution into a graphic somewhere; as we've seen, adding text can sometimes be distracting, and you will always have scale issues. If you embed a VR world in a page with <iframe>, you can always give proper attribution on the HTML side. However, this isn't really VR.

Checking image sizes and using content delivery sites

Some of the images you use, especially the ones in a <pano> statement, can be quite large. You may need to optimize these for proper web speed and responsiveness.

This is a fairly general topic, but one thing that can help is a **content delivery network (CDN)**, especially if your world will be a high-volume one.

Adding a CDN to your web server is easy. You host your asset files from a separate location, and you pass the root directory as the assetRoot at the ReactVR.init() call. For example, if your files were hosted at https://cdn.example.com/vr_assets/, you would change the method call in index.html to include the following third argument:

```
ReactVR.init(
    './index.bundle.js?platform=vr&dev=false',
    document.body,
    { assetRoot: 'https://cdn.example.com/vr_assets/' }
);
```

Optimizing your models

In `Chapter 10`, *Bringing in the Real Live World*, we built a maze that had the same *bush* model repeated for every square of the maze. If you were watching the web console, you may have noted this model being loaded over and over. It is not necessarily the most efficient way. Consider other techniques such as passing a model for the various child components as a prop.

Polygon decimation is another technique that is very valuable in optimizing models for the web and VR. With the glTF file format, you can use "normal maps" and still make a low polygon model look like a high-resolution one. Techniques to do this are well documented in the game development field. These techniques really do work well.

You should also optimize models to not display unseen geometry. If you are showing a car model with blacked out windows, for example, there is no need to have engine detail and interior details loaded (unless the windows are transparent). This sounds obvious, although I found the lamp that I used to illustrate the lighting examples had almost tripled the number of polygons than was needed; the glass lamp shade had an inner and outer polygons that were inside the model.

Now that we've gotten it published, what's next

Once we've gotten our realities built, what do we do? Where do we go?

You wouldn't be reading this book if you didn't have some idea of some kind of VR experience to build. I encourage you to play and experiment. You can even try things that you've heard are bad (such as moving points of view).

When VR started exploding again, I was briefly somewhat disgruntled; most of the things that I'd done in the generation of VR before seemed to have been forgotten; people thought "VR UIs are new!". All the while VR academic literature is literally decades old, discussing perceptual effectiveness and VR UIs, just for one area of VR.

However, this is not a bad thing. If the people flooding into VR can come up with some fresh new idea, maybe that will be the "Killer App" that everyone is looking for.

Maybe you can be the one to do this! I hope you will.

React VR is a lightweight, VR-enabled rendering system. There are still a lot of things that can be added.

Physics – making the world interact with itself

Real worlds have objects that move and interact with each other. Programming such interaction can become tedious; this is where a good physics package can excel.

Simply put, if your objects have real-world physics, they will look much more *real*.

A lot of the demos I see with physics are *bouncing ball* type demos that show objects flying around and smacking things. I think a more subtle approach to physics that is nonetheless accurate (physics engine based) will give a sense of verisimilitude in VR worlds that should not be overlooked.

There are a couple of JavaScript physics engines: **Cannon.JS** and **Oimo.js**.

Cannon.JS is a rigid body physics engine that includes simple collision detection, various body shapes, contacts, friction, and constraints. The source code and documentation is at: `http://bit.ly/CannonJS`.

The **collision detection** algorithms are themselves enough reason to use one of these packages, even if you don't foresee writing a bowling game or shooting spheres at brick walls. Collision detection can be used, for example, to determine whether a virtual avatar can navigate to a particular location in the VR world.

A blog post covering React VR and Cannon.js is at: `http://bit.ly/ReactPhysics`.

Oimo.js is a similar rigid body physics engine; it can be found at: `http://bit.ly/OmioPhysics`.

Note that Oimo.js examples show *native* three.js units, that are smaller than React VR (typically 10 to 1,000). In React VR, units are more or less 1 = 1 meter, so Oimo.js will integrate fairly smoothly.

Game play engines – letting you interact with others

There are a few websites that can package the TCP/IP code to enable multiplayer games. React VR integrates into these well, as long as they use JavaScript. Once such engine is **Lance.gg**, available at: `http://bit.ly/Lance_gg`.

It is a node-based game server. It was created to enable JavaScript developers to build real-time online multiplayer games without worrying about implementing net synchronization code. It strives to provide a smooth experience for both developers and players, regardless of lag. It has the following:

- Lance takes care of the netcode, so we can focus on the VR parts
- Can support any type of game or genre
- Optimized networking
    - TCP via websockets
    - Communication is packed and serialized into binary
    - Automatic handling of network spikes with step correction
- Intelligent sync strategies for lag handling
    - Extrapolation (client-side prediction) with step reenactment
    - Interpolation for optimal object motion
- Tools for debugging and tracing

Monetizing VR

There are several ways to make money off of VR. It is a very new art form, and a lot of applications are still being discovered. Like any new field, many things out there are experiments or funded loss leaders. The major hardware manufacturers have even built software ecosystems by funding developers.

It is a "who came first, the hardware or the killer app" situation currently. Headset sales are strong, although mobile headsets definitely lead the way, with almost ten times as many Samsung GearVR, Google Daydream, and Cardboard headsets as the higher-end models such as the Rift and Vive. The PSVR is a good system, but it can be difficult for developers who are not part of a game studio to get access to.

Don't forget, however, that you don't even need a VR headset to appreciate React VR. Most of the code you work on will be viewed in a browser without entering full VR mode, and many of your viewers may choose to do the same thing. Embedding a VR window on a website will still give a compelling experience to people even without VR equipment.

React VR may have an advantage when it comes to monetizing VR, at least from advertising.

Ways to make money off of VR are as listed:

- **Sell applications**: To do this on a website, you will probably need to implement some type of pay-to-view system. Most people do not like paywalls around websites, so this is probably best for full blown VR games, such as something built with Unity and Unreal. However, let's not discount this.
- **Being paid to build a VR experience**: Most web searches for VR Advertising will turn up these types of apps. They are almost always free to download, and are often pretty compelling. It is not, however, in my mind, a growth model for the VR producers; you can be paid fairly well to develop a VR app, but once that is done, so is your income stream. I see studio releases of VR sites that play content associated with a movie to be essentially the same concept, and an area I think React VR will be well suited for.
- **Embedding VR advertisements in your world**: One advantage of React VR is that it has access to all the layout possibilities with React itself, so this may be easier and more direct for React VR than any other VR system. One challenge is that people immersed in a VR world do not like distractions, so having advertisements pop up may have the opposite effect. Still, product placement, or billboards in your world can be fairly effective, especially if you are building some kind of virtual city.
- **Linking to products or sites from inside your VR world**: This works well for regular websites, although the challenge for VR is that you may need to take off the VR headset to really interact with what you just clicked on in the VR world. Some advertising companies have discussed building in VR advertising worlds that you will warp to from within a VR world, although so far most of these have been for traditional game engines. Still, we can expect a lot of development in this area in the future.
- **Selling off metadata**: In this model, the app itself will be free, but the VR developer will enable gaze tracking. *Hot spots* of areas within the VR world can be sold off to advertisers in the same way that clicks or impressions are sold with a more flat HTML model. This is another area of emerging standards.
- **Demo version to full version**: You can build a React VR world with models and assets taken from a full blown game engine, then put this on a web page as a tie–in or free giveaway to get people interested in your full VR app. Having industry standard formats, such as OBJ and glTF, will help do this, although a lot of the logic will have to be developed from scratch. A possibly better way is to have a free web URL and a for-pay URL behind a paywall.

- **In-app purchases**: This will be a way for things in the game to trigger purchases outside of it. For example, a video player can request a particular video be paid for, then the React VR code will play that video. In-app purchases will be fairly straightforward with React VR due to the straightforward way to integrate JavaScript.

Where VR will go in the next five years

If I knew exactly where VR would go in the next five years, I would be rich in five years, and so would you, if you invest in my predictions. Let me know how that works out.

I hope you invest in VR by developing amazing worlds, even if it isn't with React VR. I really believe in VR, and want to see it succeed this time.

That brings up what I mean by *this time*. I've been through at least one wave of VR; back then, everyone thought VR was the wave of the future. All the great things you are hearing about VR, I've heard before. I was doing VR from about 1995 to 2000 or so. VR crashed hard. There were HMDs being created, data gloves, and entire virtual worlds.

Most people say the graphics back then were too crude. There is some truth to that, but people that haven't tried VR still, say *"I will wait until the graphics get more real"* not realizing, as we've discussed and seen, it doesn't take great graphics for VR to appear *real*.

What we called VR is also a little different. Back then, seemingly ages ago, any 3D program on a PC was loosely called VR. I even predicted while the VRML language was being invented (it is now X3D), that we needed to get all this right or people would walk up to strangers from all over the world, in beautiful 3D environments, and (virtually) kill them.

In a way, I was right; in the World of Warcraft, for example, this is exactly what happens. Modern VR has everything it does due to computer gaming. All of those frag games have created a demand for cheap, high-quality video cards. You may think that a high-end video card isn't cheap, but compared to the first VR hardware, they are amazingly cheap.

3D computer games on a screen are not what we call VR today, and that is really correct. Computer games, no matter how great they look, are not as immersive as an HMD-based VR experience.

I am worried that VR might crash again; yet I don't think it will this time. The difference this time is that we all have high-powered VR devices in our pocketsour cell phones. Modern cell phones are as capable as the $100,000 Reality Engine by Silicon Graphics. We can pop a cell phone in a simple, cheap VR headset and see VR. It may not be as interactive as something with tracked controllers, but it works. Bluetooth controllers are not going away, and neither are cell phones.

VR is thus here to stay, but where will it go?

Do not wait for next year's technology

A long time ago, when I was buying my first stereo, when I was 20, and flush with what I thought was a lot of money from working the summer during my college break, I really wanted a stereo. I spent weeks pouring over specifications, listening tests, comparing features, and was generally a bit parallelized by options.

I went around to stereo stores with a wad of dough, looking to buy something.

I went to one store, and asked the sales guy what stereo system he had.

"Oh, I've got next years model," he said.

What? I thought. *Is something really great coming out?*

"Oh, so what are you waiting for?" I asked. *"What is coming out?"*

"Oh, next year I'll wait for the next year too," he said. *"You see, next year is always next year, so I never have a stereo that is obsolete,"* he said. He simply didn't ever buy a stereo.

I see his point. You might be thinking, *Wait till it gets better.*

My point is that in the last 30 years, I've listened to a *lot* more music than that salesman ever did.

You shouldn't wait to buy the next great piece of VR gear, get into it now. If something new comes out, you'll have enjoyed VR for much longer than if you had waited, and you'll know what you like a lot more. There aren't any bad decisions right now.

Better HMDs

The HMDs we have today, things such as the HTC Vive, the Oculus Rift, the PS VR, and mobile-based VR devices such as the Samsung Gear VR, the Google Daydream, and Google Cardboard, are pretty good, but they can be a lot better.

The human eye can't really be compared to a pixel display, although we know for sure that we see more detail than any current HMDs can show. We also have a wider field of view.

Current displays are roughly similar in view; 1,080 x 1,200 pixels with about 110 degrees field of view. That gives us roughly 10 to 15 pixels per degree. The human eye can see anywhere from 500 to about 1,000 pixels per inch at ten inches; this gives us about 90 to 177 pixels per degree. This will mean a nearly 20,000 or 40,000 pixel display. We're not talking about megapixels, but about gigapixels.

Can we get there in 5 years? That's a pretty high resolution, but I think we will get resolutions at least 4 or 16 times better than now.

HMDs will probably be more comfortable. I'm not sure they will get significantly smaller due to optical issues, although in 10 to 15 years, I expect that they will be the size of contacts or glasses. This is a very rough guess.

Better and more realistic graphics

Graphics cards get faster as well as cheaper all the time. In five years, we will need every ounce of that processing power to generate a display with the same visual complexity as we have now—not any better looking—due to the increase in pixels. In other words, as displays go up in pixels, making for better and wider displays, the amount of processing power to drive those goes up too, so there isn't as much of an increase in visual fidelity as you would expect. Is there a light at the end of that tunnel? Or is the light at the end of the tunnel a train going the other way? There is good news, and it is called Foveated rendering. For that, we need eye tracking, which we'll discuss in a bit.

Regardless of eye tracking and foveated rendering, we'll see more realistic rendering and more realistic looking humans. Will it be dramatically better? Will it look real? If you remember from the beginning of our book, graphics don't need to look like real life to seem real, so although I'm looking forward to better graphics, I don't think VR is reliant on them.

Easier content creation and more high-end content

So far, we have just discussed technical changes in VR. There are a lot more things that I think will happen, that will have a much larger effect on VR. Regardless of how the images are generated, sound, look, or even feel, we will need the so-called "Killer App". Right now, most VR that makes money are games. Once the larger game development studios see a future in VR, they will develop more AAA games (triple A games mean games with large budgets, often tens or hundreds of millions of dollars and large teams, including artists, developers, designers, authors, and project managers). Three AAA games are scheduled to come out shortly after this book is published: Doom VR, Fallout 4 VR, and Skyrim VR. Once we have large games with tens or hundreds of hours of gameplay, if it is compelling (and I believe it will be very compelling), we will see VR take off.

In the next five years, I think this will surely progress even further. I expect to see large persistent worlds, **Massively Multiplayer On-line Role Play Games** (**MMORPGS**) become a staple of VR. Instead of playing a game in the World of Warcraft, you will be *in* the World of Warcraft. Wow! (pun intended).

On the content side, we will also see more high-end creation software that is also in VR. Currently, the more complex creation tools, such as Max, Maya, and Blender, make the best models that you see in VR, but they are themselves conventional apps. Today, we see some apps, such as *Tilt-brush*, that let us design objects in VR. I expect higher–end CAD will have a ubiquitous VR mode themselves.

HMDs can become hot, heavy, and fatiguing after a while (mainly due to convergence accommodation conflict as discussed earlier). I don't see all work being done in VR, but it will help at the initial stages as well as in checking models.

What is quicker: to look at two objects on the screen and drag them around with the mouse, or just grab them with your hands and move them? Imagine sculpting with magic putty that you have an *undo* command. You can't do that with real clay, but you will be able to in VR.

Eye tracking

What is the eye tracking that I alluded to earlier? It is a sensor inside the HMD that looks at where your eyeballs are pointed. There are a few advantages to this kind of scanning, mainly social and rendering.

Social advantages are immense, in my opinion. When you look at someone's avatar, which is an in–game representation of another person, they can look very stiff and emotionless. Human beings detect an immense amount of emotion from their eyes; with eye tracking, your avatar can show some of these expressions. One simple test showed a dramatic improvement by simply putting cartoon eyeballs—just a black dot in a white ball—and have those eyes look around as the user was looking. The avatars, even though cartoons, looked much more real.

The rendering improvements with eye tracking, as briefly mentioned earlier, are a type of rendering called foveated rendering. With the eye tracker, instead of filling every pixel with high-detail objects, we can just show what you are looking at with high detail. The rest of the eye typically does not see in as much detail as right where your eyeball is pointed. Our rods and cones in the eye are tightly distributed in the center, and are much less dense at the outer edges of our eye. Foveated rendering makes use of that by showing less detail away from the center point of your gaze.

This really works and can significantly speed up graphics; you don't need to compute what you don't display. This was first demonstrated at the annual **Special Interest Group for GRAPHics (SIGGRAPH)** conference in 2016.

Audio improvements

Most people, when it comes to VR audio, are worried about how well the headsets work, or if they block out the sound of your cat screeching when you sit down on the couch without taking off your HMD. (Let's hope not!) There is a lot more to VR audio though; our ears do an amazing thing with pinpointing where a sound is coming from with only two sensors (normally, it takes three sensors to detect both distance and direction of any 3D source). How do our ears do that? It's done with something called a HRTF. Currently, we do have the technology to calculate HRTFs in real time. However, *what* HRTF to calculate is not that easy to determine. This is no surprise; people are unique.

Everyone's HRTF is different; if we play back a sound that is generated using my HRTF, I will hear a noise with my eyes closed as if it was coming directly from the spot the designer intended. If you hear the same noise with the same headset, you may think it sounds fake, or is coming from a different direction. This is just a reality of how we process sound.

There are some solutions currently—either measuring your HRTF in a chamber specially designed to calculate this or possibly using additional speakers in a headset. Time will tell which of these techniques will be the best; this is still an open area.

Along with the HRTF calculations to localize (pinpoint) the sound, we need more and better ways in software to locate that sound.

I would think in five years, whatever physics systems we are using for our virtual worlds may be able to generate the proper sound effects, not just play back a canned noise. For example, if you hit a concrete wall, maybe the software can generate the thud noise, at the right location and the right sound, considering how thick the wall is, and other parameters. Currently, we just play canned noises at the right location (which is still amazing, but can use some improvement). That is something I would like to see.

Controlling VR

Today's controllers usually consist of two handheld devices with multiple buttons. Most have a simple mechanical way to vibrate via software. There is a huge area of innovation possible. The VR industry has been working for decades on sophisticated devices that allow better haptics, smaller, and more accurate controllers, and data gloves. Why use a controller when you can just reach out and grab things?

- **Haptics** are any interaction involving touch. This doesn't just mean touching or holding your mouse; it can be anything from feeling a click or shake when you move your controller (the current state of the art), but it can also mean a device that pushes back when you move it. These have been demonstrated for years, and there are commercial off-the-shelf products that can do things such as allowing you to feel a surface. These will become more common and more of mass-produced, consumer-level devices.
- **Data gloves** are devices that you wear that allow every finger joint and movement to be tracked in VR. They have been available for decades. There are even systems (the Leap Motion device) that will let you reach out with your real hand, and have that interact in the virtual world. I believe that this is an area with a lot of potential in the next few years.
- **Whole body** controllers will allow your entire virtual body to be visually present, accurate, and tracked in the VR world. This is another area with a lot of potential. There are even a few prototype suits that provide full body haptics. Imagine putting on a suit and being able to feel and touch the world, not just wave a wand through the images.

Social and legal issues and solutions

If you can put a virtual statue in the middle of a public space, is that vandalism? What about painting on the side of a business in AR or VR? At first, you might think this is perfectly fine; I myself might like to see a model of some sci-fi thing in the middle of the park, that people can interact with. What if that model is of a Confederate war hero who was in favor of slavery? What if malcontent neighbors virtually tag your house with slanderous allegations?

Within social VR, we can harass people in ways just not possible in real life. If someone moves into your space, you can push them back, but in VR, bad behavior may be very easy to do. VR environments will need to take these kinds of things into consideration.

If we have guards in place to prevent virtual desecration, how do we decide what is right and what is wrong, especially in public spaces? VR can be similar to the real world—libel is libel, yet VR also offers some unique possibilities. If you are a southern gentleman, you may want to see rebel statues, and you can. The young person next to you may instead see George Washington Carver. We can all just get along; or can we? What if the guy next you wants to display chem trail deposition?

I do think persistent virtual worlds will flourish, and we will come up with innovative and interesting solutions to the preceding issues. Just remember that many people who don't like technology, or who fear it generally don't understand it. If we can create any worlds we want, we just have to want to create worthwhile worlds.

Please do!

Summary

In this chapter, we learned how to unleash our realities onto the internet. Specifically, we covered how to do version upgrades, and if we need to, how to do *rip and replace* upgrades. We discussed when to do an upgrade. We really should have discussed coding standards earlier, as it's never too soon to start, but first we had to get some React VR syntax down, so we covered this before we set our code on the world. We further discussed how to use ESLint and other linters to help you code well. Once you have good clean code, we talked about how to package your development React VR content for the web as well as how to make it fast through optimization and **Content Delivery Networks** (**CDNs**).

We discussed how to further make your websites real (through physics), play games as well as how to monetize them.

You now know everything you need to learn to use React VR on the web. I'm looking forward to finding out what you create!

Index

3

360 Video 18
3D concepts
  about 50
  coordinates 50
  matrix 58
  points 54
  rendering 60
  transforms 55, 56
3D models
  obtaining 130
  references 131
3D primitives
  about 72
  Box 72
  cylinder 72
  plane 73
  sphere 74
3DOF 220

6

6DOF 220

A

A-Frame 37
accommodation-vergence conflict 216
AmbientLight 79
Animated API
  about 165
  code 172
  teapot, spinning 170
  teapots, flying 167
animation
  URL 165
Augmented Reality (AR) 88
Axios

URL 202

B

base React VR components
  creating 90
base stations 22
Blender
  about 117
  references 134
  teapot 134, 143
Box 72

C

camelCase 256
camera 87
Cannon.JS
  URL 263
Cartesian coordinate system 51
code
  organizing 253, 254
  React VR coding style 256
  standards, checking 255
  third-party dependencies 257
coding style 256
collision detection algorithms 263
Command Line Interface (CLI) 39
common light properties
  color 79
  intensity 79
components 68
Computer Aided (Design/Drafting/Drawing) (CAD) 114
Computer Aided Design (CAD) 53
Constructive Solid Geometry (CSG) 115
content delivery network (CDN) 261
coordinates
  about 50

rotations 53
Cross-Origin Resource Sharing (CORS)
  about 199
  URL 206
Curiosity 199
cylinder 72
CylindricalPanel 75

D

deck plates
  fixing 154, 158
  React VR, finishing 158
Degrees of Freedom (DOF) 27, 220
DirectionalLight 81
Document Object Model (DOM) 66

E

edges 121
Equirectangular projection 93
ESLint
  URL 255
Euclidean space 51
European Space Agency (ESO) 95
events 69

F

fast frame rate 27
Fetch
  URL 202

G

Gaze button
  URL 238
GL Transmission Format (glTF)
  about 75
  using, for models 232
glTF export
  URL 237
graphics libraries
  OpenGL 36
  WebGL 36
Graphics Processing Units (GPU) 34

H

hardware, VR
  rendering 27
Head Mounted Display (HMD) 15, 28
Head Related Transfer Function (HRTF) 177
high-end controllers
  about 21
  HTC Vive 21, 22
  Oculus Rift 21, 23
HTC Vive 22
HTML 33

I

images
  building 212, 216
Immersion 16
Inertial Measurement Units (IMUs) 23
Irfanview 98

J

JavaScript 35
JSON
  about 200
  limitations 201
JSX 37

L

Lance.gg
  about 264
  URL 263
Lighthouses 22
lights
  about 78
  AmbientLight 79
  common light properties 79
  DirectionalLight 81
  PointLight 82
  SpotLight 83
linter 255
Linux headset 32
LiveEnvCamera object 87

M

MAAS API
  URL 206
Mac headset 32
Mars
  API, searching 202
  NASA Web APIs 208
  references, for weather 202
  styles, defining 211
Massively Multiplayer On-line Role Play Games
    (MMORPGS) 269
matrix 58, 60
Maze
  building 224
  floors, adding 228
  glTF file format, using for Models 232
  library code, including from other projects 225
  pseudo random number generators 225
  render() 226
  type checking 228
mobile headset 30, 31
mobile VR 26
multimedia
  sound 84
  video 84, 86

N

NASA Web API
  URL 208
Native Views
  extending 196
  URL 197
Node.js
  about 35
  download link 38
  installation 37, 38
  post installation 39
Non-Uniform Rational B-Spline (NURBS) 115

O

Oculus Rift 23, 25, 26
Oimo.js
  URL 263
Open Source Virtual Reality (OSVR) 29

OpenGL 36

P

PascalCase 256
PC headset 31
pedestals
  building 107
Physically based Rendering (PBR) material
  about 152, 232
  base color 152
  bump map 152
  decal 154
  diffuse map 152
  glossiness 153
  height map 153
  normal map 153
  reflectivity 153
  roughness 153
  specular map 153
  transparency 153
plane 73
Pointlight 82
points 54
polygon decimation 262
polygon modeling, with Blender 117, 118
polygons 114, 116, 120
Poser models
  references 131
preflight check 206
props 69

R

raycasters 239
React native modules
  about 181
  code, summing 188
  interacting, with React VR 185
  three.js cube demo, creating 182
React VR
  about 35, 37, 66, 262
  components 68
  core components 67
  events 69
  installing 39, 40, 42, 43, 45
  JSX 66

layout and style 70
physics 263
properties 68
React native modules, interacting 185
rip and replace upgrade 252
state 69
third-party dependencies 250
upgrade, determining 253
upgrading 248, 249
versus, React 66
React
reference 36
refactoring 255
rendering
about 60
testing 61
working 62
Room Scale 22, 222
rotations 53

S

shaders 123
sound
about 84, 177
creating 178
props 85
references 178
Special Interest Group for GRAPHics (SIGGRAPH)
270
sphere 74
Spherical panorama 94
SpotLight 83
status UI
building 212, 216
stereo and parallax
using, in Virtual Reality 15, 16
stereoscopic depth perception 11
Substance Designer
URL 100
Superagent
URL 202

T

Take Command Console (TCC) 39
teapot

in Blender 134
in in Blender 143
UV maps, fixing 143, 152
texture 123
texture mapping 117, 123, 124, 125, 126, 127,
128, 129
three.js 36
transforms 55, 56

V

vectors 54
vertices 121
video 84, 86
VideoControl 77
View object 88
Virtual Reality (VR)
360 Video 18
about 7, 13
AR 18
audio improvements 270
controlling 271
easier content creation 269
eye tracking 269
FR 18
future 266
graphics 268
high-end content 269
high-end controllers, for Linux 21
high-end controllers, for Mac 21
high-end controllers, for PC 21
history 20
HMDs 268
interacting with world, through controllers 20
legal issues and solutions 272
monetizing 264, 265
references, for software 34
social issues and solutions 272
SR 18
stereo and parallax, using 15
technologies 267
viewing 28
working 8, 9, 10, 11, 12, 14, 17
XR 18
visualization
techniques 191, 196

VR app
  background image, creating 93, 94, 95, 96, 97, 98
  base React VR components, creating 90, 91, 92
  creating 89
  objects, adding 105, 107
  objects, defining as class 103, 104
  pedestals, adding 107, 109, 110
  VR components, adding 98, 100
  VR world design 90
  world, creating on ground 98
VR components
  about 68
  cameras and scenes 68
  lights 68
  multimedia 68
  VR physical components 68
VR headset
  Linux headset 32
  Mac headset 32
  mobile headset 30
  options 29
  PC headset 31
  types 30
  warnings 29
VR Locomotion
  about 219
  artificial locomotion/rails 222
  blinks 221
  gaze detection 221
  ghost effect, avoiding 223
  room scale 221
  teleportation 221
  Tracked 6DOF controller movement paradigms 221
  treadmills 221
  types 220
  Vehicles/Cockpit locomotion 221
VR programming
  about 33
  HTML 34

VR stuff
  about 71
  CylindricalPanel 75
  Model 74
  VideoControl 77
  visible objects 71
  VrButton 77
VRButton
  about 78
  events, handling 241
  props, handling 241
  raycasters 239
  state, handling 241
  updates, creating 242
  using 237

W

web server
  attribution, obtaining 261
  bundle, publishing 258
  content delivery sites, using 261
  image sizes, checking 261
  models, optimizing 262
  React VR, packaging for release 259
  releases, obtaining 261
web services
  setting up 200
WebGL 36
WebVR
  about 222
  browser, installing 45, 47
windows on world systems 19
World of Warcraft 19
world, VR app
  cluttering 98, 100
  lighting up 101
  pasting, in Plane and Box 102

Y

YogaLayout
  reference link 70